PRAISE FOR PREVIOUS EDITIONS OF

Mississippi
Off the Beaten Path®

"This guide to the unique places of Mississippi invites you to forgo the well-worn interstates and seek out adventure on some of the lesser-known rabbit trails. *Mississippi Off the Beaten Path* is an easy-to-follow reference for those who want to soak in the culture of the Magnolia State, from the annual Slugburger Festival in Corinth to the site of actress Jayne Mansfield's fateful last ride."

—*Ole Miss Alumni Review* (Oxford, Miss.)

"The book provides maps and detailed directions to the out-of-the-way gems that make Mississippi a one-of-a-kind destination. *Mississippi Off the Beaten Path* is packed with interesting trivia about the Magnolia State and includes numerous sidebars recounting Mississippi's most colorful traditions, myths, and legends."

—*The Southern View* (Jackson, Miss.)

"Local author Marlo Carter Kirkpatrick takes a different fork in the road. Kirkpatrick's . . . *Mississippi Off the Beaten Path* spices up the journey with locales—as well as personal experiences, trivia, and tales—that lean toward the offbeat and Southern gothic."

—*The Clarion Ledger* (Jackson, Miss.)

Help Us Keep This Guide Up to Date

Every effort has been made by the author and editors to make this guide as accurate and useful as possible. However, many changes can occur after a guide is published—establishments close, phone numbers change, hiking trails are rerouted, facilities come under new management, etc.

We would love to hear from you concerning your experiences with this guide and how you feel it could be improved and be kept up to date. While we may not be able to respond to all comments and suggestions, we'll take them to heart, and we'll make certain to share them with the author. Please send your comments and suggestions to the following address:

The Globe Pequot Press
Reader Response/Editorial Department
P.O. Box 480
Guilford, CT 06437

Or you may e-mail us at: editorial@GlobePequot.com

Thanks for your input, and happy travels!

INSIDERS' GUIDE®

OFF THE BEATEN PATH® SERIES

Off the
Beaten Path®

FIFTH EDITION

mississippi

A GUIDE TO UNIQUE PLACES

MARLO CARTER KIRKPATRICK

INSIDERS' GUIDE®

GUILFORD, CONNECTICUT
AN IMPRINT OF THE GLOBE PEQUOT PRESS

The prices, rates, and hours listed in this guidebook were confirmed at press time. We recommend, however, that you call establishments to obtain current information before traveling.

INSIDERS' GUIDE®

Text design by Linda Loiewski
Maps created by Equator Graphics © The Globe Pequot Press
Illustrations by Julie Lynch
Spot photography throughout © Buck Miller/Superstock

ISSN 1540-157X
ISBN 0-7627-3529-5

Manufactured in the United States of America
Fifth Edition/First Printing

Acknowledgments

Mississippi Off the Beaten Path couldn't have been written without the insights, contributions, and cooperation of friends and colleagues statewide.

As usual, I owe the knowledgeable staff at the Mississippi Division of Tourism a huge and heartfelt "thank you." Special thanks go to Cheryl Eley of that organization, who has served as a prompt, reliable, and enthusiastic source of information for me ever since I began writing about Mississippi more than a decade ago.

I'm also deeply grateful to the many chamber of commerce and convention and visitors bureau directors and their personnel, who responded to my inquiries and, in many cases, personally guided me around their cities and towns. Thanks are also due to scores of bed-and-breakfast and restaurant proprietors who were so accommodating, and to countless local residents who petted my dog and pointed me in the right direction.

And finally, my heartfelt thanks—and my heart itself—go to Stephen Kirkpatrick, my favorite traveling companion.

THE NORTHEASTERN HILLS

■ Oxford

■ Tupelo

■ Clarksdale

■ Columbus

■ Greenville

THE MISSISSIPPI
RIVER DELTA

THE EASTERN PLAINS

■ Meridian

★ Jackson

■ Vicksburg

THE
HEARTLAND

■ Natchez

■ Hattiesburg

SOUTHERN
MISSISSIPPI
AND THE
GULF COAST

Biloxi
Gulfport ■ ■

Contents

Introduction

The geography that makes up the state of Mississippi is easily defined. Rolling northern hills and sweeping eastern plains. A pastoral heartland hugged by the Father of Waters. The fertile river delta and sun-drenched southern beaches.

But the real essence of the state is harder to put into words, for Mississippi is not merely a landscape but a state of mind.

Mississippi is nicknamed the "Hospitality State," and it's true that most of the people you'll meet here don't have to know your name to lend you a hand or stop and chat for a while. In fact, Mississippians seem to feel compelled to explain themselves, to make sure you leave with an enlightened view of this place they call home.

After all, perceptions of Mississippi are usually based on outdated stereotypes of "boss hog" sheriffs lying in wait for unfortunate travelers, sharecroppers dwelling in shacks without benefit of indoor plumbing, and rednecks running about the countryside clad in white sheets. Native Mississippians tend to view every out-of-state visitor as a personal crusade—they may not be able to change the whole world's opinion, but give them half a chance and by golly, they'll change yours.

Even left to your own devices, you'll soon discover the stereotypes are just that. Far from a haven for rednecks and racists, Mississippi is made up of bustling cities and quaint town squares, breathtaking natural wonders, and a rich culture like no other.

In fact, Mississippi has produced more writers, musicians, and poets per square mile than any other state. Mississippians are fond of saying, "We may not be able to read, but we sure can write." Works by William Faulkner, Eudora Welty, Richard Wright, Nevada Barr, Willie Morris, Greg Iles, and John Grisham would certainly seem to back up that claim. Mississippi is the birthplace of country music, the blues, and Elvis, the King of Rock 'n' Roll. Almost everything you hear on the radio has its roots in Mississippi.

And yet the state remains outside the limelight. Other than the casinos that line the Mississippi River and Mississippi Gulf Coast, the state really doesn't have any "manufactured" attractions. Things here are genuine and authentic, preserved rather than re-created. And once you've had your fill of the amusement parks and souvenir stands that make one place seem just like the last place or the next place, you'll find Mississippi a welcome change. The turnstiles and ticket takers give way to welcome mats and warmhearted people. Smoggy skylines are replaced by sweeping river views. "Hospitality" is a smile, a gesture, a friendly word.

Mississippi Off the Beaten Path will guide you through the state's diverse geography and its uncommon culture. You'll explore towns tucked away in the rolling hills and travel alongside the mighty Mississippi River that gave the state its name. You'll experience the sometimes harsh realities of life in the delta and the carefree frivolity of life on the beach. You'll converse with ladies in hoop skirts and walk on battlefields where the fate of the nation was determined.

You'll stop in odd little towns with odd little names like So-So, Why Not, Hot Coffee, Panther Burn, and D'Lo—short for a town once deemed "too damn low." There's even a microscopic community named "It" (there's not much there, but you'll know It when you see It). You'll develop an appreciation for natural phenomena like kudzu and Spanish moss, and an appetite for grits and catfish. Who knows, you may even hear yourself saying "y'all."

Care has been taken to ensure this book is as accurate as possible. Part of their quirky nature, however, is that off-the-beaten-path attractions are frequently subject to change. Ticket prices, days and hours of operation, and telephone numbers may change without notice; establishments may close; and people may move on. If you find any discrepancies in *Mississippi Off the Beaten Path,* please accept my apologies for any inconvenience or disappointment. Then, please write or e-mail me or the publisher and tell us what you have learned. Who knows, you may discover Mississippi's next great hidden attraction.

No matter where your Mississippi adventures take you, one thing is certain. You'll experience a land, a people, and a culture like no other.

And perhaps best of all, you won't have to wait in line, make reservations, or know the right people. In many cases, you won't even have to buy a ticket.

All you have to do is find it.

Mississippi at a Glance

TRANSPORTATION

Major Interstates in Mississippi

I–20 (east/west)

I–55 (north/south)

I–59 (southwest/northwest)

I–10 (east/west)

PRIMARY HIGHWAYS IN MISSISSIPPI

U.S. 80	U.S. 78
U.S. 49	U.S. 82
U.S. 45	U.S. 61
U.S. 98	

RULES OF THE ROAD

- **Speed Limit:** The speed limit on Mississippi interstate highways is 70 miles per hour. The state highway speed limit is 65 miles per hour on four-lane highways and 55 miles per hour on two-lane highways unless otherwise posted.
- **Mandatory Seat-Belt Law:** Operator and front-seat passengers in any motor vehicle designed to carry ten or fewer passengers are required to wear seat belts. People traveling with children under the age of two are required to restrain the child in an approved child-passenger restraint device or system. Violation of this law will result in a fine of not more than $25.
- **Emergency Assistance:** Contact the Mississippi Highway Patrol at (800) 843–5352, (601) 987–1212, or dial *47 (*HP) on your mobile phone.
- **Natchez Trace Parkway:** The speed limit on the Natchez Trace Parkway is 50 miles per hour and is strictly enforced. Hauling and commercial trucking are not allowed. Charter buses may receive special permits by contacting the Natchez Trace Parkway headquarters at (662) 680–4025 or (800) 305–7417.
- The *only* gas station on the parkway is located at Jeff Busby Park, milepost 193.1.

Be alert for animals wandering onto the parkway.

COMMERCIAL AIRLINE SERVICE

Delta, American, Northwest, and Southwest Airlines, as well as a number of airlink carriers, provide service into and within Mississippi. Commercial airports are located in Columbus, Greenville, Gulfport, Hattiesburg, Jackson, Meridian, and Tupelo.

Additional gateways in adjacent states include Memphis International Airport (Tennessee), New Orleans/Moisant International Airport (Louisiana), and Mobile/Bates Field Airport (Alabama).

TRAIN SERVICE

Amtrak services the Mississippi cities below. For more information, call (800) 872–7245.

Bay St. Louis	Hattiesburg	Meridian
Biloxi	Hazelhurst	Pascagoula
Brookhaven	Jackson	Picayune
Greenwood	Laurel	Yazoo City
Gulfport	McComb	

RIVERBOAT CRUISES

The **Delta Queen Steamboat Company** of New Orleans runs overnight paddlewheel cruises up and down the Mississippi River. Cruises vary in length and theme, include stops in several Mississippi river towns, and are scheduled year-round. For more information, call (800) 543–1949 or visit www.cruiselines.net/deltaqueen/.

STATE SYMBOLS

- **Flower and Tree:** Magnolia
- **Bird:** Mockingbird
- **Fish:** Largemouth bass
- **Wildflower:** Coreopsis
- **Land mammal:** White-tailed deer
- **Water mammal:** Bottle-nosed dolphin
- **Water fowl:** Wood duck
- **Stone:** Petrified wood
- **Beverage:** Milk
- **Toy:** Teddy bear
- **Motto:** *Virtute et armis* (By valor and arms)
- **Nicknames:** Magnolia State, Hospitality State

CLIMATE

Mississippi experiences a mild, yet noticeable change of seasons. Temperatures are moderate in the spring, fall, and winter; summer highs may be uncomfortable for travelers unaccustomed to the southern heat.

January's average low is forty-five to fifty degrees. Spring and autumn temperatures fall anywhere from the low sixties to mid-eighties. From June through September, temperatures reach the upper nineties with very high humidity.

Accepted dress year-round is casual and comfortable.

TIME ZONE: Central Standard

FOR MORE INFORMATION

For more information on Mississippi attractions and events statewide, contact the Mississippi Division of Tourism Development at (800) 927–6378 or visit the Web site at www.visitmississippi.org.

For information on specific cities and towns, contact the tourism organizations listed on the next page.

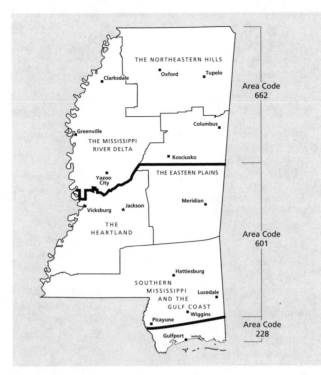

MISSISSIPPI CALLING ZONES

Many cities, towns, and convention and visitors bureaus also maintain Web sites, with more being added every day. In the ever-changing world of the Web, sites come and go and site names change frequently. If the community you're interested in does not have a Web site listed here or if the Web site listed is no longer operational, try entering the name of the community in any search engine.

MISSISSIPPI WELCOME CENTERS

Conveniently located on major interstates and highways entering the state, Mississippi's welcome centers offer free in-state hotel, motel, bed-and-breakfast, and campground reservation service.

Welcome center travel counselors will also provide free maps, brochures, and other travel information. Each welcome center features public telephones, RV waste disposal facilities, and twenty-four-hour restrooms and weather information.

Welcome center hours are 8:00 A.M.–5:00 P.M. seven days a week. Welcome centers are well-marked, with signs posted on major routes into Mississippi.

Aberdeen Visitors Bureau
(662) 369–9440 or (800) 634–3538
www.aberdeenms.org

Batesvile/Panola Partnership
(662) 563–3126 or (888) 872–6652

Hancock County Tourism Bureau
(Bay St. Louis area)
(228) 463–9222 or (800) 446–9048
www.hancockcountyms.org

Booneville Area Chamber/Tourism
(662) 728–4130 or (800) 300–9302
www.boonevillems.com

Rankin First
(Brandon area)
(601) 825–2268
www.rankinchamber.com

Brookhaven/Lincon County Chamber of Commerce
(601) 833–1411 or (800) 613–4667
www.brookhavenchamber.com

Canton Convention and Visitors Bureau
(601) 859–1307 or (800) 844–3369
www.cantontourism.com

Clarksdale-Coahoma County Chamber and Industrial Foundation and Tourism Commission
(662) 627–7337 or (800) 626–3764
www. clarksdale.com

Cleveland Chamber of Commerce/Tourism
(662) 843–2712 or (800) 295–7473
www.visitclevelandms.com

Clinton Chamber of Commerce
(601) 924–5912 or (800) 611–9980
www.clintonchamber.org

Columbus–Lowndes County Convention and Visitors Bureau
(662) 329–1191 or (800) 327–2686
www.columbus-ms.org

Corinth Area Tourism Promotion
(662) 287–8300 or (800) 748–9048
www.corinth.net

Washington County Convention and Visitors Bureau
(Greenville area)
(662) 334–2711 or (800) 467–3582
www.thedelta.org

Greenwood Convention and Visitors Bureau
(662) 453–9197 or (800) 748–9064
www.gcvb.com

Grenada Tourism Commission
(662) 226–2571 or (800) 373–2571
www.grenadamississippi.com

Mississippi Gulf Coast Convention and Visitors Bureau
(Gulf Coast area, Biloxi, Gulfport)
(228) 896–6699 or (888) 467–4853
www.gulfcoast.org

Hattiesburg Convention and Visitors Bureau
(601) 268–3220 or
 (800) 63–TOURS (638–6877)
www.hattiesburg.org

Hazlehurst Chamber of Commerce
(601) 894–3752

DeSoto County Tourism Association
(Hernando and Horn Lake areas)
(662) 429–0505
www.desotocountytourism.com

Holly Springs Chamber of Commerce
(662) 252–2515
www.visithollysprings.org

Indianola Chamber of Commerce
(662) 587–4454 or (877) 816–7581
www.indianolams.org

Tishomingo County Tourism Council
(Iuka area)
(662) 423–0051 or (800) 386–4373
www.tishomingo.org

Metro Jackson Convention
and Visitors Bureau
(Jackson area)
(601) 960–1891 or (800) 354–7695
www.visitjackson.com

Kosciusko-Attala County
Chamber of Commerce
(662) 289–2981
www.kosciuskotourism.com

Jones County Chamber of Commerce
(Laurel area)
(601) 428–0574 or (800) 392–9629
www.edajones.com

Lauderdale County Tourism Bureau
(Meridian area)
(601) 482–8001 or
(888) TOURS–20 (868–7720)
www.visitmeridian.com

Pike County Chamber of Commerce
(McComb area)
(601) 684–2291 or (800) 399–4404
www.pikeinfo.com

Natchez Convention and
Visitors Bureau
(601) 446–6345 or (800) 647–6724
www.cityofnatchez.com

New Albany Tourist Council
(662) 534–4354 or (888) 534–8232
www.ucada-newalbany.com

Ocean Springs Chamber
of Commerce
(228) 875–4424
www.oceanspringschamber.com

Oxford Tourism Council
(662) 234–4680 or (800) 758–9177
www.touroxfordms.com

Jackson County Area Chamber
of Commerce
(Pascagoula)
(228) 762–3391
www.jcchamber.com

Community Development Partnership
(Philadelphia/Neshoba County)
(601) 656–1000
www.neshoba.org

Port Gibson/Claiborne County
Chamber of Commerce
(601) 437–4351
www.claibornecountyport.com

Ridgeland Tourism Commission
(601) 956–1225 or (800) 468–6078
www.visitridgeland.org

Tate County Economic Development
Foundation/Tourism
(Senatobia area)
(662) 562–8715

Starkville Visitors and
Convention Council
(662) 323–3322 or
(800) 649–TOUR (649–8687)
www.starkville.org

Tunica Convention and
Visitors Bureau
(662) 363–3800 or
(888) 4–TUNICA (488–6422)
www.tunicamiss.org

Tupelo Convention and
Visitors Bureau
(662) 841–6521 or (800) 533–0611
www.tupelo.net

Vicksburg Convention and
Visitors Bureau
(601) 636–9421 or (800) 221–3536
www.vicksburgcvb.org

Clay County Economic Development
Corporation
(West Point)
(662) 494–5121
www.wpnet.org

Yazoo County Convention
and Visitors Bureau
(662) 746–1815 or (800) 381–0662
www.yazoo.org

STATE PARKS

Mississippi's twenty-eight state parks are ideal for a weekend getaway or an extended outdoor adventure. Located throughout the state, each park offers its own amenities, from nature trails to float trips, fishin' holes to golf courses. The parks also feature a variety of accommodations, including primitive and developed campsites, rustic cabin rentals, and full-service hotels.

For more information on Mississippi's state parks, call (800) GO–PARKS or visit www.mdwfp.com/parks.asp.

GOLF

Mississippi's diversity of courses and mild year-round climate make the state a favorite among golfers. Opportunities range from simple nine-hole courses to spectacular resort courses created by Jack Nicklaus, Arnold Palmer, Davis Love III, Jerry Pate, and other renowned designers.

Mississippi has a golf course to meet every level of challenge—and every budget. For a complete list and detailed descriptions of golf courses in Mississippi, contact the Mississippi Division of Tourism at (800) 927–6378 or www.visitmississippi.org.

HUNTING AND FISHING

Mississippi is a sportsman's dream. Hunters from around the nation come to the state in pursuit of turkey, quail, dove, waterfowl, and Mississippi's most popular game animal, the prolific white-tailed deer. Fishing enthusiasts find lakes and streams brimming with bass, bluegill, crappie, and catfish, or can head to the Gulf Coast for the deep-sea challenge posed by mackerel, cobia, sea trout, and red snapper.

For a comprehensive list of hunting and fishing lodges, outfitters and guides, and detailed information on hunting seasons, license fees, and requirements, contact the Mississippi Department of Wildlife, Fisheries and Parks at (601) 432–2400 or (800) 546–4868. You'll find more information on hunting and fishing in the *Mississippi Hunting and Fishing Guide* and *Mississippi Outfitters Guide,* two free publications offered by the Mississippi Division of Tourism. To request your copies, call (800) 927–6378. For more information, a list of Mississippi outfitters, and links to outfitters' Web sites, visit www.outfitters.org.

The Northeastern Hills

The Northeastern Hill country stretches from the edge of the Mississippi Delta to the foothills of the Appalachian Mountains. Traveling west to east, the land gradually becomes more and more hilly, more and more remote, until civilization becomes nothing more than a distant memory. Rich in history, heritage, and scenic beauty, this is the land that inspired both the complex genius of William Faulkner and the raw emotion that permeates the music of Elvis Presley.

This region includes portions of both Interstate 55 and the Natchez Trace Parkway. Both routes take visitors on a north-to-south journey through the area, but the adventures encountered along each path couldn't be more different. From the modern cities that line I–55 to time-capsule towns along the Tennessee and Tombigbee Rivers, the Northeastern Hills offer a new and different adventure just over the next crest.

The I–55 Corridor

The towns and cities that line I–55 share the fast-paced, modern personality of Memphis, Tennessee, often referred to as "the largest city in north Mississippi." Even the smaller cities along I–55 boast a sophistication that comes from living just

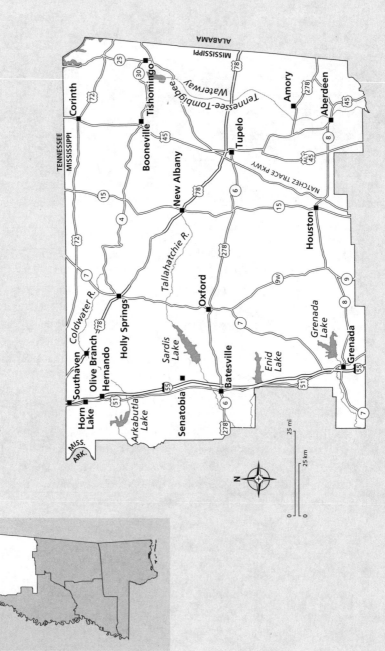

barely off a very well-beaten path. Of course, whizzing past the exits at 70 miles per hour is not the best way to soak up the local ambience. Take a short detour from the impersonal asphalt, and you'll find a wealth of unsung treasures mere minutes from the fast lane.

Begin by following I–55 South out of Memphis into **DeSoto County,** named for Hernando de Soto, the Spanish conquistador who became Mississippi's first "tourist" in 1541 and discovered the mighty river for which the state is named. As you travel DeSoto County, you'll spot frequent markers along a route dubbed the **Hernando de Soto Memorial Trail.** As de Soto's exact path has long been lost to history, this scenic route is designed to showcase the area's attractions and doesn't attempt to follow in the famous explorer's footsteps.

Pick up the de Soto Trail just south of Memphis near the communities of **Horn Lake** and **Walls.** Most historians believe it was somewhere near the sites of these towns that Hernando de Soto first gazed upon the Mississippi River. Just west of the intersection of Goodman Road and Mississippi Highway 301, you'll spot a small flower shop marked by a sign inviting you to SHOP IN ELVIS' HONEYMOON COTTAGE. Now home to **The Flower Patch,** this unassuming structure was indeed the spot where Elvis Presley brought his young bride Priscilla for their 1967 honeymoon. The cottage was once a part of Elvis's sprawling Circle G Ranch. Elvis and Priscilla went horseback riding on the property, and the King of Rock 'n' Roll was often spotted riding his motorcycle up and down Goodman Road.

For years the honeymoon cottage was a private residence; fans had to be content to gawk and snap photos from the street. Since The Flower Patch

MARLO'S FAVORITE ATTRACTIONS IN THE NORTHEASTERN HILLS

Brussel's Bonsai Nursery,
Olive Branch

The Square,
Oxford

The Grove at Ole Miss on Football Saturdays,
Oxford

The University of Mississippi,
Oxford (I confess to some alumnus bias here)

Antebellum Home Tours,
Holly Springs and Aberdeen

Rabid Elvis Fans,
Tupelo to Memphis

Memphis, Tennessee
(my hometown and "the biggest city in north Mississippi")

The Writing on the Wall at Taylor Grocery,
Taylor

moved in and opened the structure to the public, the Elvis faithful have come in droves to walk the same floors once trod by the King. According to shop owner Debbie Henson, fans have offered to purchase pieces of the building, and have even cut souvenir squares from the cottage's red carpet. Henson has set up a small display area of Elvis-related newspaper clippings and photos, but for most fans, the mere fact that Elvis once owned the property is reason enough to visit. Call (662) 781–2344 for more information, or to order a bouquet in honor of the King.

Just east of Horn Lake on Mississippi Highway 302, the bustling community of **Olive Branch** is one the fastest-growing cities in the United States. In the 1990s there was talk of bulldozing Olive Branch's old downtown area. Saved from demolition by visionary developer Bill Cruthirds, the old downtown was instead renovated and reopened as **Olive Branch Old Towne.** Today, Old Towne is a quaint area of more than twenty antiques and gift shops surrounding the open-air Pigeon Roost Plaza. Visitors can easily spend an afternoon browsing among the china, furniture, clothing, home accessories, and other unique merchandise in Old Towne's boutiques. During spring, fall, and the Christmas season, Pigeon Roost Plaza hosts twilight concerts showcasing bluegrass performances, gospel concerts, barbershop quartets, and local talent.

Gulliver would feel right at home at **Brussel's Bonsai Nursery.** Brussel's showcases the oriental art form of "bonsai," the cultivation of miniature trees. Founded by Brussel Martin in 1972, the nursery is the largest importer and grower of fine bonsai in the United States. Several members of Brussel's staff have studied this ancient art form under Japanese masters and are happy to provide visitors a glimpse into the painstaking world of bonsai. The nursery offers hundreds of specimens, accessories, and tools for sale, and features elaborate display gardens filled with tiny trees decades—and sometimes more than a century—old. You'll find Brussel's at 8365 Center Hill Road, just east of Olive Branch off Goodman Road (Highway 302). For more information or a mail-order catalog, call (800) 582–2593 or visit www.brusselsbonsai.com.

North Mississippi is best known for Elvis Presley lore, but the area is also home to another rock-and-roll legend. The **Jerry Lee Lewis Ranch**—marked by distinctive security gates emblazoned with pianos and the words "The Killer"—is just south of Horn Lake in Nesbit. As famous for his multiple marriages and tumultuous personal life as for hit songs like "Great Balls of Fire," Lewis was the subject of a feature film starring Dennis Quaid. A tour of the ranch includes a look at Jerry Lee's pianos, walls of gold records, fan memorabilia, and the "Killer's Kar Kollection," as well as Lewis's piano-shaped swimming pool, complete with black and white "keys."

Mississippi's Playing Your Song

Mention Mississippi music, and most people think of the blues or Elvis Presley. But the songs don't stop there. Whether you tune in to a country, pop, rhythm and blues, or classical station, you're virtually guaranteed to hear a voice from Mississippi.

Mississippians who've made their voices heard include Steve Azar, Brandy, Jimmy Buffet, Bo Diddley, Pete Fountain, Mickey Gilley, W. C. Handy, Faith Hill, Robert Johnson, B. B. King, Elvis Presley, Leontyne Price, Charlie Pride, LeAnn Rimes, Jimmie Rodgers, Fingers Taylor, Son Thomas, Paul Thorn, Ike Turner, Conway Twitty, Muddy Waters, Tammy Wynette, and the members of the group 3 Doors Down.

Another famous Mississippian doesn't sing himself, but came up with a ground-breaking idea that forever changed the world of music. He's Bob Pittman, the founder of MTV.

The ranch is open for tours Monday–Friday 10:00 A.M.–4:00 P.M. and is closed on major holidays. Admission is $15.00 for adults and $7.00 for children. The Jerry Lee Lewis Ranch is located at 1595 Malone Road. From I–55, take exit 284 (Pleasant Hill Road). Head east to Malone Road and turn right. Three houses down on the right, the Ranch is easily recognized by its graffiti-plastered fence, which bears hundreds of messages from The Killer's loyal fans. For more information, call (662) 429–1290.

Next, head south of Nesbit and follow the signs to downtown Hernando, where the focal point is the ***DeSoto County Courthouse.*** Inside, the story of Hernando de Soto, from his voyage to America through his death and burial in the Mississippi River, is depicted in sweeping oil murals hanging in the court-house gallery. Painted on canvas by American muralist Alonzo Newton Wells, the murals were completed in 1902 and hung for decades in the old Gayoso Hotel in downtown Memphis. Donated to DeSoto County and installed in the court-house in 1953, they carry an estimated value of $700,000. Visitors are invited to view the paintings Monday through Friday during normal business hours.

The courthouse was once a hot spot for "quickie" marriages, earning quaint little Hernando the nickname "Las Vegas of the Mid South." Marriage laws were once much more relaxed in Mississippi, and Hernando became a magnet for lovebirds from Memphis who just couldn't stand the three-day wait-ing period required in Tennessee. In more recent years the courthouse served as the setting for real-life dramas for lawyer-turned-blockbuster novelist John Grisham. Before his phenomenally successful legal thrillers allowed him to quit his day job, Grisham kept law offices in nearby Southaven and sometimes met with clients and legal associates in the marbled corridors of the courthouse.

Learn more about Grisham, Jerry Lee Lewis, Elvis, and Hernando de Soto's ties to the area during a visit to the *Historic DeSoto Museum.* The museum brings the colorful histories of all of DeSoto County's towns together in one facility. Along with exhibits on notable residents and events, the museum features an antebellum log cabin used as a field hospital during the Civil War. The Historic DeSoto Museum is located at 111 East Commerce Street. For more information, call (662) 429–8852.

Continue your exploration of the past with a visit to one of DeSoto County's many antiques shops. More than a dozen shops are scattered around Southaven, Olive Branch, Nesbit, and Hernando, offering treasure hunters a wide selection of furniture, glass, collectibles, and accessories. For a complete list of antiques shops, contact the DeSoto County Tourism Association, (662) 429–0505. A favorite stop for shoppers and art lovers is *Joseph Eckles Stoneware* (2650 Scott Road, Hernando; 662–429–1621), where the handmade pottery includes dinnerware, vases, bird feeders, and decorative pieces.

Wrap up your visit with a ride along Delta View Road, 10 miles northwest of Hernando. The unspoiled beauty that Hernando de Soto first gazed upon centuries ago is found again in a panoramic view of the Mississippi River Delta, the South's richest farmland. The mood and mystery of the delta come together on a steep bluff where the land drops off sharply, then stretches flat and fertile as far as the eye can see.

Overnight visitors to DeSoto County should plan a stay at Nesbit's *Bonne Terre Country Inn and Cafe,* a charming bed-and-breakfast inn situated on one hundred scenic, secluded acres just twenty-five minutes from Memphis. *Southern Living* magazine describes Bonne Terre as, "not just a place you stay for the night . . . It's a destination, a place to go and stay and savor." After a visit there, you're sure to agree. Each of the fifteen rooms at Bonne Terre (French for "good earth") features a balcony or patio overlooking the five-acre lake, swimming pool, pecan tree grove, or wildflower garden. Enchanting individual decor, French and English antiques, in-room fireplaces, whirlpool tubs, and fresh flowers contribute to each room's welcoming ambience. Favorite pastimes at Bonne Terre include fishing in three lakes, strolling in the herb and flower gardens, picnicking in the pecan grove, or simply relaxing poolside. Weekday rates begin at $165.

The inn's elegant *Bonne Terre Cafe* offers sumptuous dishes with a European flair. Creative beef, seafood, and poultry entrees are complemented by organically grown vegetables and fresh herbs from the inn's own garden. Tempting appetizers, sinful desserts, and an excellent wine list are sure to please even the most discriminating palate. A double-sided fireplace, open-style European kitchen, and panoramic view of the lake and woods enhance the dining experience. Bonne Terre Cafe is open for lunch on Thursdays and for dinner Monday–Saturday, and hosts a Sunday jazz brunch featuring live entertainment the first Sunday of every month. Prix fixe dinner packages can include round-trip limousine service. For reservations (required) at the Bonne Terre Cafe, call (662) 781–5100. For room reservations and rates at the Bonne Terre Country Inn, call (662) 781–5100 or visit www.bonneterre.com.

Comfortable accommodations are also available at several fine bed-and-breakfast inns in Hernando. A stay at the contemporary **Sassafras Inn** (785 Highway 51, 662–429–5864 or 800–882–1897, www.memphis.to) includes use of an indoor pool and sauna, home theater and game room, and all the sassafras tea you can drink. Billed as "the prettiest house in DeSoto County," **Dockery House** (3831 Robertson Gin Road, 662–449–5427, www.dockery house.com) offers one guest room and a loft in an authentically restored 125-year-old Victorian farmhouse. **Magnolia Grove Bed and Breakfast** (140 East Commerce Street, 662–429–2626 or 866–404–2626, www.magnoliagrove.com) features three guest rooms in an elegant turn-of-the-twentieth-century southern mansion and serves dinner by candlelight in the mansion dining room.

For bed-and-breakfast with a rustic touch, visit **Brigadoon Farms,** a sprawling country retreat in Olive Branch. Proprietor Jeanette Martin began developing this rural refuge as a form of grief therapy following the death of her husband. Today, the Brigadoon Farms retreat and conference center encompasses tranquil nature trails, picturesque lakes ideal for fishing and pedal boating, and a relaxing hot tub and swimming pool. Accommodations are available in the farm's Country Goose Inn, a log lodge overlooking the lake; the Honeymoon Cottage, a modern house overlooking the swimming pool; and the Bunk House, a spacious facility ideal for youth or other groups. Brigadoon Farms is located at 350 Highway 305. For information and rates, call (662) 895–3098 or (877) 895–3098, or visit www.brigadoon farms.com.

Continue south on I–55 to the DeSoto/ Tate County border, where signs point the way to **Arkabutla Lake.** Some two million outdoor enthusiasts visit Arkabutla each year, drawn to the lake for fishing, swimming, and water-skiing, and to its wooded shores for camping, hiking, and hunting.

trivia

Arkabutla native James Earl Jones is famous for his resonating voice. Jones can be heard daily reminding news junkies, "This is CNN," but he's best known as the voice of the dreaded Darth Vader in the *Star Wars* trilogy.

The 12,700-acre lake is the windiest lake south of Chicago, making Arkabutla a favorite for sailing and wind-surfing. A strong wildlife management program has also made Arkabutla a popular area for

MARLO'S FAVORITE ANNUAL EVENTS IN THE NORTHEASTERN HILLS

ABERDEEN

Spring Pilgrimage,
April,
(662) 369–9440 or (800) 634–3538

CALHOUN CITY

Biblical City,
December,
(662) 637–2257

CORINTH

Slugburger Festival,
July,
(662) 287–1550

GRENADA

Grenada Lake's "Thunder on Water"
Safeboating Festival,
June,
(800) 373–2571,
www.thunderonwater.com

HOLLY SPRINGS

Spring Pilgrimage,
April,
(662) 252–2943

OXFORD

Double Decker Arts Festival,
April,
(800) 758–9177
www.doubledeckerfestival.com

Football Season at Ole Miss,
September–November,
(662) 915–7554

RIPLEY

First Monday Trade Day,
Weekend prior to the first Monday of
each month,
(662) 837–4051

TUPELO

Elvis Presley Festival,
June,
(662) 841–6598 or (888) 273–7798,
www.tupeloelvisfestival.com

WATER VALLEY

Water Valley Watermelon Carnival,
August,
(662) 473–1122

wildlife watching. Pack your binoculars and keep an eye out for wood ducks, turkeys, quail, rabbits, and white-tailed deer.

Make your next stop on I–55 **Senatobia** and the **Front Street shopping area,** a historic district lined with one-of-a-kind, locally owned boutiques. For unusual home accessories and gifts, try **The Loft, Traditions, Gifts and Interiors,** or **Ultimate Expressions.**

If your garden is in need of a focal point, consider a wooden swing, glider, or park bench handmade by local, ninety-plus-year-old craftsman **Wesley Woolfolk.** Visit Woolfolk's front-yard "gallery" at 207 North Park Street, or give the craftsman a call at (662) 562–7371.

For a bona fide shopping extravaganza, plan a visit to nearby **Coldwater** on the first full weekend of June, August, or October. **Coldwater Trade Days,** the largest flea market in a seven-county area, cranks up three times a year with more than 300 booths and 30,000 rabid shoppers.

After a full day of bargain hunting, consider an overnight stay at one of the area's bed-and-breakfast inns. Nestled on a quiet, shady street in downtown Senatobia, **Spahn House** offers modern accommodations in a restored 1904 town house. Rates begin at $75. Call (662) 562–9853 or (800) 400–9853, or visit Spahn House on-line at www.SpahnHouse.com. Located in Coldwater 2 miles off I–55, **Wynnewood Bed and Breakfast** features wooded walking trails, cane-pole fishing in a fully stocked catfish pond, a swimming pool, and an adult-size tree house surrounded by native birds and wildlife. Accommodations are in a two-room cottage or secluded, rustic cabin. Call (662) 622–5563 or visit www.wynnewoodbedbreakfast.com.

Continuing down I–55 South, make sure your arrival in **Como** coincides with dinner time. This tiny town's biggest claim to fame is the **Como Steakhouse,** a beef-lover's delight housed in the old town post office on Main Street. You can watch as the cook prepares your juicy steak over an open grill in the dining room, or you can cook your own and take $1.00 off the tab, which is usually less than $20.00. The Como Steakhouse fires up the grill Tuesday–Saturday 5:00–10:30 P.M.

From Como it's just 5 miles south to **Sardis,** another quiet little town where "action" is for the most part limited to skiing and swimming at **Sardis Lake.** There is the **Heflin House Museum,** constructed in 1858 and now operated as a historical museum by the Heflin House Heritage Association. The house is open for tours the third Sunday of every month 1:00–4:00 P.M., and hosts an annual Christmas tea the first Sunday of December. Rental cabins and camping are available at **John W. Kyle State Park** overlooking Sardis Lake. Call (662) 487–1345.

Success Can't Spoil a Bluesman

Even after his international success as a blues musician and recording star, "Mississippi" Fred McDowell continued to work pumping gas at a Como, Mississippi, Stuckey's store. When his agent asked him why, McDowell replied, "All my friends are here, so you know I'm going to be here."

Because he never got around to installing a telephone in his home, McDowell also used the Stuckey's as a makeshift office. Other employees could be heard calling out to the pumps, "Hey, Fred! We got Paris, France, on the phone for you!"

If you're traveling in the fall, you may want to continue along I–55 South as far as **Grenada** for the **National Fox Hunt Chase and Futurity.** Held the last weekend of October through the first weekend of November, this annual adventure brings as many as 500 hunters, complete with horses and more than 1,000 hounds, to Graysport Landing on Grenada Lake. Tally ho!

A **Historic Grenada Walking and Driving Tour Guide** is available from the Grenada Tourism Commission. Highlights include the **Confederate Cemetery,** where one hundred eighty unknown soldiers are buried; the **Yellow Fever Cemetery,** created by a dreadful 1878 epidemic that claimed eighty percent of the city's population; and **Golliday House,** an antebellum home that briefly served as headquarters for Confederate President Jefferson Davis during the Civil War and was the scene of a still-unsolved murder in the 1930s.

Another of Grenada's antebellum landmarks is the site of a modern attraction. The **First Street Gallery** (223 First Street, 662–227–9349) displays paintings, sculpture, pottery, and other fine and folk art, some available for purchase. The gallery is housed in the restored Grenada Bank building originally constructed in the 1840s.

'Til Death Do Us Part

The city now known as Grenada was established in 1836 by the union of the towns of Pittsburgh and Tullahoma. While the two communities were actually joined in a marriage ceremony—complete with an officiating minister—it was not a case of love at first sight.

Originally settled in the early 1830s, the towns were separated only by a surveyor's line, known today as Line Street. Neither town would concede one inch to the other. Each operated its own ferry across the Yalobusha River, a mere mile apart. When Pittsburgh established the area's first newspaper, Tullahoma enticed the cash-strapped editor to move it to their city by paying off his mortgage. Pittsburgh, however, still claimed the area's only post office—until, that is, the residents of Tullahoma stole it, actually moving the building and its contents across the city line in the dark of night.

Eventually both sides wearied of the rivalry, and in 1836, agreed to consolidate. The union would take the form of a wedding ceremony, followed by a community barbecue.

The ceremony was performed on July 4, 1836, but before the barbecue got cold, arguments broke out over which name the new town would be known by. A wise wedding guest suggested starting over with a new name. Grenada was chosen in honor of Granada, Spain, the citizens shared a reconciliatory toast, and the town has enjoyed an atmosphere of matrimonial bliss ever since.

No trip to Grenada is complete without a stop at the **Grenada Lake Visitors Center,** which features a large observation deck overlooking the 38,000-acre reservoir, the largest lake in Mississippi. A twenty-minute multimedia presentation chronicles the construction of the Grenada Dam, and exhibits describe local history and wildlife. Fishermen and -women will want to make a stop at the **Pro Lures and Minnetonka Moccasins Outlet** (17125 Highway 8 West) before hitting the lake in search of crappie, bass, catfish, or bream.

Big cat fanciers—make that fanciers of *big cats*—should plan a side trip to **Cougar Haven.** Owner David Mallory has turned the rural property surrounding his home into a sanctuary for more than twenty lions, tigers, and cougars, and one rare lion/tiger mix known as a liger. Mallory rescues the cats from owners who have neglected or abused them, or in some cases, from well-intentioned owners who simply weren't prepared for the demands of caring for a large, exotic "pet."

"I support people's right to own big cats, but only if they're willing to take care of them," Mallory explains.

Taking care of Cougar Haven's twenty-plus residents is no simple matter. The cats consume some fifteen cases of chicken per week. Add a modest stipend for their caretaker, and the basic bill comes to a whopping $400 per week, not including the cost of the cats' enclosed shelters or their veterinary care. But for Mallory, caring for the cats is not a dollars-and-cents proposition, but a labor of love.

"I try to meet the cats' emotional needs as well as their physical needs," he explains. "Most of the animals who come here have been abused. I want to give them the best quality of life possible."

Mallory works as a full-time logging contractor; Cougar Haven operates on donations from sanctuary visitors and animal lovers. A contribution of as little as $1.00 per person buys a look at the magnificent cats and an informative talk with Mallory, who's happy to spend as much time as you'd like telling you about the animals that have become his passion.

You'll find Cougar Haven just outside Grenada, at 39 Dobbs Road in the **Gore Springs** community. Mallory gives tours by appointment, which he's usually happy to schedule on the spur of the moment. Call (662) 226–0746 to set up a visit and get directions to Cougar Haven. Here, kitty kitty kitty . . .

Tiny Gore Springs is also the cat's meow for antiques buffs. The hamlet's **Country Road Antiques** is five buildings and 20,000 square feet of antique furniture, glassware, jewelry, and bric-a-brac. Owners Peggy and Earl Gillon promise a warm welcome, "whether you're buying, browsing, or just lost." And if all that antiquing wears you out, you're welcome to enjoy a cold co' cola, relax in the old-fashioned porch swing, and discover for yourself why the

Country Road Antiques motto is, "Antique furniture, cold drinks, comfortable chairs, and ails listened to."

To get to Country Road Antiques from Grenada, follow Highway 8 East approximately 16 miles, then turn left onto Dividing Ridge Road. Follow Dividing Ridge Road right through the fork 1.7 miles from Highway 8. Signs are posted along the way. Country Road Antiques is open 8:00 A.M.–5:00 P.M. Monday–Saturday.

Overnight visitors to Grenada should indulge in a stay at **The Cottage Inn,** a delightful bed-and-breakfast owned and operated by New Orleans-trained chef Paul Verneuille and his lovely wife, Rosa. Housed in a beautifully restored, century-old Victorian cottage, the inn offers luxurious accommodations and a decadent southern breakfast prepared by Chef Paul. Optional indulgences include a four-course surf 'n' turf dinner, aromatherapy treatments, hand and foot massages, and relaxing soaks in the hot tub. Rates begin at $85. The Cottage Inn is nestled in the heart of the Grenada historic district at 329 Margin Street. Call (662) 417–4823 or visit www.thecottageinn.net.

From Grenada, head back north on I–55 a short distance until you reach Highway 7, then travel northeast toward the Central Crests.

The Central Crests

The gently rolling hills to the east of the interstate seem far removed from the hustle and bustle of urban life. This is Faulkner country, a timeless realm of Civil War battlefields, well-tended historic homes, and picturesque town squares. Most of the more than 500 Civil War battles waged on Mississippi soil were fought in this area, making the few antebellum towns that survived the Union torch all the more impressive. With a rich legacy of history, heritage, and literature, this peaceful area of gently rolling hills is widely regarded as a center for American southern culture.

That said, who could be more of a cultural icon than Elvis Presley? For serious Elvis fans, **Mike McGregor's Leather and Jewelry Shop** is a must-see. Owner Mike McGregor was once the leather craftsman for the King. Visitors to his shop can purchase replicas of Elvis's famous belts and jewelry (ostentatious would be an understatement) and hear stories from the King's glory days. You'll find the shop on Highway 7 just past **Water Valley.**

The dog days of August may not seem like the best time to visit Mississippi—unless you happen to be visiting Water Valley during the annual **Watermelon Carnival.** The juicy festivities here date back to the early 1930s. When the town's economy suffered from a dramatic drop in cotton prices, local farmers chose watermelons as their new cash crop. The chamber of commerce organized a carnival to introduce the world to Water Valley watermelons, and a tradition was born. Today the three-day "melonbration" includes a music festival, golf tournament, motorcycle parade, arts and crafts show, the crowning of the Watermelon Queen, and, of course, all the chilled, juicy watermelon you can slurp up. For this year's dates, call (662) 473–1122.

Railroad buffs and hobos at heart should plan a stop at the **Water Valley Casey Jones Railroad Museum,** a heartfelt tribute to the legendary engineer and folk hero killed in the crash of engine number 382. Housed in the restored Water Valley Depot, the museum showcases the extensive railroad memorabilia and photography collection of the late Bruce Gurner of Water Valley, a retired railroader and schoolteacher who spent almost fifty years researching the legend of Casey Jones and the history of the Mississippi Division of the Illinois Central Railroad. Gurner began collecting Casey Jones memorabilia in 1955 and continued until his death in 2002. In his later years, Gurner spoke of the day when he could "ask Casey in person why he didn't jump." The Water Valley Casey Jones Railroad Museum is open Thursday, Friday, and Saturday 2:00–4:00 P.M. and by appointment. Climb aboard at 105 Railroad Avenue. Call (662) 473–3828 or visit www.watervalley.net/users/caseyjones/home.htm.

Continue on Highway 7 North from Water Valley into **Oxford,** a postcard-pretty college town and literary center listed in the books *The 100 Best Small Towns in America* and *The 100 Best Small Art Towns in America* and called a "thriving New South arts mecca" by *USA Today* and "the best place in the South to retire" by *Money* magazine. Oxford's folksy town square, graceful antebellum homes, tree-shaded boulevards, and quintessential southern college campus have been immortalized in more pages than the city has residents.

Begin a literary tour of Oxford with a trip down Highway 6 West and a look at the big yellow Victorian on the left. It's the part-time **home of John Grisham,** former Mississippi state legislator and best-selling author of *The Firm, The Client, A Time to Kill, The Chamber, The Testament, The Brethren, A Painted House, The Summons, The King of Torts,* and other legal thrillers. The estate includes a full-size baseball diamond upon which Grisham once coached a local Little League team.

Of course, Oxford's dust jackets don't stop with Grisham. Willie Morris, Barry Hannah, and Larry Brown all felt their

trivia

Mississippians are fond of saying, "We may not be able to read, but we sure can write." Works by Mississippians Margaret Walker Alexander, Nevada Barr, Ellen Douglas, William Faulkner, Shelby Foote, John Grisham, Carolyn Haines, Thomas Harris, Beth Henley, Greg Iles, Willie Morris, Eudora Welty, Tennessee Williams, and Charles Wilson would certainly seem to justify that claim.

genius stirred by Oxford's landmarks and landscapes, but it was Nobel Prize–winner William Faulkner who first put Oxford on the literary map.

Even if you haven't thought of Faulkner since high school English class, a trip to Oxford will have you searching for your old paperbacks. Faulkner modeled the mythical Yoknapatawpha County, the setting for his tales of glory and decadence in the South, after Oxford and Lafayette County. As a child, Faulkner lived in a small cottage at the corner of South Eleventh and Buchanan Streets, but **Rowan Oak,** Faulkner's antebellum home at the bend of Old Taylor Road, is the place where his genius came to life. The house remains much as Faulkner left it, with his black manual typewriter on display in the study and the outline of his Pulitzer Prize–winning novel, *A Fable,* scrawled on the wall. Rowan Oak is open for tours, with days and hours varying by season and sometimes tied to local events. Call (662) 234–3284 or (662) 915–7073 for visitor hours. Even when the house isn't open, the tree-shaded grounds and adjacent Bailey's Woods are the perfect place to enjoy a quiet afternoon stroll.

During his lifetime, Faulkner was regarded as a bit of a character around town. He served briefly as the University of Mississippi's postmaster and was reportedly the worst postmaster in the school's history. Faulkner himself generally agreed with this assessment, explaining that he "didn't care to be at the beck and call of any fool who could afford a postage stamp." Rowan Oak is owned by the University of Mississippi, where Faulkner was briefly enrolled as a lackluster student. The university's **J.D. Williams Library** displays Faulkner's 1949 Nobel Prize, first edition prints of his books, and early handwritten manuscripts. The inscription on the library's wall, "I decline to accept the end of man. I believe that man will not merely endure, he will prevail," was pulled from Faulkner's Nobel Prize acceptance speech. Faulkner is buried in nearby **St. Peter's Cemetery** at the corner of Jefferson Avenue and North Sixteenth Street. Faithful readers and aspiring writers leave dog-eared paperbacks—and the occasional bottle of bourbon—on the author's grave.

Oxford's rich literary heritage is showcased in two annual conferences, the **Faulkner and Yoknapatawpha Conference** and the **Oxford Conference for the Book.** Both events attract aspiring writers and renowned authors from around the world; past speakers have included John Grisham and Stephen King. Call the Institute for Continuing Studies at (662) 915–7282 or e-mail cstud ies@olemiss.edu for conference speakers and dates.

Much of the activity in Oxford is focused on the town square (known simply as **"The Square"**), where the focal point is the imposing **Lafayette County Courthouse,** which played a starring role in Faulkner's *The Sound and the Fury.* Faulkner fans will also want to visit **City Hall,** where a bronze statue of the literary genius gazes out over the courtyard.

The Square is also home to a number of restaurants and specialty and antiques shops. Excellent dining choices located on or near The Square include *City Grocery* (152 Courthouse Square), the *Ajax Diner* (118 Courthouse Square), the *Henry Cafe and Jubilee Lounge* (1006 Jackson Avenue East), and *Proud Larry's* (211 South Lamar Boulevard), which is also the best place in Oxford for live music.

A stroll around The Square isn't complete without a visit to *Square Books* (160 Courthouse Square), a favorite hangout of Oxford's many famous and aspiring writers and widely regarded as one of the South's premier bookstores. Square Books packs the calendar with signings and readings from best-selling and soon-to-be-best-selling authors year-round. Located five doors down from the main store, *Off Square Books* is a sister store featuring thousands of reduced price and remaindered titles, as well as rare, out-of-print, and collectible books.

Fall and spring Thursday evenings 5:30–6:30 P.M., Off Square Books hosts a standing-room-only crowd for the live broadcast of *Thacker Mountain Radio* (www.thackermountain.com), a quirky program that showcases two of Oxford's greatest treasures: literature and music. Described as "Prairie Home Companion" meets the South, Thacker Mountain Radio features authors reading from their latest works and live music performed by local and national talent. Tickets aren't required; you're welcome to walk in and choose a folding chair. If you can't stop by for the show, tune in locally to WOXD 95.5 FM for a distinctive radio program like no other in the country.

For reading recommendations and a calendar of events at Square Books, Off Square Books, and Thacker Mountain Radio, visit www.squarebooks.com.

Even for non-bibliophiles, shopping opportunities abound on The Square. The *Southside Gallery* (150 Courthouse Square) brings the international art scene to Oxford with exhibits by noted painters, photographers, and folk artists. African-American art and pottery are among the offerings at *S&J Art Gallery and Collectibles* (1010 Jackson Avenue East). *Mississippi Madness on the Square* (141 Courthouse Square) offers gourmet foods and gift baskets, and *University Sporting Goods Company* (105 Courthouse Square) is the place to shop for Ole Miss apparel. You'll also want to browse in the *J. E. Neilson Company Department Store* (119 Courthouse Square), the oldest continuously operating department store in the South.

Anywhere you go in Oxford, you're bound to run into a student or two. The city fathers chose the name "Oxford" in 1837 in hopes of improving their chances of landing Mississippi's first public university. Their efforts were successful; the *University of Mississippi,* known affectionately as "Ole Miss," was founded in Oxford in 1848.

A (Religious) Conversion on the 10-Yard Line

It's been said that in the South, football is a religion, and Saturday is the day of worship. Northeastern and mid-Atlantic cities can have their basketball; in the South, college football reigns supreme.

Of course, casual spectators may question whether Heaven really cares about the outcome of a football game. For these naysayers, devout Mississippians have but one reply—November 19, 1983.

On that fateful day, the University of Mississippi Rebels and the Mississippi State University Bulldogs met for the annual intrastate bloodletting known as the Egg Bowl. State dominated the first half, but Ole Miss rallied in the second, battling to a precarious 24 to 23 lead in the fourth quarter. Not to be denied, the Bulldogs drove to the Rebel 10-yard line, and with seconds remaining, lined up to kick the game-winning field goal.

The kick was up . . . it had the distance . . . it split the uprights . . . and then, miraculously, a strong gust of wind *blew the winning kick back outside the goal posts.*

The ball fell harmlessly back to earth. MSU kicker Artie Cosby stared in disbelief. The Ole Miss team began a wild celebration that lasted into the night. Fans on both sides fell to their knees.

Headlines the next day screamed "The Immaculate Deflection!" and the 1983 Egg Bowl—and its supernaturally influenced kick—made history and highlight reels for years to come.

Perhaps the University's most famous feature is the ten-acre, parklike retreat known simply as ***The Grove.*** Normally a peaceful spot for strolling, counting tulips, or relaxing in the shade, The Grove is packed with enthusiastic tailgaters on ***Southeastern Conference football*** weekends, most of whom put out their best silver and finest table linens—along with a brass candelabra or two—in honor of the pregame festivities. For really *big* games and Homecoming, waiters, bartenders, and big-screen TVs are the norm. If you attend a football game at Ole Miss, don't come in blue jeans. Football is serious business in Oxford, with an unwritten student dress code that demands blue blazers and ties for gentlemen and skirts and high heels for ladies. Attire has relaxed a little since the 1950s and 1960s, when women often sported full-length furs for ninety-degree September kickoffs.

The University has closed its doors only once—when the entire male faculty and student body marched away to fight in the Civil War. The wounded from the fierce battles of Corinth and Shiloh were treated in the university's buildings, and legend has it that spiteful Union troops rode their horses through the university's most hallowed halls. A handful of the university's original buildings survived the 1864 torching of Oxford, including the *Lyceum,* a white-columned Greek Revival structure that houses the administrative offices and serves as the campus focal point and university logo. Also of interest is 1889 *Ventress Hall,* where stained-glass windows honor the University Greys, a company of faculty and students who were wiped out in the Battle of Gettysburg.

The *Barnard Observatory* was built to house a magnificent telescope ordered with great excitement by the university science department but never delivered due to the outbreak of the war. Today, the observatory houses the *Center for the Study of Southern Culture,* a teaching and research center dedicated to the study of the South. Researchers at the center produced the highly acclaimed *Encyclopedia of Southern Culture,* an eight-and-a-half-pound tribute to everything Southern. Bone up on your southern culture with a visit to the Center's Web site at www.olemiss.edu/depts/south/.

The *University of Mississippi Blues Archive* is the only research facility in the country dedicated to the study of the blues. The archive includes the personal collection of blues legend and Mississippi native B. B. King. Call (662) 915–7753 for an appointment to view the artifacts and photographs or listen to any of the more than 50,000 soulful recordings.

University Museums usually promotes its Greek and Roman antiquities, but the average person would probably tell you the *real* attraction there is the *Amazing, Ingenious, and Grotesque Display.* Housed in its own "cabinet of curiosity," this Ripleyesque collection includes a wreath made entirely of human hair, an unidentified "critter" fashioned into a purse, and a pair of fleas dressed as a bride and groom posing for wedding photos under a magnifying glass.

University Museums also houses an extensive collection of paintings by former Oxford resident Theora Hamblett. Hamblett launched her artistic career at the age of fifty-five, painting scenes from her childhood, dreams, and religious visions. A growing collection of southern folk art includes works in textiles, wood, clay, paint, and natural materials, and the museums' collection of World War I posters is one of the most complete in existence. You'll find University Museums on the edge of campus at the corner of Fifth Street and University Avenue. Hours are 9:30 A.M.–4:30 P.M. Tuesday–Saturday, and 1:00–4:00 P.M. Sunday. Admission is free. Call (662) 915–7073.

trivia

The University of Mississippi gospel choir made national headlines in 2001 when its debut CD, "Send Up the Praise," was nominated for a Grammy Award.

Monument to the Movement

When James Meredith became the first African-American to enroll at the University of Mississippi in 1962, his arrival on campus was signaled by rioting, tear gas, and the deployment of the National Guard. Nearly forty years later, the university launched a fundraising campaign to erect a permanent memorial on campus honoring Meredith and other heroes of the civil rights movement in Mississippi.

The $150,000 project will be funded through donations from students, businesses, and private citizens, and through state and federal arts grants. The completed memorial will be placed between the historic Lyceum and the John D. Williams Library at the heart of the Oxford campus—the same spot where James Meredith fought to make history in 1962.

For an off-the-beaten-path dining experience, head 10 miles east of Oxford to the microscopic community of **Yocona.** The old beige house just east of the Yocona Community Center is the **Yocona River Inn,** a country store turned catfish house turned upscale restaurant. Outside, you'll be greeted by a small, hand-painted sign and the warm glow of porch lights. Inside, the wood-paneled walls are lined with a hodgepodge of old china, toys, and antique soft drink bottles, creating a cozy atmosphere. The Yocona River Inn's menu changes weekly, and although you might expect the fried catfish option, the artistic appetizers, upscale salads, and scrumptious steaks, wild game, and pasta selections are a welcome and delicious surprise. The restaurant doesn't serve wine or liquor, but you're welcome to bring your own.

To find Yocona from Oxford, head east on University Avenue, go under the Highway 7 underpass, and take a right onto Highway 334. Travel 8.4 miles into the Yocona community (a small cluster of nondescript buildings—don't blink or you'll miss it), then look for the old beige house on the righthand side. The address is 842 Highway 334. Reservations are *not* accepted, but for more information—or directions if you get lost in the sticks—call (662) 234–2464. The navigationally impaired should visit www.yocona.com and print a map before heading out.

If you stay overnight in Oxford, try one of the town's bed-and-breakfast inns. Delightful, moderately priced accommodations are available at **Puddin Place** (662–234–1250), and the **Oliver Britt House** (662–234–8043), both conveniently located near the University and the town square. Rates at the inns begin at around $60 for weekdays, $65 for weekends, and $76 for those all important football weekends.

If you don't mind a short drive through the peaceful countryside, book a memorable night or weekend at the ***Holly Ridge Farm Bunkhouse.*** Owners Hollaman ("Holly") and Linda Raney have converted one side of their working horse barn into a charming guesthouse with a rustic, cowboy motif. The two-bedroom Bunkhouse includes a small kitchen and shares a wall with the friendly horses and fragrant hay on the other side (don't worry—the bed-and-breakfast side of the barn is completely free of whinnying and horsey aromas). After a good night's sleep in the absolute quiet of the country, saddle up and join your friendly, outgoing hosts on a guided trail ride through their 160 wooded acres.

The Bunkhouse is just 5 miles from Oxford but feels a century away, and after a restful night in the barn, you may never want to sleep in a hotel again. For rates, reservations, and a map to the Bunkhouse, call Holly and Linda at (662) 236–7733 or (662) 236–4001.

Seven miles southwest of Oxford, tiny ***Taylor*** has carved out quite a reputation as an artists' colony. This minuscule community is home to writers, sculptors, photographers, painters, potters, basket weavers, furniture makers, musicians, and a blacksmith, most of whom live and work within walking distance of one another. The community's many artists display and sell their work in the ***Taylor Arts Gallery*** founded by Marc Deloach and Christine Schultz, mail carriers for the Taylor post office. Marc and Christine are themselves a husband-and-wife artistic team. Marc makes cypress furniture; Christine is a freelance writer and photographer. The couple met at a reading at Oxford's Square Books and put a contract on a white-frame house in Taylor eight days later. The Taylor Arts Gallery is just across the road from their home.

The couple doesn't own a television set, preferring to spend most of their free time on their art. But since opening the gallery, Marc does confess to a heightened interest in college sports.

trivia

Football greats Brett Favre, Archie Manning, Deuce McAllister, Steve "Air" McNair, Walter Payton, Jerry Rice, and Wesley Walls all hail from Mississippi. Football frenzy in the state reached new heights in 2001, when Archie Manning's son Eli took over quarterbacking duties at the University of Mississippi. Eli was the number one pick in the 2004 NFL draft.

"I've started keeping up with Ole Miss football," he confesses. "If they win, people seem to be in more of a buying mood."

"Downtown" Taylor is anchored by a wonderful combination of cholesterol and artwork known as the ***Taylor Grocery.*** Once a country grocery store that served catfish in the back, Taylor Grocery has removed the old shelves and merchandise and devoted the entire, ramshackle building to the art of preparing and serving fried catfish and perfectly grilled steaks, operating under the motto, "Eat or we both starve." While the steaks are delicious, traditionalists prefer to stick with the catfish that made the place famous—a deep-fried indulgence that actually does your heart good every once in a while.

trivia

In 2000, the University of Mississippi became the second Mississippi university awarded a chapter of Phi Beta Kappa, the prestigious liberal arts honorary association. Millsaps College, a private institution in Jackson, was awarded a Phi Beta Kappa chapter in 1988.

Both the catfish and the steaks come with a side order of magic markers and an invitation to add your own clever maxims to Taylor Grocery's graffiti-plastered walls, floors, furniture, and ceiling. If you're lucky enough to visit this mecca for fish-lovers and aspiring poets, be sure to scribble a witty message for those who come after you. And don't forget to check the walls for words of wisdom from U.S. Senator Thad Cochran, actress Lauren Hutton, singer Jimmy Buffet, and aspiring writer Marlo Carter.

After a visit to Taylor, take Highway 7 North from Oxford to **Holly Springs.** This pretty little town is home to some sixty **antebellum homes and churches,** spared destruction because the ladies of Holly Springs devoted themselves to distracting the Union soldiers sent to torch the town. In this charming setting of white-columned homes and colorful gardens, hoop skirts seem almost mandatory, but the only time they're considered appropriate street attire is during the annual **Spring Pilgrimage.**

The original Holly Springs Pilgrimage allowed visitors to tour twenty-three homes for a quarter. Today, the pilgrimage offers tours of seven homes, which rotate from year to year, guaranteeing repeat visitors new tours each spring. Approximately 5,000 pilgrims visit Holly Springs during the three-day event, usually held the second weekend in April. For next spring's dates and ticket prices, call the **Holly Springs Tourism Bureau** at (662) 252–2515.

trivia

The movies *Cookie's Fortune* and *Big Bad Love* were filmed in Holly Springs.

Located at 104 East Gholson Avenue, the Tourism Bureau offers self-guided walking and driving tour maps, and brochures featuring historic homes, churches, and landmarks. Of particular interest is **Walter Place,** which served as quarters for Julia Grant while her husband Ulysses occupied the town. In her memoirs, Mrs. Grant wrote of the "sea of army tents" outside Walter Place. When Holly Springs was raided by Confederates under the command of General Earl Van Dorn, the troops were forbidden to enter the house as long as Mrs. Grant was quartered inside. In return for this display of chivalry, Grant placed a safeguard on the house preventing any invasion by Union troops for the remainder of the war— and unwittingly establishing Walter Place as a safe haven for Confederate soldiers and spies. Walter Place is open for tours by appointment. Call (662) 252–2515.

Also of interest is **Hamilton Place,** where the mistress of the house hosted parties, teas, and concerts for the Union troops, hoping to take their minds off their torches. One Union general particularly enthralled with her musical gifts told her, "You and your piano can take credit for saving Holly Springs." You'll also want to drive by **Airliewood,** where General Grant established headquarters and his restless troops shot every picket off the iron fence; **Dunvegan,** where the landscaping includes pine trees planted in 1845; and **Wakefield,** home of a brazen belle who actually went so far as to *marry* a Union soldier, a scandal still discussed in Holly Springs today. **Montrose,** the lushly landscaped home of the Holly Springs Garden Club, is open for tours during limited hours and by appointment. The **Montrose Arboretum** on the grounds encompasses more than fifty species of native trees labeled with common and botanical names. For tour hours or to arrange an appointment, call (662) 252–2515.

History buffs will also want to stop by the **Marshall County Historical Museum,** three floors and twenty-two viewing rooms filled to the rafters with artifacts and displays. The building itself was constructed in 1903 as a dormitory for the old Mississippi Synodical College, the first junior college for women in the state. A $2.00 admission fee buys a look at Chickasaw Indian artifacts,

Airliewood

Graceland Too

Even if you're not an Elvis Presley admirer, you'll find Graceland Too, home of the self-proclaimed "Number One Elvis Fan," to be a memorable stop. Paul McLeod and his son, Elvis Aron Presley McLeod, have transformed their home into a virtual shrine to the King of Rock 'n' Roll.

Father and son have amassed a huge collection of Elvis memorabilia, including records, concert tickets, and flowers from Elvis's grave. Most impressive is the Graceland Too archive, a vast collection of more than 20,000 newspaper clippings and articles related to Elvis. Father and son also take turns manning a fleet of VCRs and television sets, recording any reference to the King. Graceland Too is located at 200 East Gholson Avenue in Holly Springs. There is no telephone and there are no set operating hours. According to Paul McLeod, Graceland Too is open anytime you want to stop by and pay the $5.00 admission fee.

vintage clothing, Civil War relics, antique toys, and a display detailing events from the 1878 yellow fever epidemic, which claimed more lives in Holly Springs than the Civil War. Notable artifacts include a condolence card from Mrs. Jefferson Davis to a Mississippi war widow, and an 1869 income tax return listing a total tax liability of $27.95. The museum is located at 220 East College Street, and is open Monday–Friday 10:00 A.M.–5:00 P.M., Saturday 10:00 A.M.–2:00 P.M.

Nearby **Hillcrest Cemetery** (Elder Street and South Market Street) is the final resting place of hundreds of yellow fever victims and of Hiram Revels, the country's first black United States senator. Thirteen Confederate generals and a number of Civil War soldiers are also buried at Hillcrest.

A Holly Springs attraction of a different sort is the **Kate Freeman Clark Museum,** a collection of more than 1,000 paintings by a single Holly Springs native. The collection is believed to be one of the world's largest single collections of paintings by a single artist. Clark's paintings were shown in Chicago, Boston, Philadelphia, and New York, but she refused to sell even one, perhaps because her mother told her it would be "like selling a child." Instead, Clark willed the entire collection to the town of Holly Springs, including sketches, still lifes, landscapes, even a colorful bird painted on a real leaf. The museum is open by appointment for a charge of $2.00; drop-ins are usually welcome. To arrange a visit, call Bea Green at (662) 252–2838.

The **Ida B. Wells Art Gallery** (220 North Randolph Street) showcases work by African and African-American artists. The collection is housed in the historic Spires-Boles home, the birthplace of journalist and antilynching activist Ida B. Wells. For visiting hours and more information, call (662) 252–3212.

Holly Springs's **Rust College** (150 East Rust Avenue) is the second-oldest private college in Mississippi and the oldest African-American college in the state. Founded in 1866, the institution represented one of the first post–Civil War efforts made by the national Freedmen's Bureau to educate African-American children and adults and to train African-American teachers. The college is located on the site of the former slave auction grounds of Holly Springs. Each year, the Rust College graduating class holds a candlelight ceremony at a gazebo where the auction block once rested. Tours of Rust College are available by appointment. For more information, call (662) 252–2491 or (662) 252–2515.

If all that sightseeing leaves you hungry, stop by **Phillips Grocery** (541 East Van Dorn Avenue) where the burgers were named among the nation's best by *USA Today*. Located next door to the old railroad depot, Phillips was originally opened as a saloon in 1882 by Oliver Quiggins, a former Confederate soldier. The establishment did a thriving business serving the constant flow of train passengers, many of whom arrived in Holly Springs from the North. The colorful Quiggins delighted in ordering his "Yankee" customers to take off their hats, explaining in no uncertain terms, "I've always been a Southern gentleman and I used to shoot you during the war, so you'll take off your hat if you expect service in my place."

Gardening enthusiasts and birdwatchers will enjoy a side trip to the lovely **Strawberry Plains Audubon Center** (285 Plains Road). Located 3 miles north of Holly Springs on Highway 311, Strawberry Plains is a 2,500-acre preserve and nature center bursting with native plants, flowers, birds, and butterflies. The headquarters for the Mississippi Audubon Society, the center offers birding hikes, nature walks, and educational programs year-round. The first Saturday in September, more than 1,000 visitors descend on Strawberry Plains to celebrate the spectacular migration of thousands of hummingbirds.

Strawberry Plains welcomes visitors during daylight hours Monday–Friday. A winding country road leads visitors through the lushly landscaped grounds to **Davis House,** a stately antebellum mansion that's open for tours during the

Walnut's Original Keg Party

The tiny north Mississippi town of Walnut was originally known as Hopkins, but was rechristened in 1872 when a keg of whiskey was mistakenly delivered to nearby Hopkinstown. The train was forced to backtrack an hour to correct the error. The townspeople changed the name on the spot to avoid further mix-ups, celebrating the new name with toasts from the recovered keg.

Holly Springs Pilgrimage. For more information about programs and events at Strawberry Plains, call (662) 252–4143.

If you're in this area on the Saturday or Sunday prior to the first Monday of the month, take Mississippi Highway 4 out of Holly Springs into **Ripley,** then follow Mississippi Highway 15 South to the **First Monday Trade Day.** Best described as "fifty acres of economic chaos," this colorful monthly flea market attracts as many as 1,500 vendors and 30,000 shoppers. A Ripley tradition since 1893, First Monday vendors peddle everything from antiques to food to livestock. For vendor reservations, call (800) 4–RIPLEY. For other information, call (662) 837–4051.

From Ripley, take Highway 15 North to U.S. Highway 72 East and the history-rich town of **Corinth.** The city's location at the junction of two railroads made Corinth a strategic prize in the Civil War. More than 300,000 soldiers and 200 generals occupied the city between 1861 and 1865. Generals William T. Sherman and Ulysses S. Grant both spent time in the Corinth area, and the 1862 siege of Corinth broke the record for the largest concentration of troops in the western hemisphere. Julia Grant, the general's wife, was also a wartime visitor. According to local historians, Mrs. Grant, accompanied by her own slave, set up quarters in a local plantation house. When she left she stripped the place clean, taking even the doors and window glass with her.

By the spring of 1862, Union troops were entrenched so close to Corinth they could hear the rattle of supply trains and the beat of Confederate drums inside the fortified city. Vastly outnumbered, Confederate General P. G. T. Beauregard decided to retreat to nearby Tupelo. The evacuation was conducted with the utmost secrecy. Dummy cannons guarded the line, campfires burned, and buglers serenaded the deserted works. When Union troops cautiously entered the city at daybreak, they discovered only a deserted town.

The Battle of Corinth took place in October 1862, when the Confederates attempted to retake the town in what was to become the bloodiest battle in Mississippi history. Hand-to-hand fighting engulfed the city, and the Confederates were driven out of Corinth.

The site of the Battle of Corinth includes the **Corinth National Cemetery,** the final resting place for Union soldiers killed in some twenty battles in Mississippi and Tennessee.

Battery Robinett, the scene of fierce fighting in the fall of 1862, is the site of the National Park Service's $9.5 million **Civil War Interpretive Center.** Opened in 2004 as the Corinth Unit of Shiloh National Military Park, the 12,000-square-foot center is home to an auditorium, museum, research room, and interpretive courtyard. Interactive exhibits will tell the compelling story not only of the 1862 battle but also of the plight of citizens left to forage for themselves in an occupied city.

The center runs a fifteen-minute video on Corinth and the War, offers a self-guided historic tour brochure and map to important historic sites, and sells Civil War prints and other memorabilia. The center is open Monday–Saturday 9:00 A.M.–5:00 P.M. and Sunday 1:00–5:00 P.M. Call (662) 287-9501.

It's difficult to take a drive through any part of Corinth without crossing the ring of **earthworks** that encircled the city during the war. These hastily constructed ridges of earth formed a protective buffer for the weary soldiers to sleep behind. While the earthworks are found all over town—even running through the occasional front lawn—the larger, more intact sites require a short hike through the woods off Shiloh Road. The 4-foot-high mounds don't look especially impressive until you consider they were constructed by hungry, tired soldiers working in the dark with handheld shovels the size of garden trowels. Many of the more remote sites haven't changed in the 140-plus years since the war. If a soldier from 1862 woke up today in the wooded area off Shiloh Road, he'd still know exactly where he was.

roscoeturner andgilmore

One of Corinth's most colorful residents was the high-flying Roscoe Turner, an early stunt pilot famous not only for his daring aerial maneuvers, but for his copilot—a pet lion dubbed Gilmore.

Both Turner and Gilmore received national recognition—Turner was the first (and so far, the only) Corinth native to appear on the cover of *Time* magazine, and Gilmore, now handsomely stuffed, occupies a spot in the Air and Space Museum in Washington, D.C.

Built in 1857, the **Curlee House** served as headquarters for Confederate Generals Braxton Bragg and Earl Van Dorn and for Union General Henry Halleck. Today the house is owned by the city and is open for public tours 9:00 A.M. to 5:00 P.M. Monday–Saturday and 1:00–5:00 P.M. Sunday. Winter tour hours are 9:00 A.M.–4:00 P.M. Monday–Saturday and 1:00–4:00 P.M. Sunday. The Curlee House is located at the corner of Childs and Jackson Streets.

At the opposite end of Bunch Street at the Kilpatrick Street intersection, you'll find the **Fish Pond House.** Although it's not open to the public, the Fish Pond House's most interesting architectural feature is easily viewed from the street. The roof is topped by a copper-lined basin used to catch rainwater—the latest marvel in indoor plumbing when the house was built in 1856.

If you have any questions about Corinth history, the volunteers at the **Northeast Mississippi Museum** at Fourth and Washington Streets are sure to have the answers. The museum displays Civil War relics, Indian artifacts, and local memorabilia, but its biggest asset is a friendly staff of volunteers who delight in spinning tales for out-of-town guests. There's no admission fee, but donations are welcome. The only strict requirement is that you must sign the guest register. Visit the museum Monday–Saturday 10:00 A.M.–5:00 P.M. or Sunday 2:00–5:00 P.M. During the winter, the museum is open Monday–Saturday 10:00 A.M.–4:30 P.M. and Sunday 2:00–4:30 P.M. Call (662) 287-3120.

Downtown Corinth is a handsome commercial district of Italianate, Colonial Revival, and Art Deco architecture. You'll discover a number of interesting shops in the area, including **Waits Jewelry.** The store was founded by Ernest Waits, a multitalented entrepreneur born in 1870. Mr. Waits's wife still runs the store today and is happy to answer any questions except those regarding her age. The shop's most remarkable feature is not its merchandise, but the hand-painted murals that circle the high ceiling. Mr. Waits himself painted the landscapes, which depict a day from late afternoon until sunrise and the seasons from August to August. According to his wife, Mr. Waits had never painted before he began the elaborate murals and used "places in his mind" as the models for the work.

trivia

There's literally "something in the water" in northeast Mississippi. The state's record striped bass, flathead catfish, and walleye were all pulled from local lakes and rivers.

Downtown is also home to **Borrum's Drug Store** (604 Waldron Street), the oldest continually operated drugstore in Mississippi. Founded in 1869, Borrum's still serves up thick grilled cheese sandwiches and frosty coke floats from a gleaming soda fountain. The drugstore is run by Camille Borrum Mitchell, who was the first female pharmacist in Corinth. Locals gather beneath the deer heads at Borrum's to watch Ole Miss football games and exchange gossip. Visitors may even hear a tale or two about Sheriff Buford Pusser, whose life was chronicled in the *Walking Tall* movie series. Pusser was sheriff of McNairy County, Tennessee (just across the state line) and was a frequent visitor to Corinth.

Next door to Borrum's is the cheerful **Waldron Street Market** (606 Waldron Street), the place to shop for quirky picture frames, pillows, and jewelry. Waldron Street Market also carries Mississippi-made foods and artwork, including **Hinkle Creek Pottery** crafted by mother and daughter potters and Corinth residents Lynn Barnwell and Rebecca McCalla.

With so much Civil War history in the area, it's no wonder that **C&D Jarnagin,** the nation's largest supplier of uniforms to Civil War reenactors, is also located in downtown Corinth. C&D Jarnagin does not operate a showroom but does schedule appointments for serious reenactors interested in purchasing historically accurate uniforms, footwear, hats, and accessories. Call (662) 287–4977 to schedule a visit or request a catalog. Merchandise is also available through the company's Web site, www.jarnaginco.com.

Finally, no stroll around downtown would be complete without a snack from **Dilworth's Tamales,** a Corinth tradition since 1890.

Corinth hosts several colorful festivals, the most notable of which is the **Slugburger Festival,** which celebrates that unique southern delicacy, the slugburger. Not to be confused with the garden pest of the same name, the slugburger is a part-beef, part-breading concoction made popular during the Depression when families were hungry and meat was scarce. The origin of the name is subject to some local debate, with theories ranging from "slug" as slang for a nickel, the burger's original cost, or another word for "fake," as in fake meat. In spite of its less-than-appetizing name, the slugburger attracts some 15,000 hungry fans to the July festival held in its honor. For this year's dates, call the **Corinth Area Tourism Promotion Council** at (800) 748–9048.

Overnight guests to Corinth may choose one of several bed-and-breakfast inns, where rates begin at around $50. Civil War buffs who didn't get their fill in Corinth may want to take a side trip to **Shiloh,** just across the Tennessee state line. Call (731) 689–5275 for more information on the **Shiloh National Military Park.**

For a break from the war altogether, take U.S. Highway 45 south of Corinth, then go 9 miles east on Mississippi Highway 356 to the **Jacinto Courthouse.** Once the political and cultural center of northeast Mississippi, Jacinto was founded in 1836 as the county seat of Old Tishomingo County. In its heyday, Jacinto was home to a boys' boarding school, a busy stagecoach stop, numerous churches, and even more plentiful bars and taverns.

Jacinto was home to two classes of people—those who drank, fought, and committed adultery, and those who went to church, to temperance meetings, and to bed early. Court was the main source of entertainment for both groups, and the two-story brick courthouse—built in 1854 at a whopping cost of $7,199.72—was the town's focal point.

But just as construction on the courthouse was completed, Jacinto's population began to decline. People moved to cities where the railroad created jobs and business opportunities, and the Civil War claimed many of the residents who stayed behind. The final bell tolled for Jacinto in 1870, when one-million-acre Tishomingo County was divided into the present Alcorn, Prentiss, and Tishomingo Counties. No longer a seat of government, Jacinto faded into a ghost town.

Today the town is maintained and operated by the Jacinto Foundation. Tour buildings include the courthouse museum, an 1850s doctor's office, and a country store. The courthouse is open daily, except Monday, May–September and on weekends in April, October, and November. Official hours are 1:00–5:00 P.M. Tuesday through Friday and Sunday, and 10:00 A.M.–5:00 P.M. Saturday. For more information, call (662) 286–8662.

The Appalachian Foothills

The Appalachian Mountains begin in the extreme northeastern corner of the state, creating a rugged terrain of rocky outcroppings, thick woodlands, and bubbling streams that run cool and clear even in the heat of a Mississippi summer.

The most remarkable feature of the Appalachian Foothills is the complete solitude, deafening quiet, and total lack of urbanization. In this tranquil, unspoiled section of Mississippi, Mother Nature is the main attraction.

From Corinth, take Highway 72 East to Highway 25 North, then follow Highway 25 to *J. P. Coleman State Park.* Bordered by the *Tennessee River* and beautiful *Pickwick Lake,* J. P. Coleman is a popular resort attracting outdoor enthusiasts from northeast Mississippi and nearby Memphis, Tennessee. The area is home to the largest inland marina in the United States and a scenic waterfall frequented by boaters. Call (662) 423–6515 for more information or cabin rental reservations.

trivia

Whether they're headed for the river, the lake, or the beach, Mississippians love the water. The state averages one boat for every ten people.

From J. P. Coleman it's just a short drive south along Mississippi Highway 25 to *Iuka.* The land around Iuka is woodsy, hilly, and completely unspoiled, characterized by a peace and quiet so complete that urban dwellers may find it a bit unnerving. Named for a Chickasaw Indian chief drawn to the area by its healthful mineral springs, Iuka was a popular spa of the 1880s. The water was bottled in the early 1900s and won first place in the 1904 World's Fair. The *Iuka Mineral Springs Park* on Highway 172 East offers travelers a taste of the same sparkling water Chief Iuka discovered centuries ago.

The *Old Tishomingo County Courthouse* (circa 1889) at the corner of Fulton and Quitman Streets houses a collection of Indian relics, Civil War artifacts from the 1862 Battle of Iuka, and other collections related to local history. The museum is open weekdays 10:00 A.M.–4:00 P.M. and Saturday 10:00 A.M. to 2:00 P.M. Lunch is also the best time to check out *Ellie's Snack Bar,* which specializes in slugburgers. Ellie's has been in operation in the one-room building at 108 Front Street since the early 1940s.

Head south on Highway 25 about 1 mile outside the Iuka city limit, turn right on County Road 187, and follow the signs to **Woodall Mountain,** the highest point in Mississippi. At an elevation of 806 feet, Woodall Mountain doesn't require crampons or bottled oxygen, but the view is scenic, the landscape is unspoiled, and the tranquil atmosphere is perfect for a quiet picnic.

Return to Highway 25 and head south to **Tishomingo** and **Tishomingo State Park.** The park offers a unique landscape of imposing rock formations and fern-filled crevices found nowhere else in Mississippi. Massive boulders blanketed in moss jut out from the steep hillsides, and colorful wildflowers border winding trails once walked by the Chickasaw Indians. The historic **Natchez Trace Parkway** runs directly through the park.

Visitors may stay overnight in rustic cabins clinging to the boulder-studded hillsides, then explore a 13-mile nature trail that winds along rocky ridges with spectacular views, through shallow canyons, and beside the rushing waters of Bear Creek. Hikers beware—a walk on the **swinging bridge** high above the creek is not for the faint of heart. A **float trip** about 6 miles long down Bear Creek is offered April–October. Rappelling and disc golf are also popular park attractions. For information and cabin rental reservations, call (662) 438–6914.

From Tishomingo, take Mississippi Highway 30 West to **Booneville** and **The Quilt Gallery.** He's never sewn a stitch himself, but Claude Wilemon has quite a talent for quilt design. Wilemon works with local seamstresses who transform his designs into one-of-a-kind quilts, all of which are displayed in his home and all of which are for sale. The Quilt Gallery is located in Burton, east of Booneville on Mississippi Highway 30. Look for the big stone house on the right and a sign marked QUILT SHOP. The gallery is open 7:00 A.M.–5:00 P.M. Monday–Saturday, and for $1.00 you can also tour the thirteen-room house. Call (662) 728–3302 for an appointment, or just drop in.

Antiques hounds will want to take a drive along Church Street, where treasures await discovery at **Boone's Camp Antique Mall, Downtown Antiques,** and a handful of equally eclectic shops. Bibliophiles can while away the hours in **Latte Books** (108 South Main Street), a bookstore/coffee shop combination that offers a delectable selection of both. But if you drop by on a Tuesday night, don't expect a library-like atmosphere. Tuesdays are open mike night, a big hit with the local community college crowd.

Like most Mississippi towns, Booneville boasts a Civil War "So-and-So slept here" landmark. The white frame **Cunningham House** (located behind the restored depot that houses the Booneville Chamber of Commerce) played host to General Nathan Bedford Forrest the night before the 1864 Battle of Brice's Cross Roads.

From Booneville it's just a short drive south on US 45 to **Baldwyn** and the **Brice's Cross Roads Battlefield.** Located 6 miles west of Baldwyn on Mississippi Highway 370, the former Civil War battlefield is a National Park Service site.

The Battle of Brice's Cross Roads took place in June 1864, when Confederate General Nathan Bedford Forrest organized his cavalry for an attack on Union General William T. Sherman's supply line. Union forces moved out of Memphis to stop him, and the opposing units met at Brice's Cross Roads. The outnumbered Confederates attacked vigorously and forced the Union troops back. Union forces began a careful withdrawal, but as the troops crossed Tishomingo Creek a supply wagon overturned, panicking the soldiers and turning their orderly retreat into a full-blown rout. More than 1,500 Union soldiers were captured and nearly as many were killed during the wild flight back to Memphis. A soldier described the scene as a horrible melee in which "live and dead mules were mixed up with live and dead men in the mud and water." The remains of a Federal soldier trampled in the retreat were discovered impacted in the creek bed nearly one hundred years later.

The Confederate victory was a brilliant success for Forrest, a colorful military genius who based his strategies on the maxims, "Get there first with the most men," and "Shoot at everything blue and keep up the scare."

Today, well-marked trails and interpretive markers guide visitors through the park, which includes Civil War cannons, a monument, and the Bethany Confederate Cemetery. Audio tapes of a driving tour are available at the visitors center, which houses a battlefield diorama and interactive exhibits and screens a video program narrated by noted Civil War historian and author Shelby Foote. The visitors center at 607 Grisham Street is open Tuesday–Saturday 9:00 A.M.–5:00 P.M. and Sunday 12:30–5:00 P.M. Admission to the visitors center is $3.00 for adults and $1.00 for children. For more information, call (662) 365–3969.

From Baldwyn, follow Mississippi Highway 30 West into **New Albany.** More often associated with nearby Oxford, Nobel Prize–winner William Faulkner was born in New Albany. The house is no longer standing, but a historic marker designates the site.

If lunchtime finds you craving a good old-fashioned hamburger, head for **Latham's Hamburger Inn,** located at 106 West Main. Take a seat on a wooden swivel stool rescued from an old trolley car and sample one of Latham's super-secret-recipe burgers, a New Albany tradition since 1927. Visitors have been known to request a frozen supply of burgers for the road.

New Albany also offers some interesting sights outside the main part of town. As you approach the intersection of Mississippi 15 North and County

Road 82, look for the small, white picket fence next to the railroad tracks. The fence marks the **Grave of the Unknown Frenchman.** In the 1880s, convict labor was used to build the railroads. According to legend, a wrongly accused Frenchman working on the chain gang received word his wife was dying. Desperate to reach her side before it was too late, he made a break for freedom, was shot and killed by a guard, and was buried where he fell.

Rivers and Rails

The cities and towns in the Rivers and Rails section of Mississippi sprang up as shipping hubs along the railroads and the Tennessee and Tombigbee Rivers, a heritage still celebrated there today.

This is an area where festivals revolve around "railroad days" and bands play on the rivers' banks, where museums display old train whistles and elegant old neighborhoods have their roots in the cotton-shipping trade.

Today the focus of commercial shipping is the **Tennessee-Tombigbee Waterway,** a 234-mile transportation route, scenic passage, and recreational area connecting the inland South with the Gulf of Mexico. The Tenn-Tom is a haven for sportsmen, boaters, campers, and other outdoor enthusiasts; the communities along its banks are dotted with boat ramps and campgrounds offering direct access to the water.

But perhaps first and foremost, this area is Elvis Presley's homeland. From New Albany, take U.S. Highway 78 East to **Tupelo.** A modern industrial center listed in Hugh Bayless's *The Best Towns in America,* Tupelo is best known as the birthplace of Elvis Presley, the King of Rock 'n' Roll. No matter which route you follow into the city, it's impossible to miss the many directional signs that point visitors toward the **Elvis Presley Birthplace and Park.** Vernon Presley, Elvis's daddy, borrowed $180 to construct the two-room, shotgun-style house where the King of Rock 'n' Roll was born. Two years later, the Presleys were evicted when they couldn't scrape together enough money to repay that modest loan.

trivia

Built in 1937, Tupelo's **Church Street School** was hailed as one of the most outstanding designs of its time. A scale model of this Art Moderne structure was displayed at the 1939 New York World's Fair as "the ideal elementary school."

The flowered linoleum, worn furnishings, and sepia-toned family portrait are a sharp contrast to the flashy cars, sequined jumpsuits, and extravagant lifestyle more often associated with Elvis. The entire structure is only 450 square feet, and the guide at the door is quick to mention that Graceland, Elvis's estate in Memphis, holds a sofa longer than this entire house.

When Elvis hit the big time, he returned to his hometown for a benefit concert to raise money to build a park for disadvantaged children. The fifteen-acre property purchased for the park included Elvis's first home, and today more than 60,000 tourists and fans take the exit off US 78 to Elvis Presley Boulevard each year, headed for the tiny shotgun shack at the end of the road.

The guest book bears signatures from visitors from all over the United States and dozens of foreign countries. Most of their comments echo the sentiments of a visitor from England who wrote, "You were my idol. Rest in peace."

Worshipping the King

In the summer of 1982, I entered the workforce as a tour guide at Jimmy Velvet's Elvis Presley Museum in Memphis. A personal friend of the King of Rock 'n' Roll, Velvet remodeled an old gas station across the street from Graceland and filled it with a hodgepodge of photos, costumes, jewelry, and furniture, all of which once belonged to Elvis. Fans from around the world paid $3.00 for me to lead them through the "exhibit hall" and snap their photos in front of Elvis's baby blue Lincoln Continental or perched on the edge of his king-size bed.

The following summer, I graduated to working at Graceland itself, where my job duties included calming guests who claimed to have seen Elvis's ghost lurking on the staircase, providing tissues for fans who still "can't believe he's gone," and shaking hands with Priscilla Presley, who donned dark glasses and hid in the crowd during a top-secret, undercover inspection tour. The hottest selling item in the gift shop? Bags of dirt from Graceland, each accompanied by a "certificate of authenticity."

But even two summers immersed in Elvis doesn't qualify me as a true fan of the King. "Fan," after all, is short for "fanatic," which is really the only way to describe the hordes of people who travel from around the world to see where Elvis lived and died.

Even today, more than twenty-five years after his death, fans wait in line for hours to tour the house, the cars, and the airplanes. They invest their hard-earned cash in T-shirts bearing his likeness and dirt from his flower beds. They tattoo his name on their bodies and name their children "Elvis Aron Presley Jones." They are obsessed.

So what was it about the boy from Tupelo that changed people's lives and continues to touch them today? Was it his unforgettable voice? His smoldering eyes? His undulating pelvis? His tragic, early death? Or was it purely and simply charisma?

No one has ever been able to pinpoint the quality that made a poor country boy a King, but one thing is certain. If you could bag that with a certificate of authenticity, it'd be a bargain at any price.

A museum behind the birthplace houses clothing, costumes, photographs, records, and other Elvis memorabilia donated by longtime Presley family friend Janelle McComb. Dozens of photos depict Elvis as a schoolboy and young adult. Some of the earlier shots reveal a little-known secret: Elvis was actually a dark blond who dyed his hair black. Among the quirkier artifacts are "souvenirs" recovered from Elvis's hotel room by an enterprising pair of fans who paid hotel security $40 for admittance to the room after the King checked out. Their spoils included two used coffee cups (still stained) and a damp bath towel that was sealed in plastic and stored in a deep freezer to preserve its moisture. Also displayed is a letter from then-President Jimmy Carter to Presley's family upon the death of the superstar, in which the president described Elvis as "unique and irreplaceable. His death deprives our country of a part of itself."

"Elvis at 13"

Perhaps most poignant is a quotation from the King himself. Stenciled on a wall are Elvis's own words, "I could never become so rich that I would forget what it's like to be poor." Elvis lived up to those words; many of his concerts were benefits, and the museum itself is housed in a former youth center Elvis established for children in the neighborhood where he grew up.

As he strolled the grounds of his birthplace with his friend Janelle McComb shortly before his death, Elvis mentioned that he would like to see a small chapel erected somewhere on the grounds. After Elvis's passing, McComb launched a personal crusade, raising donations from friends and fans to construct the intimate Memorial Chapel that now graces the grounds. Though many weddings have been held beneath the stained glass windows, the birthplace guide is quick to mention that contrary to rumor, there is not and will never be an Elvis impersonator on site to perform marriages. Like the rest of the park, the chapel is marked by an aura of dignity and peace.

In 2002, the Elvis Presley Birthplace and Park unveiled a bronze **statue of "Elvis at 13."** Sculpted by North Carolina artist Michiel Van der Sommen, the statue depicts Elvis in overalls carrying his guitar, much as he would have looked when the family relocated from Tupelo to Memphis in 1948. Future plans for the birthplace include a story wall to feature "quotes and quips" from friends of the King.

Admission to the birthplace is $2.50, admission to the museum is $6.00, and $7.00 buys a look at both. The Elvis Presley Birthplace and Park is open Monday–Saturday 9:00 A.M.–5:00 P.M., Sunday 1:00–5:00 P.M. Call (662) 841–1245.

Die-hard fans of the King should stop by the ***Tupelo Convention and Visitors Bureau*** (399 East Main Street or call 800–533–0611) and pick up a map to several sites on the ***Elvis Presley's Early Years Driving Tour.*** The 2-mile tour features several Elvis-related sites, each marked by a bronze plaque featuring the performer at age thirteen. Stops include ***Lawhon Elementary*** and ***Milam Junior High Schools,*** where Elvis was a student; ***Johnnie's Drive In,*** where Elvis often stopped for a cheeseburger and an RC Cola; and the site of the old ***Mayhorn Grocery,*** where the future King of Rock 'n' Roll was inspired by the blues.

Perhaps the most popular stop along the route is ***Tupelo Hardware*** (114 West Main Street), where Elvis purchased his first guitar. As the story goes, Elvis's mother, Gladys, brought him to the store in 1946 to buy a bicycle, but a rifle caught young Elvis's eye. Mother and son compromised on a guitar, and the rest is rock-and-roll history. Today, Tupelo Hardware is a major stop for the Elvis faithful, with busloads of fans pouring into the store at all hours. Radio shows have been broadcast live from the very counter where the young Elvis forked over his $7.75, and the staff has long since learned that a typical day at work involves as much rock and roll as hammer and nails. Souvenir T-shirts, postcards, and guitar-shaped key chains are emblazoned with the message, "Where Gladys bought her son his first guitar."

Tupelo's year-round Elvis frenzy reaches its peak the first weekend in June, when Elvis fans, music lovers, locals, and folks who just enjoy a good party descend on the town for the annual ***Elvis Presley Festival.*** For a schedule of festival events and a list of this year's headliners, call (888) 273–7798.

Believe it or not, there *is* more to Tupelo than Elvis. Children and adults alike will enjoy a visit to the ***Tupelo Buffalo Park,*** where the residents include just about everything *but* a hound dog. This mini-zoo is home to a lion, a Bengal tiger, a giraffe, monkeys, snakes, goats, rabbits, horses, iguanas, and a pair of hedgehogs. The real attractions, however, are the massive, shaggy bison grazing on the park's 145 acres. The largest bull tips the scale at 2,500 pounds; at more than 250 head, the herd itself is the largest east of the Mississippi River. Visitors board a Monster Bison Bus—a school bus equipped with a monster truck kit—and ride through the herd, which shares its range with a handful of water buffalo, a few Texas longhorns, and a pair of yaks. The bus stops at a feeding station, where visitors have the opportunity to stand inside a safely enclosed pen and hand-feed the bison. The bus tour lasts about forty-five minutes, leaving plenty of time for kids to explore the park's playground and petting zoo. Along with T-shirts and caps, the Buffalo Park gift shop sells bison meat and hides (sorry, no blue suede shoes).

The buffalo roam at 2272 North Coley Road, just north of the Tupelo Regional Airport and across from the Tupelo Furniture Market. Tours are available Monday, Thursday, and Friday 9:00 A.M.–6:00 P.M., Saturday 9:00 A.M. to dusk, and Sunday 1:00–4:00 P.M. Admission is $10.00 for adults and $8.00 for children; group rates are available. For more information, call (662) 844–8709 or (866) 27BISON, or visit www.tupelobuffalopark.com.

If you thought the Monster Bison Bus was an unusual vehicle, wait until you visit the *Tupelo Automobile Museum,* which showcases more than one hundred antique, rare, and celebrity cars dating from as early as 1896. The personal collection of Tupelo businessman and car connoisseur Frank Spain, the automobiles are valued at more than $6 million. Spain's collection includes an 1899 Knox; a rare Duesenberg; one of only fifty-one Tuckers ever built; Tony Curtis's 1964 Leslie from the film *The Great Race;* Liberace's Corvette; a never-driven Dodge Viper; and, in a nod to Tupelo's most famous native son, a 1976 Lincoln Mark IV once owned by Elvis Presley. Spain began his collection more than thirty years ago, and with a few exceptions, has at least one car for every year in which the automobile has existed.

Spain's personal favorite? A 1948 Jaguar.

His wife Jane's favorite? "As long as it has air conditioning and it's an automatic," she says, "I don't really care."

Approximately one hundred meticulously restored, running automobiles are displayed in chronological order; open restoration bays allow visitors to see works-in-progress. Take a tour through automotive history Tuesday–Sunday 10:00 A.M.–6:00 P.M. Admission is $10.00 for adults, $8.00 for seniors and AAA members, and $5.00 for children under twelve, who must be accompanied by an adult. The Tupelo Automobile Museum is housed in a 120,000-square-foot facility at 275 East Main Street.

The opening of the Tupelo Automobile Museum helped launch Tupelo's newest spring festival, a classic car show christened the *Blue Suede Cruise.* For a list of activities and this year's dates, call (800) 533–0611.

Like most of north Mississippi, Tupelo was the site of a fierce Civil War battle. The Battle of Tupelo is remembered in a small park on West Main Street. After the disastrous Union rout at Brice's Cross Roads, General Sherman ordered General A. J. Smith to "Go out and follow (Nathan Bedford) Forrest to the death, if it costs 10,000 lives and breaks the Treasury." Smith drew the Confederate forces under Forrest and General Stephen D. Lee into battle at Tupelo.

Dinner with Dr. Nash

If you're in Tupelo at dinner time, grab a bite at *Jefferson Place* (823 Jefferson Street). Operating in a renovated house built in the 1930s, this casual, cozy bar and grill is a favorite hangout of many Tupelo residents—and one Tupelo ghost.

This spirited diner has been known to move tables, chairs, and glasses of beer, pat waitresses on the back, and occasionally laugh aloud, all in the presence of a dining room full of witnesses. According to Jefferson Place's former owner, Kacky Brown, this mischievous ghost is "Dr. Nash," the friendly spirit of a former Tupelo physician.

Prior to his demise, Dr. Nash occupied a home at 205 Gloster Street (now another popular Tupelo eatery). When Ms. Brown opened a dress shop in the good doctor's former residence, the ghost made his first appearance in the boutique's tea room, rocking in his favorite chair, laughing at the shop's patrons, and rummaging around in the attic. When Ms. Brown and her late husband Ed bought the house across the street and turned it into Jefferson Place, Dr. Nash relocated along with them.

In 1995, Ms. Brown sold the restaurant to current owner Robert Bristow, who'll be happy to seat you near Dr. Nash's regular corner table. If you stop by Jefferson Place for dinner on a Tuesday night, chances are good you'll run into Kacky Brown, who'll be pleased to regale you with tales about—and maybe even to introduce you to—her old friend the ghost.

A misunderstood direction cost the Confederates the battle—an incident that one of Forrest's men described as "making the General so mad he stunk." Smith, however, was short of supplies, and many of his troops were suffering from heat exhaustion. The Union troops hastily retreated, leaving their own wounded behind.

As Generals Lee and Forrest discussed the day's events around the campfire, Lee wondered aloud why the other Confederate generals couldn't match Forrest's success in battle. "Well General," Forrest is said to have replied, "I suppose it's because I'm not handicapped by a West Point education."

The one-acre *Tupelo National Battlefield* features a large memorial honoring both armies, cannons, and an interpretive marker and map. The *Oren Dunn City Museum,* also located on West Main Street, displays relics from the battle, as well as Indian artifacts and NASA exhibits.

History and nature are the focal points at the *Natchez Trace Parkway Visitors Center.* A scenic route more than 8,000 years old maintained by the U.S. Department of the Interior, the fabled *Natchez Trace Parkway* is headquartered in Tupelo. The visitors center offers information to Trace travelers and houses exhibits related to the Parkway's history. Three miles north of the visitors center is a preserved segment of the original Trace, which leads to the *graves of thirteen unknown Confederate soldiers.* Local legend has it the men were executed by their own commander, the ill-tempered Braxton Bragg. You'll find the visitors center at the intersection of West Main Street and the Natchez Trace Parkway just north of town.

For a unique shopping experience and one-of-a-kind gifts, visit *The Main Attraction and Coffee Bar* (214 West Main). Grab a cappuccino from the Elvis Coffee Bar, then browse shelves, walls, and racks packed with vintage clothing, funky furniture, lava lamps, beaded curtains, Moroccan hand drums, and off-the-wall refrigerator magnets. The Main Attraction also offers a spectacular assortment of jewelry, from very inexpensive to high-dollar pieces made with exotic stones.

The Flowerdale Marketplace (2025 McCollough Boulevard) features an eclectic selection of antiques, rugs, furniture, home and garden accessories, and gifts from more than thirty-five vendors. *Carmita's Café at Flowerdale* is the perfect place to unwind over a light lunch, admire your purchases, and chat with friendly owners Carmita and Michael West. You'll find a similar-yet-still-unique shopping experience at the *High Cotton Market and Café* (1292 North Veterans Boulevard), where an afternoon's browsing comes with dessert and coffee on the side.

Other unique shops include *Serendipity* (623 West Main Street), where the gifts with attitude include one-of-a kind jewelry, sushi-print pajamas, and "party panties"; and *Wicks N More* (134 South Industrial Road), which stocks hundreds of locally poured candles in every size, shape, and scent. Most of Tupelo's specialty shops and boutiques are open 10:00 A.M.–6:00 P.M. Monday–Saturday.

For a truly vast selection of upscale merchandise, oddities, and "junque," visit the *Tupelo Gigantic Flea Market.* This flea market lives up to its name, attracting more than 30,000 shoppers and vendors from a dozen states, and selling everything from oriental rugs to puppies. The Tupelo Gigantic Flea Market is open the second weekend of every month except February and August in the climate-controlled buildings of the Tupelo Furniture Market. Speaking of furniture, Tupelo is the second-largest furniture manufacturing location in the world; retail outlets scattered around town offer a wide selection of furniture at reasonable prices.

Tupelo is home to several wonderful restaurants, but only one can make the claim, "Elvis ate here." As noted in an affidavit on the wall, *Johnnie's Drive-In* (908 East Main Street) was a teen-aged Elvis's favorite source of cheeseburgers. The oldest restaurant in Tupelo, Johnnie's has won almost as many fans as the King himself. Revered for its burgers and barbecue, the restaurant has been owned by only two families since opening in 1945. The decor is still vintage 1950s, and Johnnie's still offers curb service.

Celebrity artwork adorns the walls at **Vanelli's** (1302 North Gloster), a festive, friendly, Greek and Italian joint bursting with pizza, pasta, and personality. You'll be greeted at the door by accordion-playing owner Bill Kapenekas ("colorful" is an understatement), then led to a cozy table for a meal that will have you loosening your belt a notch. Between courses, Bill will lead you on a guided tour of his art collection, which includes limited edition prints and originals by John Lennon, Joan Baez, and other famous musicians.

trivia

In 1959, Mary Ann Mobley became the first Miss Mississippi to win the Miss America crown. Mary Ann was followed by three more Miss Americas from the state – Lynda Lee Meade (1960), Cheryl Prewitt (1980), and Susan Akin (1986).

An unusual choice for lunch is **The Cottage Shoppe and Tobacconist** (208 North Spring Street). Patrons (fourteen max) relax at a handful of tables tucked into a cozy corner of this tiny tobacco and coffee shop. In addition to gourmet lunches and sinful desserts, the shop sells fine tobacco and cigars, and flavored coffees by the cup or the pound. If owner Austin Haley looks familiar, it's probably because you've seen him on television. Haley returned to Tupelo after a New York acting career that included roles on the long-lived soap operas *One Life to Live* and *Another World*.

If you're staying in Tupelo overnight, choose delightful, unusual accommodations at the **Mockingbird Inn,** where each room represents a different global destination. Guests may wake up in Africa, Paris, Athens, Venice, Mackinac Island, Sanibel Island, or Bavaria. The rooms do have one thing in common—guest books filled with praise for innkeeper Sharon Robertson's scrumptious home-cooked breakfasts. The inn is conveniently located in the heart of town at 305 North Gloster. Rates at the Mockingbird begin at $89. For reservations, call (662) 841–0286.

From Tupelo, take US 278 west to **Pontotoc.** This gracious community features a number of lovely old homes and historic sites. The homes aren't open for tours, but driving-tour maps are available at the **Pontotoc County Chamber of Commerce** located at 109 North Main Street. Sites on the tour include antebellum homes, Civil War battlegrounds, and sites related to the Chickasaw Indians. An interesting display of Chickasaw artifacts and rare historical documents is also featured in, of all places, the local McDonald's. Pick up a burger and take a look at an arrowhead at 145 Highway 15 bypass.

Pontotoc is also home to **Westmoreland's,** an eclectic collection of early twentieth-century farm tools, clothing, quilts, and furnishings. The antiques were all collected by Mildred Westmoreland, whose motto is, "It's more than just old junk, it's American history." Housed in Ms. Westmoreland's home on Highway 9 North, the collection is open by appointment. Admission is $5.00. Call Ms. Westmoreland at (662) 489–7673 to arrange a visit.

From Pontotoc, take Mississippi Highway 41 South to U.S. Highway 278 and the railroad town of *Amory.* Named after Harcourt Amory, a shareholder in the railroad company, the town was founded as a train service stop between Memphis and Birmingham. Nearby Aberdeen was first considered as the stopping point, but the residents of that town, concerned about the noisy train whistles and the "riffraff" associated with the railroad, voted against it.

Follow the signs to the *Amory Regional Museum,* located in an old hospital building. Admission is free and a friendly tour guide will be happy to walk you through the many exhibits related to local history. Displays include Indian artifacts, a military room, and railroad memorabilia housed in an old train car. The most fascinating exhibits, however, are those related to the old hospital itself. Formerly the Gilmore Sanitarium, the museum displays medical equipment from the 1800s through the 1960s. A rate card describes the services of Dr. B. C. Tubb, a prominent local physician of the early 1900s who charged $1.00 for an office visit and $2.00 for house calls. An infant-sized iron lung, original scrub room, and instrument sterilizer that still smells of disinfectant may look primitive to the modern visitor, but once represented state-of-the-art medical equipment.

A log cabin restored and moved to the museum grounds offers a glimpse of small-town life in the 1840s. The cabin is furnished in the style of the period and includes a children's sleeping loft reminiscent of the *Little House on the Prairie* TV series. When you sign the guest register, check for an entry from January 1996 that reads, "I was born in this cabin in 1932." The Amory Regional Museum is open Tuesday–Friday 9:00 A.M.–5:00 P.M. and weekends 1:00–5:00 P.M. Call (662) 256–2761.

From the museum, go 1 block over to Main Street and head toward downtown Amory and *Bill's Hamburgers.* The menu at Bill's includes hamburgers, hamburgers, and just for variety, hamburgers. It's hard to get confused at Bill's—your only choice is with or without onions. The restaurant has changed hands several times, but the menu has remained the same since 1929. Bill's is on Main Street at Vinegar Bend.

Amory may look like a sleepy southern hamlet, but every other year celebrities from Nashville, New York, and Hollywood descend on the town for the *Stars Over Mississippi* fundraising event. Created by Amory native Sam Haskell, executive vice president and worldwide head of television for the William Morris Agency, the event funds college scholarships for needy

Mississippians. Entertainers who have appeared at Stars Over Mississippi include actors Ray Romano, Whoopi Goldberg, Gerald McRaney, and Delta Burke; supermodel Kathy Ireland; and country superstar duo Brooks & Dunn. For the next Stars Over Mississippi lineup, visit www.starsovermississippi.org.

The charming river town of **Aberdeen** is less than 20 miles south of Amory off Mississippi Highway 25. Located on the banks of the **Tombigbee River,** Aberdeen was one of the busiest ports of the nineteenth century. Huge shipments of cotton crowded the city's docks, and for a time Aberdeen was the second-largest city in Mississippi. Wealthy merchants and planters competed in the building of elaborate mansions, purchasing their furnishings in Europe and shipping them up the Tombigbee by steamboat.

trivia

"Mississippi" is Choctaw for "Father of Waters," referring to the mighty river for which the state is named. The earliest known written version of the name was the French "Michi Sepe."

Today Aberdeen's main attraction is a collection of elegant old homes showcasing architectural styles from Greek Revival to Victorian to Neoclassical. All told, Aberdeen boasts more than 200 homes and buildings listed on the National Register of Historic Places.

Several of the homes are open every April during the **Aberdeen Spring Pilgrimage. The Magnolias,** a palatial, 1850 Greek Revival mansion donated to the city by a local resident, is open for tours daily. Call (662) 369–7956 to reach the attendant, or contact the **Aberdeen Visitors Bureau** at (662) 369–9440 or (800) 634–3538.

Located at 124 West Commerce Street across from City Hall, the visitors bureau also offers a self-guided driving tour brochure and map of Aberdeen titled *A Search for Gold.* The tour takes visitors past several beautiful homes, including an area of magnificent Victorians known as **Silk Stocking Row.**

The **Old Aberdeen Cemetery** is the site of a tale worthy of Ripley's Believe It or Not. It seems Ms. Alice Whitfield was knitting—a popular pastime in 1854—when she died in her rocking chair. According to local legend, Ms. Whitfield was then buried in the rocking chair, knitting and all. The cemetery, located at the corner of Whitfield and Poplar Streets, also includes a number of Civil War–era gravesites. The cemetery and its residents come alive during the Pilgrimage, when local high school students host a candlelight tour called **Lies and Legends of Old Aberdeen Cemetery.**

Antiques buffs should plan a stop at **Petunia's,** a quaint shop doing business in an old cottage at 100 West Canal Street. Petunia's is owned by a

Hollywood makeup artist who's also an Aberdeen native; his mother runs the shop for him between visits.

If you're visiting the second weekend in December, continue on Highway 8 West to **Calhoun City** and a trip back in time. The **Biblical City** re-creates a typical town in the Holy Land around the time of Christ. Visitors can tour the temple, the tavern, or even the jail, passing the time with tax collectors, census takers, and merchants of the day. The focal point of the Biblical City is a live nativity scene, complete with real animals. Virtually every soul in Calhoun County plays a role in this annual re-creation. Attracting an average of 5,000 visitors every year, the Biblical City boasts a higher population than Calhoun City. The Biblical City comes alive 6:00–9:00 P.M. the second Thursday, Friday, and Saturday of December. Call (662) 637–2257.

The Natchez Trace Parkway

The **Natchez Trace Parkway** stretches diagonally across Mississippi, cuts a corner through Alabama, then winds to an end in Nashville, Tennessee, following an unspoiled route through lush forests, beside sparkling streams, and into the heart of America's frontier past.

This timeworn scenic path, more than 400 miles long and 8,000 years old, was originally "traced out" by buffalo, then trekked by Indians, and finally trampled into a rough road by trappers, traders, and missionaries. French maps dated as early as 1733 include the Natchez Trace; British maps of the same period refer to it as the "Path to the Choctaw Nation." From 1800 to 1820, the frontier brimmed with trade and new settlements, and the Natchez Trace was the busiest highway in the southwest.

But by the late 1820s, the speed of steamboats made travel along the Natchez Trace impractical, and the once-busy road dissolved into the brush. In 1909, the Daughters of the American Revolution spearheaded a campaign to mark the Old Trace, and their work culminated in the Natchez Trace Parkway, a national highway maintained by the National Park Service.

Today's highway closely follows the original trail. The uniquely southern penchant for sharing good tales preserved the colorful legends surrounding the Trace, and historic markers

trivia

The Natchez Trace Parkway is one of only fourteen National Scenic Byways and one of only six All-American Roads in the country. Both designations were awarded by the Federal Highway Administration in recognition of the Trace's historic value and scenic beauty.

Little-Known Facts about the Northeastern Hills

The oldest book in the United States, an ancient Biblical manuscript, is housed at the University of Mississippi.

On December 7, 1874, the Jesse James Gang held up Corinth's Tishomingo Savings Bank, escaping with $15,000.

Elvis Presley was scheduled to play in Corinth in 1954, but had to cancel due to low ticket sales.

Tupelo was one of only four cities in the United States that celebrated the first official Mother's Day in 1908.

The state of Mississippi has produced twenty-nine Rhodes Scholars—twenty-four from the University of Mississippi, four from Millsaps College, and one from Mississippi State University.

Lee County, Mississippi is the world's leading producer of upholstered furniture and the second-largest manufacturer of all furniture sold in the world. More than 5,000 Lee County residents are employed in furniture manufacturing by more than one hundred companies.

In April 2000, Corinth native Gus McLeod became the first pilot to fly over the North Pole in an open-cockpit airplane. His feat was documented by National Geographic Television. McLeod attributed his lifelong interest in aviation to Roscoe Turner, another famous aviator from Corinth.

along the way detail the path's romantic history. Indian mounds, ghost towns, and nature trails beckon from just off the paved road.

Visitors exploring northeast Mississippi via the Natchez Trace will encounter wildlife, enjoy natural beauty free of commercial traffic, and pass historic sites too numerous to list. A few words of caution for first-time Trace travelers—stick to the 50-mile-per-hour speed limit, which is constantly monitored and always enforced. And while the Trace is tranquil and uncrowded by day, it can seem a little dark and spooky at night. Small towns and cities are located at frequent intervals just off the parkway, but there are no commercial establishments and only one gas station on the Trace itself. Finally, night travelers should keep an alert watch for deer, which are known to bolt into the road unexpectedly.

Traveling north to south on the Trace through northeast Mississippi, visitors pass many of the attractions mentioned previously in this chapter. The parkway runs directly through *Tishomingo State Park* located in the extreme northeastern corner of the state. Near mile marker 293.4 are wayside exits for the ***Tennessee-Tombigbee Waterway,*** a 234-mile scenic passage and recreational area connecting the inland South with the Gulf of Mexico.

The Trace is headquartered in ***Tupelo*** (see earlier in this chapter), home of the ***Natchez Trace Parkway Visitors Center.*** A museum located within the visitors center houses artifacts and displays chronicling the history and development of the Old Natchez Trace and the modern parkway. A scenic nature trail located on the property provides a welcome break from the road.

Places to Stay in the Northeastern Hills

The following is a partial listing of the many hotels, motels, and bed-and-breakfast inns in the area not mentioned in the text.

Lincoln Ltd. is a full-time reservation service for bed-and-breakfast inns statewide. For reservations in any area of Mississippi, call (800) 633–6477 or (601) 482–5483.

ABERDEEN

Cypress Lakes Lodge
(bed-and-breakfast)
1208 Hillcrest,
(662) 369–8241

AMORY

The Old Place
(bed-and-breakfast)
60036 Country Barn Road,
(662) 256–4707
www.theoldplaceBandB.com

BELMONT

Belmont Hotel and Bed & Breakfast
121 Main Street,
(662) 454–7948

CORINTH

The Generals' Quarters
(bed-and-breakfast)
924 Fillmore Street,
(662) 286–3325
www.thegeneralsquarters. com

The Samuel D. Bramlitt House
(bed-and-breakfast)
1125 Cruise Street,
(662) 396–4979
www.bramlitthouse.com

GRENADA

Stone Canyon Resort Bed & Breakfast
1255 Fort Hill Road,
(662) 227–1211 or
(662) 229–0020

HOLLY SPRINGS

Fort Daniel Hall
(bed-and-breakfast)
184 South Memphis,
(662) 252–6807

Somerset Cottage
(bed-and-breakfast)
310 South Cedar Hills Road,
(662) 252–4513

OXFORD

The Tree House
(bed-and-breakfast)
53 County Road 321
(off South Lamar Boulevard),
(662) 513–6354 or
(877) 849–8738
www.thetreehousebandb.com

Places to Eat in the Northeastern Hills

The following is a partial listing of the many restaurants in the area not mentioned in the text.

ABERDEEN

Cottage Tea Room
(sandwiches, salads, desserts)
109 East Washington Street,
(662) 369–1157

CORINTH

Cross City Grille
(casual)
307 East Waldron Street,
(662) 287–7282

ALSO WORTH SEEING

BATESVILLE

Factory Stores of Mississippi

HOLLY SPRINGS

Dunn's Shooting Grounds, Inc.
(clay bird range, plantation quail hunting)

Wall Doxey State Park

OLIVE BRANCH

Maywood Beach and Pool

SARDIS

John W. Kyle State Park

TUPELO

Elvis Presley Lake and Campground

Tombigbee State Park

Trace State Park

Tupelo Artist Guild Gallery

MEMPHIS, TN

Beale Street

Graceland (Elvis Presley Home)

SHILOH, TN

Shiloh National Military Park

GRENADA

Jake 'n Rips
(barbecue, catfish)
1525 Sunset Drive,
(662) 227–9955

Mo' Suga
(steaks, seafood)
4817 South Main Street,
(662) 226–0450

**Roxie's Square Table
Spoon** (New Orleans style)
97 First Street,
662) 229–0809

HOLLY SPRINGS

Fort Daniel Hall
(elegant dinners in an
antebellum home)
184 South Memphis Street,
(662) 252–6807

OXFORD

Doe's Eat Place (steaks)
1536 University Avenue,
(662) 236–9003

SENATOBIA

Penny's Pantry
(light lunches, desserts)
136 North Front Street,
(662) 562–5570

TUPELO

**Finney's Sandwich
& Soda Shop**
(sandwiches, soda fountain;
don't miss the signature
potato salad)
1009 West Main Street,
(662) 842–1746

Gloster 205
(fine dining)
205 North Gloster Street,
(662) 842–7205

The Eastern Plains

The Eastern Plains span rich black prairies, pastoral cattle farms, sacred Indian homelands, and bustling industrial centers.

Tradition runs deep here, whether it's found in a carefully restored antebellum home, a hallowed Indian mound, or a modern company's success story.

The stops here have more in common than just freshly painted front porches, and it's more than just the sights and scenery that make this region special. The Eastern Plains are blessed with a singular culture centuries in the making and a rich history that's mellowed into legend.

The Golden Triangle

The small cities of Columbus, West Point, and Starkville make up the region known locally as the Golden Triangle. The three cities work together to promote themselves, capitalizing on the rich diversity of activities and attractions available in this small geographic area.

A tour of the Golden Triangle begins in *Columbus,* a pretty little town of *antebellum homes* and antiques shops near the Mississippi–Alabama line. Entering Columbus from U.S. Highway 82 West, take the Main Street exit and make your first stop

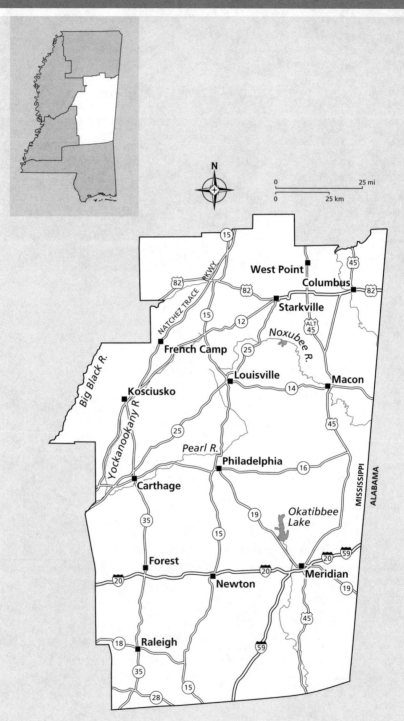

the *Tennessee Williams Home/ Mississippi Welcome Center.* This cheerful gray-and-yellow Victorian built in 1878 was the first home of the famous playwright who introduced the world to Blanche DuBois and penned Marlon Brando's most memorable line—"Stelllla!" Inside, a friendly staffer will provide you with maps, a walking- and driving-tour brochure, and tickets to Columbus tour homes. The Welcome Center is open Monday–Sunday 8:00 A.M. to 5:00 P.M.

The city's two historic districts showcase one of the greatest diversities of antebellum architecture in the South. Shaded streets are lined with carefully preserved examples of Greek Revival, Italianate, Federal, and Gothic Revival–style mansions and cottages. At least two homes are open for tours any day of the week. Pick up the tour schedule and purchase tickets at the Tennessee Williams Birthplace. Tickets range from $6.00 to $7.50 per person per home, depending on the home. Homes are open 10:00 A.M.–4:00 P.M. Monday–Saturday and 2:00–4:00 P.M. Sunday.

Tour homes include *Amzi Love,* built in 1848 and continuously occupied by generations of the Love family ever since; *Highland House,* rebuilt in 1909 after the original home was burned to the ground by a jealous housekeeper; the *Lee Home and Museum,* former residence of Confederate General Stephen D. Lee; and *Temple Heights,* supposedly haunted by an eccentric ghost named Elizabeth. Also on the tour is *Rosewood Manor,* built for a northern-born bride who refused to occupy it, insisting that a ravine near the house would leave her susceptible to "the vapors." Several of the tour homes double as bed-and-breakfast inns. Call (800) 327–2686 or (662) 328–0222 for rates and reservations, or contact the individual bed-and-breakfasts listed at the end of this chapter.

All of Columbus's tour homes boast their share of history and charm, but the most fascinating home on tour is the magnificent *Waverley Plantation,*

MARLO'S FAVORITE ATTRACTIONS IN THE EASTERN PLAINS

Waverley Plantation,
Columbus

Friendship Cemetery,
Columbus

The aroma at the Ole Country Bakery,
Macon

L. V. Hull's House,
Kosciusko (look for the shoe tree with my name on it)

Neshoba County Fairgrounds
Philadelphia (air-conditioned cabins only)

A whirl on the Dentzel Carousel,
Meridian

theghostof
waverleyplantation

When Robert and Donna Snow purchased the old Waverley Plantation in the early 1960s, they knew they were buying a piece of history. They didn't know they were also inheriting a former resident.

The Snows had lived in Waverley for about two years when the ghost made her first appearance. Donna Snow heard a child crying, sometimes calling for her "mama." A small indentation began appearing on the upstairs bed, about the size of a child napping. The Snows once sat in the room for an entire afternoon and actually saw the bedclothes straighten themselves when the ghost child "awakened." The little girl has appeared only once, dressed in a ruffled nightgown and standing on the stairway. To this day, her identity remains a mystery.

appropriate subject matter for everything from *This Old House* to *Unsolved Mysteries*. Waverley was built in 1852 and served as home to the original builder's family until the last descendant died in 1913. For nearly fifty years Waverley sat vacant. Then, in 1962, Robert and Donna Snow fought their way through the overgrown grounds, stepped into the graffiti-plastered foyer, and fell in love. The Snows bought Waverley and began the painstaking process of restoration.

It was a daunting task. Vines had crept in through the broken windows, birds and bats called the cupola home, and every wall was covered with graffiti. The late Donna Snow once remarked that "you weren't anyone unless you had written your name, the date, and who you loved on the wall. I've been privy to every love affair from 1913 to 1962." Remarkably, the vandals and curiosity seekers left the house largely intact. Of the original 718 staircase spindles, only three were missing. Just two panes were broken in the front door glass, and the only damage to two towering, gilded mirrors was a crack inflicted during a Civil War dance.

Room by room, the Snows restored Waverley to its former glory. Today it's hard to believe the opulent mansion was once an abandoned ruin. From the first floor foyer (so spacious it doubles as a ballroom), two curved, freestanding staircases rise to join balconies on the second, third, and fourth floors. Sixteen windows surround the mansion's lofty cupola, 65 feet above the entry.

Waverley and the incredible story of its restoration—and its ghost—have been featured on a number of television shows, including *Bob Villa's Restore America–Castles of the Confederacy* and *Larry King Live.*

Waverley is located 10 miles north of Columbus and 15 miles east of West Point on Mississippi Highway 50 near the Tombigbee River. The house is open for tours seven days a week 9:00 A.M.–5:00 P.M. Admission is $7.50. Call (662) 494–1399.

Twelve antebellum homes are open during the annual ***Columbus Spring Pilgrimage*** held the first two weeks of April. In addition to the obligatory hoop skirts and blooming gardens, the Columbus extravaganza offers a look at period crafts, with demonstrations ranging from antique doll restoration to lace making to china painting staged in several of the tour houses. Pilgrimage tickets are $15 per three-home tour package. Several antebellum churches that served as Civil War hospitals also open their doors for free tours during pilgrimage week. Pilgrimage also brings the return of the ***Chattanooga Star***, a paddlewheeler offering sightseeing excursions along the scenic Tennessee-Tombigbee Waterway. The *Chattanooga Star* departs from Riverside Park in downtown Columbus. Cruises run only during the pilgrimage, and tickets are available at the boat only. Excursions are $8.00 for adults and $6.00 for children. For more information, including daily cruise schedules, call (800) 327–2686.

For complete information on all pilgrimage events, call the Columbus Convention and Visitors Bureau at (800) 327–2686 or visit www.columbus-ms.org.

Y'all Come Back Now, Ya Hear?

I've lived in Mississippi for more than a dozen years now, and the natives still say they can tell I'm "not from around here." My hometown is Memphis, Tennessee—a city, it seems, that's too far north for me to have a truly southern accent.

The much-maligned, equally celebrated, and often-imitated southern drawl is as indigenous to Mississippi as grits and humidity. Visitors may poke fun at the slow, fluid pace of our speech, but can anyone really find the fast-paced, short-clipped, now-now-now! cadence of a Yankee tongue more pleasing than the soothing, melodic, drippin'-with-molasses rhythm of a genuine, southern-fried voice asking for "moah ahs tae, plase?" ("more iced tea, please?")

In the movies, the southern drawl is used as a kind of unflattering shorthand, a lazy way to characterize ignorance, poverty, or redneckism. But we Southerners (even those of us from as far north as Memphis) are actually proud of our melodious, genteel drawl. Down here, slow, sultry, vowel-laden speech is a sign of good breeding, the hallmark that separates the Scarlett O'Haras from the no 'count riffraff.

To us, it's the northern tongue that sounds so foreign. But be warned—one of the gravest sins a visiting northerner can commit is attempting to imitate the southern style of speech. Trust me, you aren't fooling anyone.

Of course, most Yankees are able to enjoy a visit to Mississippi without bringing along a translator. Just listen a little more slowly, and you'll be able to communicate with us just fine. But if you learn only one thing about the southern way of speaking during your visit, make it this: The word "y'all" is short for "you all" and is never, ever singular.

Columbus was one of a handful of Mississippi cities never occupied by Union troops during the Civil War. In fact, the most significant war-related event in Columbus occurred on April 25, 1866, a year after the war ended. A group of war widows visiting **Odd Fellows Cemetery** decided to decorate not only the graves of their husbands and fathers but of the Union soldiers buried there as well. A newspaper account of the event read, "We are glad to see that no distinction was made between our own Confederate dead and Federal soldiers who slept their last sleep by them. . . . Confederate and Federal—once enemies, now friends receiving their tribute of respect." The gesture was immortalized in a poem titled, "The Blue and the Gray" which was carried in newspapers nationwide. News of the good deed of the ladies of Columbus quickly spread, spurring other communities to follow suit and earning Columbus a reputation as the city "where flowers healed a nation." This simple Decoration Day evolved into America's national Memorial Day, and the cemetery was renamed "Friendship."

Twelve Gables, the home where the ladies met to plan their Decoration Day, is sometimes open for tours during the Spring Pilgrimage. The Decoration Day itself is reenacted every April 25 at 4:00 P.M. in Friendship Cemetery. Costumed reenactors from the Stephen D. Lee Chapter of the United Daughters of the Confederacy lay flowers on the graves of soldiers who fell more than a century ago. Today, their gesture honors not only the Blue and the Gray but the four women who replaced the bitterness of war with the grace of forgiveness. For more information on the Columbus **Decoration Day Reenactment,** call (800) 327–2686.

Friendship Cemetery is located at the end of South Fourth Street in the South Columbus Historic District behind the Tennessee Williams Birthplace. Fourth Street is interrupted by a small warehouse district; to reach the cemetery, go 1 block over to Fifth Street and head south until Fourth Street picks up again. From Fifth Street look to your right until you spot a tall wrought-iron fence surrounding the elaborate 1800s monuments.

A stroll through the oldest section of the cemetery reveals exquisite monuments honoring loved ones of the 1800s. A few of the markers are so old their inscriptions haven't merely faded but have disappeared altogether. Several military graves are marked with swords and Confederate emblems. In the center of the cemetery, the Mississippi state flag, United States flag, and Confederate flag fly over row after row of simple markers honoring the Civil War dead. During Spring Pilgrimage, Friendship Cemetery hosts "Tales from the Crypt," a candlelight tour of the cemetery complete with costumed guides who relate true stories about Friendship's "residents." Tickets are $2.00 for nonstudents, $1.00 for students. Tours are conducted 7:00–10:00 P.M.

Located at the edge of the South Historic District on College Street, **Mississippi University for Women** was the first state-supported women's college in the country. Organized in 1884, "the W" campus includes twenty-four buildings listed on the National Register of Historic Places. In 1982, "the W" went coed and now bills itself as "Mississippi University for Women . . . And Smart Men, Too."

Friendship Cemetery

Downtown Columbus is home to some twenty antiques shops and boutiques offering one-of-a-kind gifts and collectibles. A brochure listing the many shops is available at the welcome center. Many of these specialty shops carry **Jubilations Cheesecakes,** made in Columbus and shipped to cheesecake lovers nationwide.

If you're in the market for an unusual keepsake or exquisite gift, choose a star, cross, or personalized name plaque from **Stained Glassworks, Inc.** (101 Fifth Street South). Each colorful and inspirational piece is truly unique, featuring properties created not only by the studio's talented craftspeople, but by the volatile nature of the glass itself. The Stained Glassworks showroom and gift shop is open to the public Tuesday–Saturday 10:00 A.M.–7:00 P.M. Tours of the workshop are available with advance notice. To watch the craftspeople at work, call (662) 329–2970 or visit www.stainedglassworks.org.

Columbus is the largest city on the **Tennessee-Tombigbee Waterway.** Some $50 million worth of modern recreational facilities were included in the Waterway's construction. Parks bordering the 234-mile Tenn-Tom offer nature trails, boat launches, charter excursions, and primitive and developed camping sites. Excellent water quality and a variety of game fish make the Tenn-Tom one of the nation's top fishing spots. Guide service is available, but finding a "honey hole" is usually easy, even for first-time anglers. For more information, call the **Columbus Convention and Visitors Bureau** at (800) 327–2686 or visit www.columbus-ms.org/recreation.html.

From Columbus take U.S. Highway 45 South into the tiny town of **Brooksville** and follow the comforting aroma of fresh-baked bread to the **Ole Country Bakery.** Tempting cakes, pies, and pastries line the shelves of this

"The Blue and the Gray"

America's Memorial Day was first celebrated in Columbus in 1866, when a group of war widows decided to decorate not only the graves of their own loved ones, but of the Union soldiers buried in Columbus as well. Their gesture was immortalized in the following poem, originally published in *The Atlantic Monthly* in September 1867.

"The Blue and the Gray"

By the flow of the inland river,
Where the fleets of iron have fled,
Where the blades of grave grass quiver,
Asleep are the ranks of the dead;
Under the sod and the dew,
Waiting the judgment day—
Under the one, the blue,
Under the other, the gray.

From the silence of sorrowful hours
The desolate mourners go,
Lovingly laden with flowers
Alike for the friend and the foe;
Under the sod and the dew,
Waiting the judgment day—
Under the roses, the blue
Under the lilies, the gray.

Sadly, but not with upbraiding,
The generous deed was done;
In the storm of the years that are fading,
No braver battle was won;
Under the sod and the dew,
Waiting the judgment day—
Under the blossoms, the blue,
Under the garlands, the gray.

No more shall the war-cry sever,
Or the winding rivers be red;
They banish our anger forever
When they laurel the graves of our dead;
Under the sod and the dew,
Waiting the judgment day—
Love and tears for the blue,
Tears and love for the gray.

—Frances Miles Finch

old-fashioned bakery operated by the Mennonites, a community similar to the Amish in their dress and lifestyle. A friendly woman clad in a flowered dress and apron and wearing the traditional black cap will take your order for warm baked goods or giant po' boy sandwiches. The bakery is open Tuesday–Friday 6:00 A.M.–5:00 P.M., and Saturday 6:00 A.M.–2:00 P.M., and is closed Sunday and Monday.

Continue on US 45 South 9 miles to *Macon.* Take a right onto Mississippi Highway 14 into downtown, turn right on Jefferson Street, then take the first right past the Noxubee County courthouse. The imposing redbrick building on your left is the *Noxubee County Library,* perhaps the only library in the country with bars on the windows and a hanging gallows inside. No, it's not the world's stiffest penalty for an overdue book. The library is housed in the old town jail built in 1907. The original iron doors, window bars, and working gallows all remain; the library books are stored in the old cells. Climb the thirteen steps that lead to the gallows if you dare; the librarian promises to "come find you if you scream." Bring your camera—the librarian will loan you a black-and-white striped uniform to slip on while she snaps your photo behind bars. You'll even receive a folder headlined, "Look who's in jail and loves it" in which to display your mug shot. Be a convict or a bookworm Monday, Tuesday, Thursday, or Friday 8:00 A.M.–6:00 P.M. Use your one phone call to dial (662) 726–5461 for more information.

"Goin' once . . . Goin' twice . . . Sold!" If you're in the Macon area on a Monday afternoon, stop by the **cattle auction barn** on US 45 at the northern edge of town. Even if you don't happen to be traveling with a full-size cattle trailer, hearing a live auctioneer call for bids on prized livestock is an entertainment experience you won't find just anywhere. Auctions are held every Monday at 1:00 P.M.

From Macon, take US 45 Alternate North to **West Point,** listed in Norm Crampton's *The 100 Best Small Towns in America.* This point of the Golden Triangle is built around outdoor recreation, with many of its attractions named for nearby Waverley Plantation.

You might not expect to find a championship golf course in a community of 12,000 people, but the **Old Waverly Golf Club** made *Golf Digest's* list of the top one hundred courses in America. Designed by Bob Cupp and Jerry Pate, Old Waverly attracts serious players from around the country. Cottages overlooking the course are available for overnight guests at rates ranging from $110 to $350 per night. Call (662) 494–6463 for reservations.

Avid anglers should plan a stay at **Waverly Waters.** This rustic resort offers sport fishing in a seventy-acre lake stocked with largemouth bass, bluegill, and bream. The lake is natural, with an underwater structure of tree tops, stumps, tires, and other fish habitats designed by Bill Dance. The resort also features a professionally designed sporting clay range and jogging and nature trails. Guests stay overnight in the rustic cypress lodge or in one of five cabins. Visitors must stay overnight to fish. Call (662) 494–1800 for lodge, cabin, and boat rental rates or reservations.

With outdoor recreation such a priority, it's only logical that **Mossy Oak,** a national leader in camouflage wear, is based in West Point. Serious hunters nationwide rely on Mossy Oak's "breakup," "oak shadow grass," "forest floor," and other well-designed camo patterns to keep them out of sight while they're on the hunt. Developed by sportsman Toxey Haas, Mossy Oak camo wear is designed and manufactured in West Point. Although their clothing may blend in perfectly with its surroundings, you'll have no trouble spotting the **Mossy Oak Mall** on Highway 45 South.

Non-outdoorsy types can while away an hour or two exploring West Point's well-maintained city parks and a pair of museums focusing on local heritage. The **West Point Friday House Museum** (307 East Westbrook Street) features exhibits on the city's history, including a room dedicated to West Point native and blues legend Chester "Howlin' Wolf" Burnet. The **Sam Y. Wilbite Transportation Museum** (204 Commerce Street) is a must for railroading buffs. The museum traces the history and various modes of transportation from the 1700s to the present. The highlight of the journey is a look at the largest working model railroad in the South. The Transportation Museum is open Thursday–Saturday only.

Lunch- or dinnertime in West Point calls for a trip to **Anthony's** (116 West Main Street), a grocery-store-turned-restaurant that still features the original meat coolers in the back of the main dining room. Lunch at Anthony's is a country-cooked buffet of fried chicken, lima beans, cornbread, and other assorted "Bubba food." Dinner is a more upscale affair, with a menu featuring seafood, steak, and poultry. On "Once in a Blues Moon Night," held the first Saturday of each month, Anthony's brings in a live blues band. Anthony's is open for lunch Sunday–Friday 11:00 A.M.–2:00 P.M., and for dinner Monday–Thursday 5:00–9:30 P.M., Friday and Saturday 'til 10:00 P.M.

The population of West Point triples on Labor Day weekend, when the **Prairie Arts Festival** brings more than 600 vendors and 30,000 festival-goers to downtown. The high point of the festival is a juried art show, but shoppers may also choose from flea market trinkets and fine antiques. Nonshoppers will

Little-Known Facts about Mississippi

In 1839, the Mississippi legislature passed one of the first laws in the English-speaking world protecting the property rights of married women.

Mississippi was the first state in the nation with a planned system of junior colleges.

With a white-tailed deer population of two million, Mississippi boasts more white-tailed deer per capita than any other state. Sportsmen bag an estimated 330,000 deer in the state every year. The highest scoring white-tailed deer ever taken in North America (for benefit of serious hunters, it was a 295% non-typical Boone & Crockett) was harvested in east-central Mississippi.

One-fourth of the nation's supercomputing power is housed in Mississippi.

Mississippi has a population of 2,768,619.

Some 78,000 Mississippians joined the Confederate military. By the Civil War's end, 59,000 were dead or wounded.

Mississippi has more certified tree farms than any other state.

enjoy four stages of entertainment, food, and children's activities. The Prairie Arts Festival is held the Saturday before Labor Day. The Friday night prior to the Prairie Arts Festival, West Point hosts the *Howlin' Wolf Blues Festival,* a tribute to the West Point native and blues legend.

The plains of Mississippi bear little resemblance to the Serengeti, but an overnight stay at West Point's *B. Bryan Preserve does* lend itself to dreams of Africa. Created by Dr. Frank Mello and his wife, Judy Bryan Mello, B. Bryan is a private reserve dedicated to the breeding and preservation of endangered African hoofstock. Here antelope, greater kudu, and scimitar oryx enjoy the space, privacy, and ideal climate required for breeding. A renovated, 1845 log cabin provides comfortable lodging for up to twelve overnight guests, who are treated to walking or driving tours of the preserve. For rates or reservations at this unusual retreat, call (662) 494–5575 or visit www.bbryanpreserve.com.

From West Point, take US 82 West to *Starkville,* the final point on the Golden Triangle and the home of *Mississippi State University.* Take the downtown exit, turn left on Main Street, then head straight onto the sprawling campus. The state's largest university, MSU is a national leader in agricultural research. If a groundbreaking soybean study doesn't excite you, how about wine making? A tour of the *A. B. McKay Food and Enology Laboratory* takes wine lovers through the entire process from grapes to glass and concludes with a sampling of Mississippi muscadine wines. Call (662) 325–3011 to schedule a tour and tasting.

Gardening enthusiasts will enjoy a visit to the *MSU arboretum* (662–325–2000), where a variety of annuals, perennials, blooming shrubs, and trees put on a spectacular display spring through fall. Get a close-up-and-personal look at the world of creepy-crawlers at the *Clay Lyle Entomology Museum* (662–325–2085), which features the third largest insect collection in the Southeast. A tour of the *Dunn-Seiler Earth Science Museum* (662–325–3915) may not be quite as exciting as a ride through Jurassic Park, but you will see a real triceratops skull and a saber tooth tiger head.

There's no Mickey, but a visit to the university's *Engineering Research Center (ERC)* may remind you a little of Disney. Visitors can "test drive" the ERC's virtual reality programs in the CAVE™ (Computer Automatic Virtual Environment). With advance notice, the ERC can send visitors on a virtual reality roller coaster ride, a high-speed flight through a forest, or other larger-than-life adventures. Call (662) 325–7642 (unless, of course, you suffer from motion sickness).

Don't leave campus without a hefty ball of Mississippi State's own Edam cheese. Manufactured at the dairy science plant on campus, this smooth, flavorful cheese is sold in one-, two-, and three-pound balls wrapped in red wax

MARLO'S FAVORITE ANNUAL EVENTS IN THE EASTERN PLAINS

COLUMBUS

Spring Pilgrimage/
Tales from the Crypt,
April,
(800) 327–2686

Possumtown Pigfest,
September,
(662) 328–4532

MERIDIAN

Jimmie Rodgers Memorial
Country Music Festival,
May,
(888) 868–7720

PHILADELPHIA

Choctaw Indian Fair,
July,
(601) 650–7450

Neshoba County Fair,
July,
(601) 656–8480

WEST POINT

Prairie Arts Festival,
September,
(662) 494–5121

bearing the official university seal. Mississippi State cheese is sold by mail to Edam lovers around the world and in the Cheese Sales Office in the **Herzer Dairy Science Building.** The Herzer building is located on the campus on Stone Boulevard. The cheese shop is open Monday–Friday 9:00 A.M.–5:00 P.M. Tours at the cheese- and ice-cream-making facility are available with advance notice. Call (662) 325–2338 to schedule a visit.

The **John Grisham Room** in the university's Mitchell Memorial Library houses the best-selling author's papers and publications. The collection includes literary manuscripts, legislative files, photos, signed works, and other materials from the popular author, including the original manuscript for his first novel, *A Time To Kill.* The room is open Monday–Friday 9:00 A.M.–4:00 P.M. Call (662) 325–2559.

Of course, there's more to life in a college town than just academics. Mississippi State brings the excitement of **Southeastern Conference sports** to Starkville, fielding strong teams in basketball, baseball, and football. Game days are marked not only by tailgate parties and pom-poms, but also by the incessant clanging of cowbells, a tradition dating back to the university's days as an agricultural college. If you visit MSU on a baseball afternoon, stake out a spot between the barbecue grills and lawn chairs in the **Left Field Lounge,** the place to see and be seen while cheering on the team.

While "Bulldog Spirit" may seem to completely dominate the town, Starkville is also home to a few off-campus attractions.

Kids and adults alike will enjoy a visit to **Pinedale Farms**, where the residents include sheep, goats, pigs, rabbits, and chickens, as well as such exotic animals as miniature horses, pot belly pigs, emus, and llamas. From Starkville, go west on US 82, 5 miles past Stark Road. Turn right (north) onto County Lake Road, then immediately right onto Reed Road. Continue 1.5 miles to the Pine Dale Farms entrance. Admission is $4.50, or $4.00 per person for groups of fifteen or more. Reservations are required, so call (662) 323–9543 to schedule a visit and a picnic.

If you'd like an aromatic reminder of your visit to Starkville, stop by the **Aspen Bay Company** (1010 Lynn Lane West) for a scented signature candle, and with a little advance notice, a fragrant tour of the family-owned candle factory. The Aspen Bay gift shop is open Monday–Saturday 9:30 A.M.–5:30 P.M. Call (662) 324–2231 for information about the factory tour. Upscale gifts are also available at **Giggleswick** (200 East Main Street), a Starkville shopping tradition that surely owes at least a portion of its longevity to its unusual and unforgettable name.

Overnight guests receive a warm welcome at any of Starkville's lovely bed-and-breakfast inns. Dating to 1836, **The Cedars** (662–324–7569) is the centerpiece of a 183-acre estate dotted with forests and fishing ponds. Built by one of Starkville's founding fathers in 1890, **Caragen House** (662–323–0340) is the only example of the steamboat Gothic architectural style in Mississippi. The

"Starkville City Jail"

In the mid-1960s, Johnny Cash performed a concert at Mississippi State University. Afterward, he went back to his motel and had a few drinks, then decided to go out for smokes.

Maybe it was the few drinks or the intricacies of locating smokes in an unfamiliar town, but Cash wound up parked in a local family's flowerbed. On any other night the family might have been flattered by the country star's unexpected detour, but their daughter had planned to use the ill-fated flowers in her upcoming wedding and was most distraught to find them flattened.

Cash spent the remainder of his visit to Starkville in the city jail. But far from being humbled by the experience, Cash capitalized on his run-in with the local law, penning a tune called "Starkville City Jail." Cash soon returned to Starkville to sign copies of his new album, bringing with him gifts for the entire Starkville police force.

Hickory Hill Bed and Breakfast Cabins (www.hickoryhill.net) are rustic, private cabins complete with fireplaces and front porches and surrounded by sixty-two acres of sweeping prairie lands.

The Natchez Trace Parkway

This section of the legendary *Natchez Trace Parkway* includes three major stops and dozens of smaller historic sites marked by the familiar brown and yellow signs. Don't let the European flair of town names like "French Camp" and "Kosciusko" fool you. This leg of the parkway still retains the frontier charm for which the route is famous.

From Starkville, continue on US 82 West approximately 20 miles to Eupora, where US 82 intersects the Natchez Trace. Head south on the Trace to mile marker 193.1 and *Jeff Busby Park,* a national park named for Congressman Thomas Jefferson Busby, who introduced the bill calling for the surveying of the Old Natchez Trace and the creation of the modern parkway.

Jeff Busby features nature trails, campsites, picnic areas, and a panoramic, 20-mile view from the overlook atop Little Mountain, one of the highest points in Mississippi. A well-marked nature trail identifies native plants and describes their use as foods and medicines by early settlers. Be warned—the trail looks deceptively easy, but will definitely leave you winded and ready for a cool drink from the convenience store at the park entrance. If you plan to continue along the Natchez Trace from here, gas up now. The service station at Jeff Busby is the only one located directly on the parkway.

Continue on the parkway 12 miles south of Jeff Busby to *French Camp,* a charming little village established in 1812. Nearly 200 years later, French Camp is still best described as a peaceful settlement on the rural frontier. Attractions just off the Natchez Trace include the 1846 *Colonel James Drane Plantation House,* a working blacksmith studio, and a sorghum mill that operates in the fall. The *French Camp Academy Historical Museum* displays tools, clothing, books, newspaper clippings, a 400-year-old Bible, a 1932 class ring, and dozens of photos and artifacts documenting the area's century-plus history as a Christian educational center. The French Camp information center and a gift shop selling sorghum, preserves, quilts, yard art, and other handicrafts are housed in an 1846 log cabin. And if you're strolling the settlement at noon, you'll be blessed by the peal of bells and joyous music emanating from the 1874, white clapboard French Camp Baptist Church.

Noon is also an excellent time to try the soup and sandwiches at the *Council House Cafe,* located in an authentic Choctaw Indian council house of the 1820s. Choose a table next to the fireplace, pull up a ladder-back chair, and sink your teeth into "the Big Willy"—according to my husband, the best BLT he's ever put in his mouth. The French Camp historic area is generally open 8:30 A.M.–5:00 P.M. Monday–Saturday. The cafe serves lunch 10:30 A.M.–2:30 P.M. For more information, including a sorghum-making schedule, call (662) 547–6482.

A boardwalk leads from the Colonel Drane House to the **French Camp Academy Bed and Breakfast Inn,** a quiet frontier lodge where Daniel Boone would feel right at home. Made from two one-hundred-year-old, hand-hewn log houses, the inn offers a wide back porch overlooking the Natchez Trace Parkway. When the tourists have left for the day and the sun sets slowly over the quiet Natchez Trace, it doesn't require too much imagination to picture a friendly Indian or weary trapper or missionary wandering up the road to become the inn's next guest. The ambience may be rustic, but rest assured the rooms are quite comfortable and modern. Rates begin at $75. Call (662) 547–6835 for reservations.

This tranquil setting is also home to the **French Camp Academy** boarding school. Marked by a sign reading, THE HEAVENS DECLARE THE GLORY OF GOD, the academy's **Rainwater Observatory** houses the largest telescope between Atlanta and Houston. Gaze into the heavens through one of thirteen powerful telescopes, five of which are designed for daytime viewing. A small planetarium offers educational programs for groups as large as thirty. Visit the observatory Web site at www.rainwaterobservatory.org, or call (662) 547–6377 to schedule a free visit and a look at the stars.

Back on the Trace 20 miles south of French Camp, you'll spot the sign directing you to the **Kosciusko Museum and Information Center.** Kosciusko began as a community of taverns and inns established to serve travelers on the Old Natchez Trace. Listed in Norm Crampton's *The Best 100 Small Towns in America,* Kosciusko still welcomes visitors today.

Originally known as Redbud Springs, the town's name was changed to the easy-to-remember but impossible-to-spell "Kosciusko" in the late 1830s. The state representative in charge of choosing the name recalled an ancestor's colorful tales about Thaddeus Kosciuszko, a Polish engineer who served on George Washington's staff during the Revolutionary War. Kosciuszko never visited Mississippi, yet the town was named in his honor (minus the "z"), and the most prominent display in the Kosciusko Museum and Information Center is a life-size wax statue of the Polish freedom fighter. Dirt from Kosciuszko's grave in Krakow, Poland, was used in landscaping the town of Kosciusko's **Redbud Springs Park.**

The friendly volunteers at the information center will be happy to tell you more about Kosciusko's history and to provide you with a copy of the *Towers & Turrets* brochure, a **walking and driving tour** showcasing the city's lovely

Victorian architecture and numerous historic sites. Use caution exiting the information center—the peace and tranquility of the Natchez Trace gives way to a major highway bypass just off the property, and the sudden increase in traffic can be startling.

To avoid the traffic, take a right onto the bypass from the information center, then turn left onto Jefferson Street. Continue on Jefferson into downtown, then take a right on Huntington Street to the **Kosciusko City Cemetery.** Take the BoBo Street entrance into the cemetery, then continue straight until you come upon a stone woman in Victorian dress in the center of the Kelly family plot.

When Laura Kelly died in 1890, her devastated husband sent her photo and favorite clothing to a renowned sculptor in Italy, asking that the artist immortalize his beautiful wife in stone. The Kellys' house was under construction at the time of Laura's death, and her grieving husband's next instruction was to the builder. Mr. Kelly ordered a third story be added to the house so that he could look out across the cemetery and see the statue of his beloved wife gazing back at him.

Alas, the bereaved husband was rather fickle. By the time the statue arrived in Kosciusko, he had already married Laura's sister. Nevertheless, the **Laura Kelly Statue** was erected in the family plot, prompting the townspeople to speculate what the second Mrs. Kelly must think every time she looked out the window to find her husband's first wife (her own sister) staring back at her. The **Kelly-Jones-Ivy House** still stands at 309 East Jefferson Street, though it's no longer visible from the statue site.

As you return to Huntington Street via BoBo Street, look to your left for a white marker labeled "Mother" and "Father." The names of Mr. and Mrs. W. E. Burdine's nineteen children are inscribed on the marker between their graves. With so many offspring, the prolific Burdines seem to have run out of names toward the end. Child number 17 was christened simply, "Seventeen."

As you leave the cemetery, turn right onto Huntington Street, then take the first right, Allen Street. **L. V. Hull's house** is the ninth on the right, but don't worry about missing it if you forget to count. The tiny house sits behind what is surely the most unusual example of "landscaping" in Mississippi. The yard is packed with carefully positioned, elaborately painted artifacts, including several clocks, a handful of hobbyhorses, old television sets, tires, toys, even a bomber jacket. The most common ornaments by far are Mrs. Hull's "shoe trees"—loafers, sneakers, and high-heeled pumps of every size and color displayed on tall stakes protruding from the ground. A few determined azaleas peek out from beneath this odd collection, but there's nary an inch to spare.

Visitors from as far away as Australia have visited Mrs. Hull's yard and toured her similarly decorated and equally packed house. Mrs. Hull's guest book logs more than 300 visitors a year from as many as twenty states and several foreign countries. Some call it folk art, others call it junk. Of those who voice the latter opinion, Mrs. Hull asks, "If it's just junk, why do you want to come see it?" Leave one of your own shoes for Mrs. Hull, a friendly woman who welcomes drop-in visitors at just about any hour—even when she doesn't have her teeth in. Be sure to bring along some cash—no visit is complete without an L.V. original, and virtually every item in the house and yard is for sale.

From Mrs. Hull's house, turn left onto Huntington Street, then continue past the Jefferson Street intersection to the ***Mary Ricks Thornton Cultural Center.*** Built in 1898, this beautiful Gothic structure once served as a Presbyterian church, then fell into disrepair after years of abandonment and neglect. The building was destined for demolition until the late Mary Ricks Thornton spearheaded a campaign to save it, explaining that she became involved in the restoration because, "I was married in this church in 1930, and I couldn't bear to have it torn down for a parking lot."

After months of fundraising, the Kosciusko-Attala Historical Society purchased the building and restored it for use as a cultural center. The center features ornate stained-glass windows and unusual white-over-wood pews, curved to give every churchgoer a view of the pulpit. One of the stained-glass windows is dedicated to Laura Kelly, of statuary fame. The center also features a Delta Gamma room, honoring the three Kosciusko natives and Presbyterian church members who founded the national sorority in 1873. The building hosts performances, weddings, meetings, and other events, and is open for tours by appointment. For more information, call (662) 289–2981.

Peeler House Antiques (117 West Jefferson) offers 10,000 square feet of European antiques including silver, jewelry, china, porcelain, and furniture, as well as affordably priced gifts and Gail Pittman pottery. The shop also houses ***Cafe on the Square,*** a cheerful eatery perfect for a quick lunch. But the Peeler House's most unusual delight is a full-scale, working carousel set up in a back storage area. Ask Mr. Peeler to crank it up and give you a whirl.

Peeler House formerly operated out of an 1898 Victorian mansion a couple of blocks off the town square. The building is now the ***Peeler House Bed-and-Breakfast,*** the only bed-and-breakfast in Kosciusko. The Peeler House Bed-and-Breakfast offers five guest rooms with private baths. For rates or reservations, call (662) 289–5086.

Wrap up a tour of Kosciusko with a visit to the area where the town's most famous native, Oprah Winfrey, spent her childhood. Although her birthplace is no longer standing, fans can visit the spot where Oprah gave her first public performance; at a church in the Buffalo community, Oprah recited the Easter story. Buffalo Road, now **Oprah Winfrey Road,** makes a loop off Mississippi Highway 12 and passes the church (now the Buffalo Community Center), as well as Oprah's family cemetery and the site of her birthplace.

Head east of Kosciusko on Highway 12 approximately 12 miles to the Sallis community, then take Mississippi Highway 429 South. When you spot the bright salmon farmhouse, you'll know you've arrived at the **Attala Art Gallery and Studios,** the colorful headquarters of artists Ginger and Brad Joyner. This creative couple has turned their home—a 1906 farmhouse built by Ginger's great-grandfather—into a fun, funky studio and gallery where they create and display their pottery, paintings, scented candles, and art furniture. Ginger, who earned a law degree but never practiced, focuses on paintings and thrown pottery. Brad works in slab ceramics. Both make candles, an enterprise born of necessity. "I was spending too much on candles," Ginger confesses. The couple's art spills out of the house into a handful of technicolor outbuildings. An antique fire engine and other "props" decorate the rural property. More buildings, displays, and art and pottery-making lessons are all in the planning stages.

The Joyners' work is popping up in galleries around the state, but deriving the maximum pleasure from an Attala Art candle, painting, or serving piece means meeting the artists at the source of their inspiration. Ginger, Brad, and their son Zakary are happy to share not only their art but the history of their home and the beauty of its woodsy, natural setting. Call Brad and Ginger at (504) 491–6725 or visit them online at www.attalaart.com.

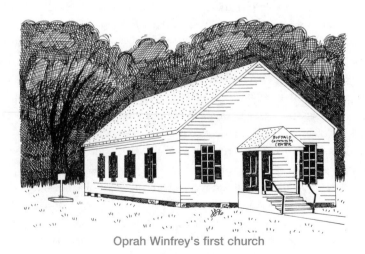

Oprah Winfrey's first church

Reservations and Rails

If you expect to find Native Americans only "out west," you'll be surprised to stumble upon a bona fide Indian reservation here in the deep South. The legends and traditions of the Mississippi Band of Choctaw Indians dominate the culture in this part of the state, reminding visitors that Mississippi history did not begin on a cotton plantation or a Civil War battlefield.

Farther south near Meridian, history is forever intertwined with the railroad. The iron horses brought east Mississippi's first settlers, whose descendants still walk its streets today.

Leave the Natchez Trace Parkway at Kosciusko and take Mississippi Highway 35 South to *Carthage,* then follow Mississippi Highway 488 to *Bryan's Country Store.* Here you'll get your first glimpse of the ancient culture of the Mississippi Band of Choctaw Indians. Bryan's sells more handwoven Indian baskets than groceries, more colorful, intricate beadwork than convenience store sundries. The baskets come in every shape, size, and color, but in only one price range—expensive. Of course, those interested in a true collector's item won't mind paying a little more for a one-of-a-kind souvenir that embodies the skill and tradition of a centuries-old people. Built in 1929, Bryan's Country Store is open 6:00 A.M.–6:00 P.M. Monday–Saturday.

From Highway 488, take Highway 16 East toward *Philadelphia* and the *Choctaw Indian Reservation.* If you were expecting the Hollywood version of an Indian village, you're in for a surprise. The Choctaw are savvy businesspeople who've brought industry, commerce, and a comfortable lifestyle to their reservation. The tribe's most spectacular venture, the multi-million-dollar *Pearl River Resort,* rises from the red dirt prairie just west of Philadelphia on Highway 16. Anchored by two dazzling casinos, the *Silver Star* and the *Golden Moon,* the resort also encompasses two luxury hotels, two award-winning golf courses, a $20 million water park, a nightly laser light and dancing water show, a full-service spa, live entertainment, fifteen restaurants, upscale shops and boutiques, and dozens of other diversions and amenities.

The members of the tribe residing on the reservation are descendants of the Choctaw who refused to leave their homeland following the 1830 Treaty of Dancing Rabbit, which ceded the last of Choctaw native land to the United States. Rather than relocate to Indian lands in the West, this small group of proud, determined Choctaw struggled against poverty and segregation to preserve their traditional culture on their native land.

Choctaw history before the coming of the "white man" and the tribe's subsequent struggles and triumphs are depicted in the *Choctaw Museum of the*

Southern Indian, a collection of exhibits and archives relating the tribe's long history in Mississippi, which dates back to the time of Christ. If you're near the reservation in July, stop for the *Choctaw Indian Fair,* a celebration of Native American culture that includes traditional dancing, crafts, stickball games, foods, and entertainment. For this year's Choctaw Indian Fair dates, call the *Philadelphia Chamber of Commerce* at (601) 656–1742 or (877) 752–2643, or the Choctaw Reservation at (601) 650–1537.

The land around Philadelphia is sacred to the Choctaw for good reason. According to Indian legend, the entire Choctaw Nation was born at the *Nanih Waiya Historic Site,* an ancient area marked by ceremonial Indian mounds and a sacred cave 20 miles north of Philadelphia off Highway 21. The Choctaw refer to the large mound at the site as the "Mother Mound." During the mass Indian exodus that followed the Treaty of Dancing Rabbit, the Choctaw who remained in Mississippi vowed "never to leave their mother as long as she stood." A flight of steep, wooden stairs leads to the top of the Mother Mound, transporting visitors to an ancient world of myth and legend. Even in the hot stillness of a summer day, it's easy to imagine the ancient Choctaw ceremonies, to hear the beat of drums and smell the smoke of campfires.

The Nanih Waiya site includes a picnic area overlooking a cypress swamp and a park office directly across from the Mother Mound. Ask at the office for directions to the cave mound, marked by legend as the very spot where the first Choctaw Indian entered the world. The cave is partially hidden in a wooded area. It's possible to step inside, but the cave floor is muddy and dark, and spelunking is not encouraged. For more information on the Mississippi Band of Choctaw Indians, including their history, culture, and businesses, visit www.choctaw.org.

Philadelphia's heritage doesn't stop with the Choctaw. A self-guided driving tour brochure of historic homes and architecture is available by calling the Philadelphia Chamber of Commerce at (601) 656–1742 or (877) 752–2643, and the *Neshoba County-Philadelphia Historical Museum* (303 Water Avenue) displays artifacts related to local history. But the town is most famous as the site of one of America's most unusual gatherings, the *Neshoba County Fair* (see sidebar, "Mississippi's Giant House Party").

Like most businesses in Philadelphia, *Peggy's Restaurant* is closed the week of the Neshoba County Fair. But if you're in town any other time of the year, stop by for a home-cooked lunch, served in Peggy Webb's home at the corner of Bay Street and Byrd Avenue. Dining is a casual experience at Peggy's—there's no sign outside, no host to seat you, and no server to take your order. Diners help themselves to an all-you-can-eat buffet groaning with fried chicken, pork chops, chicken 'n' dumplings, and other southern favorites. The food is wholesome and delicious, but the most memorable feature at Peggy's is the payment policy. Everyone here eats on the honor system. Once you've had your fill, just leave $7.00 (including tax) in the basket by the front door and be on your way. There's no bill, no receipt, no cash register, just one basket for payment and another for making change. As Peggy explains, it's less work for her, people like to be trusted, and even after forty years on the honor system, she's never once been stiffed.

Peggy considered closing her kitchen in 2000, but swayed by popular demand and her own love of cooking, she changed her mind. Peggy serves lunch for up to 200 people weekdays from 11:00 A.M. to 2:00 P.M. or until the food runs out, which is a distinct possibility on fried chicken days. To-go lunches are also available for pickup at the back door. Call (601) 656–3478.

If you miss out on lunch at Peggy's, you can always pick up a slice of hoop cheese and some slab bacon at the *Williams Brothers Store.* Founded

Mississippi's Giant House Party

The first thing you'll notice as you approach the Neshoba County fairgrounds are the houses—600 whimsical, crayon-colored cabins, most looking as though nothing more than good luck is holding them together. These ramshackle structures have usually been in the same family for generations and have been the subject of divorce disputes and contested wills on more than one occasion. The original cabins on "Founder's Square" are prime pieces of real estate, selling for as much as $100,000 each.

The price tag is only mildly astounding until you realize that for fifty-one weeks out of the year, the cabins are boarded up and the fairgrounds are deserted: That $100,000 is spent to enjoy a mere seven days at the fair in August. For that one week, the fairgrounds are jumping with a full-blown midway, harness races, musical acts, and the crowning of a teenage queen. The Neshoba County Fair is also famous for political stumping, attracting candidates for every office from dogcatcher to President of the United States.

Above all else, the Neshoba County Fair is famous for its hospitality. Many of the cabins have hosted overnight guests since the first Neshoba County Fair more than one hundred years ago. Strangers will invite you to join them for lunch or lemonade on the front porch, or even to pass the night in one of the technicolor cabins (be sure to choose one with air-conditioning—a nontraditional indulgence considered a fair faux pas as few as ten years ago). This rare display of universal hospitality has earned the fair the nickname "Mississippi's Giant House Party." For this year's dates, call the Philadelphia Chamber of Commerce at (601) 656–1742 or (877) 752–2643. Dress comfortably and bring a handheld fan.

Mississippi Burning

The most infamous chapter in Mississippi history unfolded in the summer of 1964, when three civil-rights workers vanished in rural Neshoba County.

James Chaney, Andrew Goodman, and Michael Schwerner disappeared on June 21, 1964, while investigating the burning of a black church near Philadelphia. Forty-four days later, a still-unidentified informant led the FBI to their bodies, buried in an earthen dam just outside town. All three had been shot. No one was ever convicted of the murders.

This dark period in Mississippi history was thrust back into the national spotlight in 1988, when the murders served as the basis of the highly fictionalized film *Mississippi Burning.*

While the film's release opened decades-old wounds, it also pointed out the stark contrast between the segregated Mississippi of the 1960s and the progressive Mississippi of today. And while the true story may have been compromised, the film did generate new interest in and appreciation for the work of Chaney, Goodman, and Schwerner, whose tragic deaths helped mobilize and unite all Mississippians, black and white.

Today, a monument honoring James Chaney, Andrew Goodman, and Michael Schwerner graces the grounds of Mt. Zion Church off Highway 16 East in Neshoba County—the same place where the three young men gave their lives for the cause they believed in, and forever changed the state where they died.

in 1907, Williams Brothers still retains the old-fashioned charm that led *National Geographic* to feature the "needles to horse collars" emporium in a 1937 issue. Located off Highway 16 west of Philadelphia, Williams Brothers is open Monday–Saturday 7:00 A.M.–6:00 P.M. Call (601) 656–2651.

From Philadelphia, take Highway 16 West to Mississippi Highway 39 North into rural Kemper County and follow the signs and the gravel road to ***Sciple's Water Mill,*** the oldest continuously operating water mill in the United States. The original mill was built in 1790 and was owned and operated by four families over the next fifty years. The Sciple family purchased the property around 1840 and has kept it up and running ever since. Today the mill is run by Edward Sciple, who gave up his job as a television repairman to continue the family tradition.

Sciple's Mill sits on a rocky stream surrounded by steep, tree-covered hillsides. Steps made of rock lead to the split-level building where horseshoes hang from the wooden wall and iron cowbells dangle from the rafters. Until the mid-1950s, the mill also ginned cotton and sawed lumber. Today visitors can purchase stone-ground cornmeal, and grits, or just relax down by the old mill stream.

The mill is 10 miles northwest of DeKalb off the Kellis Store Road. Several signs point the way from area highways and byways, but if you need specific directions, call (601) 743–2754. Sciple's Mill is open Monday–Friday 8:00 A.M.–3:00 P.M Visitors are welcome to stroll the grounds after hours and on weekends.

From the mill, take Mississippi Highway 39 South to **Meridian,** a historic railroad town, bustling industrial center, and the third-largest city in Mississippi.

As you drive around town, you'll notice colorful carousel horses—thirty-seven in all—prancing in front of businesses citywide. The 5-foot, fiberglass horses are part of Meridian's **Around Town Carousels Abound** program, a public art project inspired by the city's Dentzel Carousel. Each whimsical, rainbow-hued sculpture was sponsored by a Meridian individual or business, then decorated by a local or regional artist. Artists were given a stipend to cover materials, but donated their time and talents. Proceeds from the sponsorships benefited Hope Village for Children, a shelter founded by Meridian native and actor Sela Ward. Each horse was given a distinctive theme and name. You'll find "Horseplay" on the lawn of the Meridian Little Theatre, "Lightning" in front of the fire station, and "Horsecents" outside the local bank.

For a whirl on the carousel that inspired all this horseplay, follow I–20/59 to the Twenty-second Avenue exit, turn left on Eighth Street, and follow the signs to **Highland Park** (Forty-first Avenue and Nineteenth Street). Since 1909, Meridian's children (and more than a few adults) have flocked to the park for a spin on the rare **Dentzel Carousel.** Hand-carved, hand-painted ponies, goats,

You Can Take the Girl out of Meridian . . .

Golden Globe and two-time Emmy winner Sela Ward grew up in Meridian and still maintains a home in the area. Ward has proved a driving force in her hometown, spearheading renovation efforts at Meridian's Grand Opera House and founding Hope Village, a shelter for abused, neglected, and homeless children. When *Homesick,* Ward's autobiographical love letter to the South, was published in 2002, the famous actor held a book signing at the Meridian Wal Mart.

If you miss Sela Ward's latest TV or movie project, look for her in reruns of the critically acclaimed television shows *Sisters* and *Once and Again.* And if you can't find her on cable, try Weidmann's restaurant in Meridian, where the lovely Sela Ward is not only a regular but a part-owner.

Peavey Electronics—
The Sound Heard 'Round the World

Meridian's best-known business is Peavey Electronics, the world's largest manufacturer of musical amplification equipment. The company began in the early 1960s, when young Hartley Peavey built his first amplifier in the basement of his parents' home, then carried it door-to-door until he found a buyer. When he went to the local bank in search of a start-up loan, the banker told Hartley his daddy would have to co-sign for him. Today, Peavey's amplifiers, guitars, and sound systems are sold in 134 countries around the world and the company employs 2,000 workers—all of whom are paid through an account at the second bank Hartley Peavey called on.

Major artists, including Brooks and Dunn, Michael Bolton, Eddie Van Halen, Kenny Loggins, and Reba McEntire, enthusiastically endorse Peavey equipment as the finest in the world. Top recording artists often visit Meridian to test new equipment—you never know who you might bump into.

deer, giraffes, and lions whirl to cheerful circus music, accompanied by the delighted shrieks and high-pitched giggles of children and grown-ups alike. The carousel was built by Gustav Dentzel in 1895. Meridian's city fathers bought the carousel for $2,000 in 1909 and built the present carousel house following a Dentzel blueprint. About twenty Dentzel carousels exist in the United States, but the Highland Park carousel is one of only a handful still populated by the original animals, and is the only two-row, stationary Dentzel menagerie carousel in existence. The carousel spins weekends year-round from noon to 6:00 P.M. and Wednesday, Thursday, and Friday during late spring and summer from 10:00 A.M. to 2:00 P.M. The price of a ride has gone up from the original nickel to fifty cents—a worthwhile investment for the nostalgic pleasure a ride is sure to bring.

Highland Park is also home to the *Jimmie Rodgers Museum,* a tribute to the railroad worker who came to be known as the "Father of Country Music." Born in Meridian in 1897, Rodgers recorded his first song in 1927. "Sleep, Baby, Sleep" sold more than a million copies and earned Rodgers national fame as an entertainer. Tragically, Rodgers was stricken with tuberculosis at the height of his career. In 1933, he recorded his last songs, performing from a cot set up in the studio. He died later that year at age thirty-six. In 1961, Jimmie Rodgers became the first inductee into the newly formed Country Music Hall of Fame.

The Jimmie Rodgers Museum houses memorabilia from Rodgers's short but memorable career. The museum is open Monday–Saturday 10:00 A.M.–4:00 P.M. and Sunday 1:00–5:00 P.M. Admission is $5.00. Held every May, the *Jimmie Rodgers Festival* features performances by top country music stars. For this year's dates and a list of performers, call the Meridian/Lauderdale County Tourism Bureau at (888) 868–7720 or the Jimmie Rodgers Museum at (601) 485–1808.

Meridian offers tours of two historic homes, **Merrehope** and the **F. W. Williams House,** both located at 905 Martin Luther King Jr., Memorial Drive. Both homes are open Monday–Saturday 9:00 A.M.–4:00 P.M. Admission is $10.00 for both homes.

Be sure to inquire about Eugenia, Merrehope's resident ghost. Eugenia Gary died in Alabama just before her father purchased Merrehope in 1868. But if the stories are true, Eugenia moved into the house anyway—and continues to live there today. Several Merrehope visitors and employees have reported seeing a young woman in period dress moving about the house or gazing out the windows. All of the witnesses identified the specter as the same young woman whose portrait hangs in the museum room upstairs. The girl in the portrait is Eugenia Gary.

Those interested in Mississippi's civil-rights and African-American heritage may wish to pay respects at the gravesite of James Chaney. Along with fellow

Meridian's Own Phantom of the Opera

The curtain first rose on Meridian's Grand Opera House on Fifth Street in 1890. Nicknamed "The Lady" after the hand-painted portrait of an unidentified "Gibson Girl" on the proscenium above the stage, this palatial theater hosted the finest talent in the country. Touring opera and Shakespearean companies, vaudeville shows, and minstrel acts all took the stage at the lavish Grand Opera House. A young George Gershwin's signature is still visible on one of the dressing room walls.

After thirty-seven years of theatrical magic, the Grand Opera House closed, but it seems one of the performers never left. While the doors are kept locked and the curtain is down, a beautiful melody often rings through the empty theater—the crystal-clear voice of a woman singing. The sound seems to come from the empty stage, behind the portrait of the unidentified Gibson Girl. Visitors to the long-dark theater have also reported cold spots on blistering summer days, the low murmur of a voice backstage, and the sound of shattering crystal—perhaps the spirit of a long-gone diva, practicing for her next performance. Over time, the ghost has also come to be known as "The Lady."

The Grand Opera House is currently undergoing a $31 million restoration, and is scheduled to reopen in 2006. Once again, the theater will fill with patrons, the curtain will rise, and beautiful music will fill the Grand Opera House. Perhaps the return of live entertainment will put The Lady's spirit to rest. Then again, perhaps the mysterious diva has been practicing for decades, waiting for her new audience.

The King and Queen of the Gypsies

The events that brought Kelly Mitchell, the Queen of the Gypsies, to Meridian's **Rose Hill Cemetery** for burial in 1915 are unknown; perhaps she was simply in the area when she died. Whatever the reason, it was in Meridian that the Queen laid in state for twelve days while members of the tribe gathered from around the nation for her funeral. When the hearse headed out to Rose Hill Cemetery, an estimated 5,000 gypsies followed. When Emil Mitchell, the King of the Gypsies, died years later, he was buried next to his wife, along with several members of the tribe.

Today, the royal gypsy graves are visited frequently by transient tribal members, who leave fresh fruit and juices as a sign of respect. Perhaps they even converse with the spirits of the departed gypsy royals—that would explain why the gravesite has the added feature of patio furniture cemented into the plot.

If you visit the gypsy graves at Rose Hill Cemetery (Fortieth Avenue off Eighth Street) yourself, be sure to bring along some fruit and fresh-squeezed juice. You never know when you might run into a member of the family.

civil rights workers Andrew Goodman and Michael Schwerner, Chaney gave his life for the civil-rights cause in 1964 (see sidebar, "Mississippi Burning," earlier in this chapter). When local black burial grounds refused to inter Chaney's body for fear of reprisals and vandalism, he was finally laid to rest in an isolated grave in the Okatibbee Baptist Church Cemetery in southwest Lauderdale County. On the twenty-fifth anniversary of his death, a marble monument was erected at his grave. Chaney's marker bears the inscription, "THERE ARE THOSE WHO ARE ALIVE, YET WILL NEVER LIVE. THERE ARE THOSE WHO ARE DEAD, YET WILL LIVE FOREVER. GREAT DEEDS INSPIRE AND ENCOURAGE THE LIVING." To get to the cemetery from Interstate 20/59, take exit 151 (Valley Road). Travel 3.4 miles, then turn left at the church on Fish Lodge Road. The cemetery is on the right.

Commemorate your visit to Meridian with a purchase from **Hart Hall**, a century-old Victorian mansion filled to the rafters with distinctive home accessories, jewelry, tableware, and gifts. Hart Hall is located at 1521 Twenty-fourth Avenue in Meridian's Mid-Town Historic District. Call (601) 485–8942.

Other interesting shopping opportunities include **The Bead Island** (1316 Twenty-fifth Avenue), a treasure trove of jewelry, beads, and funky furniture; **The Art Connection** (3813 Eighth Street) for paintings, prints, and books by African-American artists; **The Corner Stitch** (1820 Twenty-third Avenue), an heirloom sewing, smocking, and embroidery shop located in a historic prairie-style home; **Plant the Earth** (7802 Poplar Springs Drive) for handmade soap, candles, and garden art; and **Reflections of Modern Gardens** (3700 Highway

39 North), where yard and garden items share the spotlight with fine china and Gail Pittman pottery.

Admire your purchases over dinner at **Weidmann's Restaurant** (210 Twenty-second Avenue). This Meridian tradition began in 1870, when Swiss immigrant Felix Weidmann established a fruit and vegetable stand on this same downtown corner. As the business grew, Weidmann expanded his offerings and his property, until Weidmann's Restaurant evolved into one of the area's most popular eateries. The restaurant outlived its founder, operating with only minor changes for nearly a century. In 2002, Weidmann's was purchased by popular Mississippi restaurateur Nick Apostle, chef Willie McGeehee, and a group of local investors that included actor Sela Ward. The building was completely remodeled, the menu was overhauled, and in 2003 Weidmann's reopened, quickly regaining its status as a Meridian favorite.

Railroad buffs may prefer to dine at **Montana's** (2113 Front Street), where the decor includes a 2,000-square-foot model railroad traveled by the locomotive "Queen City Big Dog." Members of the Queen City Model Railroad Club built the elaborate, working model, which encompasses more than 1,500 feet of track and more miniature details than can possibly be absorbed in a single visit. The display is open for public viewing during the restaurant's regular hours, 11:00 A.M.–2:00 P.M. Monday, and 11:00 A.M.–9:00 P.M. Tuesday–Saturday. The trains run 4:30–9:30 P.M. Thursday, and 8:00 A.M.–2:00 P.M. Saturday.

Take a welcome break from the road with a stay in one of Meridian's charming bed-and-breakfast inns. Owners Thomas and Janet McBrien run a southern bed-and-breakfast with an English and Irish flair at **The Lion and Harp** (4432 State Boulevard). For rates and reservations at this lovely Victorian inn, call (601) 485–8235 or visit www.lion andharp.com. A neoclassical beauty overlooking the city, the 1902 **Century House Bed and Breakfast** (2412 Ninth Street) offers bed-and-breakfast accommodations within walking distance of several Meridian attractions. Call (601) 482–2345 or visit www.centuryhousebnb.com.

triviafact

Meridian's E. F. Young Manufacturing Company is the oldest African-American-owned company in the United States. The firm was founded in 1933 by E. F. Young, a barber who developed and patented one of the world's first lines of black hair care products.

Another old-fashioned pleasure waits just outside Meridian in the tiny hamlet of **Causeyville.** The 1895 **Causeyville General Store and Gristmill** stocks snacks and sundries behind its old-timey counters and original fixtures, and displays antique music boxes and other instruments in its mechanical music museum. The store is open from a crack-of-dawn 6:00 A.M.–7:00 P.M. Monday–

Little-Known Facts about the Eastern Plains

Columbus was originally christened "Possum Town" in a dubious tribute to early settler Spirus Roach, who bore an unfortunate resemblance to an opossum.

The Tennessee-Tombigbee Waterway and the Great Wall of China are the only man-made objects on earth visible to astronauts in space.

Before putting down roots on the Mississippi State University campus, a sycamore tree planted outside the university's Dorman Hall flew to the moon on an Apollo mission as a sapling.

At its height in the early 1800s, the Mississippi Choctaw nation included fifty villages and more than 25,000 warriors. The word "Choctaw" means "charming voice."

Meridian's Peavey Electronics is the world's largest manufacturer of musical amplification equipment.

Famed hat maker John B. Stetson honed his skills at Dunn's Falls near Meridian. It was here the haberdasher designed his most popular creation, a men's hat known simply as "the Stetson."

Every twenty-four hours, 365 days a year, Weyerhaeuser's Columbus paper manufacturing facility produces a ribbon of paper 24 feet wide and 900 feet long—the size of a two-lane highway extending all the way from Columbus to Philadelphia, Pennsylvania.

Columbus' Sanderson Plumbing Products, Inc., is the exclusive supplier of toilet seats for the space shuttle.

The Mississippi School for Math and Science is one of only four state- supported, residential high schools for academically talented students in the nation.

Saturday, and 8:00 A.M.–5:00 P.M. Sunday. Take Highway 19 South approximately 7 miles from Meridian, watching for the right turn to Causeyville. Follow the signs approximately 5 miles to the Causeyville General Store, located at 6129 Causeyville Road. If you get turned around, call (601) 644–3102 and ask for directions.

Another interesting side trip lies just west of Meridian in *Decatur.* This rural community is home to Melvin Tingle's *Okla Museum,* a collection of primitive tools, furniture, and other historic artifacts, most related to the history of Newton County. The highlight of Melvin's collection is the Indian Basket Room, a display of more than 300 handmade Choctaw Indian baskets, some as many as 150 years old. Melvin bought his first Choctaw basket more than forty years ago, and he's still adding to the collection today. With such an extensive display of the artistic expression of this proud native race, it's only fitting that the museum be called "Okla," the Choctaw word for "people." The collection is displayed in a replica of a farmhouse Melvin built "from scratch" behind his home.

To get to the Okla Museum, follow I–20 West from Meridian and take the Hickory exit right to Highway 503 North, which will lead you into Decatur. Turn right when the road dead-ends at Highway 15; Melvin's house is about 150 yards down on the left and is marked by a small cedar shingle on a wooden post. Melvin welcomes visitors whenever he's home, but it's wise to call (601) 635–2023 before heading out for a visit.

From the Meridian area, take I–59 South 11 miles to the Savoy exit at Enterprise, then follow the signs to *Dunn's Falls.* This crystal-clear, 65-foot waterfall once served as a power source for a gristmill and for the manufacturing of Stetson hats. The historic Carroll Richardson Gristmill, complete with working waterwheel, is open for tours. Dunn's Falls also features a swimming area in the old mill pond, hiking trails, campsites, and picnic areas with grills. Dunn's Falls is open seven days a week. Hours are 9:00 A.M.–5:00 P.M. October–March, and 9:00 A.M.–7:00 P.M. April–September. Admission is $1.25.

Continue on US 45 South to *Quitman* and another famous swimmin' hole, the *Archusa Creek Water Park. Archusa Springs* was a popular resort of the 1800s built around a "medicinal" sulfur spring. Located near the Civil War–era Texas Hospital, the spring was frequented by recuperating soldiers. The hospital and resort were destroyed by Union troops in 1864. A Texas Hospital memorial marker and Confederate cemetery are located 2 miles south of

Old Man Stucky's Ghost

A man named Stucky once ran an inn in the small community of Savoy near Dunn's Falls. Stucky was rumored to have been a member of the infamous Dalton gang. Unable to put his wicked ways behind him, he robbed and murdered as many as twenty of his patrons, burying his victims beneath a wooden bridge over the Chunky River. When his dastardly deeds were discovered, Stucky was hung from the bridge, which came to be known as both "The Hanging Bridge" and "Stucky's Bridge."

What became of Stucky's ill-gotten treasure isn't certain, but according to local legend and frightened witnesses, Stucky is still searching for it. The tale of Old Man Stucky may be shrouded in mystery, but one thing is clear—if your travels bring you to Stucky's Bridge in Savoy after dark, and if you see the swinging glow of a kerosene lantern crossing the bridge, the smartest thing for you to do is *run.*

Quitman on US 45. The spring still flows into Archusa Lake today, and analyses reveal the water is still high in sulfur. Nearby Archusa Creek Water Park offers rustic cabin rentals and outdoor recreational activities in a wilderness setting.

In October the water park hosts the annual **Clarke County Forestry and Wildlife Festival,** featuring forestry competitions, arts and crafts, food, and live entertainment. For cabin rental rates and reservations or information about the festival, call (601) 776–5701.

Outdoorsy types will also enjoy a float trip down the **Chickasawhay River.** Information on canoe rentals is available from the **Clarke County Chamber of Commerce,** (601) 776–5701.

The chamber also offers a free, self-guided driving tour brochure of lovely homes, a historic mill town, and other sites listed on the National Register of Historic Places. Call for your copy or pick one up at the chamber offices at 100 South Railroad Avenue.

Places to Stay in the Eastern Plains

The following is a partial listing of the many hotels, motels, and bed-and-breakfast inns in the area not mentioned in the text.

Lincoln Ltd. is a full-time reservation service for bed-and-breakfast inns statewide. For reservations in any area of Mississippi, call (601) 482–5483 or (800) 633–6477.

COLUMBUS

Amzi Love
(bed-and-breakfast)
305 Seventh Street South,
(662) 328–5413

Backstrom's Country Bed and Breakfast
4567 Highway 182 East,
(662) 328–7213 or
(800) 689–3983
www.missbab.com

Cartney-Hunt House
(bed-and-breakfast)
408 Seventh Street South,
(662) 244–7232
www.cartney-hunthouse.com

The Griffin Home Bed and Breakfast
1305 Third Avenue North,
(662) 329–0010

Highland House
(bed-and-breakfast)
810 Highland Circle,
(662) 327–5577

Plymouth Bluff Center
(rental cabins)
2200 Old West Point Road,
(662) 241–6214
www.plymouthbluff.com

KOSCIUSKO

Peeler House Bed and Breakfast
203 North Wells Street,
(662) 289–5086

PHILADELPHIA

Pearl River Resort Silver Star Hotel & Casino and Golden Moon Hotel & Casino
(on the Choctaw Indian Reservation)
Highway 16 West,
(866) 447–3275
www.pearlriverresort.com

QUITMAN

Archusa Water Park
(cabin rentals)
540 County Road 110,
(601) 776–6956 or
(800) 748–9403

STARKVILLE

Hotel Chester
101 North Jackson Street,
(662) 323–5005 or
(866) 325–5005

Places to Eat in the Eastern Plains

The following is a partial listing of the many restaurants in the area not mentioned in the text.

COLUMBUS

Brickerton Grille
(seafood, steaks, pasta, salads)
78 Brickerton Street,
(662) 327–5474

J. Broussard's
(New Orleans–style)
309 Main Street,
(662) 243–1480
www.jbroussards.com

Proffitt's Porch
(po'boys, red beans and rice, seafood gumbo, homemade desserts)
1587 Officer's Lake Road,
(662) 327–4485

KOSCIUSKO

Cafe on the Square
(sandwiches, salads, lunch only)
117 West Jefferson Street
(inside Peeler House Antiques),
(662) 289–5165

MERIDIAN

Café Latte
(light lunches, specialty coffee)
820 Twenty-second Avenue,
(601) 482–3663

The Hungry Heifer
(emu burgers, Cajun catfish, eclectic specialties)
1310 Fourteenth Street,
(601) 483–2509

Luigi's
(Italian)
1910 Highway 19 North,
(601) 693–0100

PHILADELPHIA

The Magnolia
(casual)
103 Walnut Street,
(601) 389–6700

STARKVILLE

Abner's Famous Chicken Tenders
(chicken, tortilla wraps, salads)
518 South Montgomery Street,
(662) 338–0098

The Little Dooey
(barbecue)
100 Fellowship Street,
(662) 323–6094
www.littledooey.com

ALSO WORTH SEEING

COLUMBUS
Lake Lowndes State Park

Rosenzweig Art Center

LOUISVILLE
Legion State Park

MACON
Noxubee National Wildlife Refuge

MERIDIAN
Meridian Museum of Art

MORTON
Roosevelt State Park

PHILADELPHIA
Dancing Rabbit Golf Course

Geyser Falls Water Park

Golden Moon Casino

Silver Star Casino

QUITMAN
Clarkco State Park

The Mississippi River Delta

According to writer David Cohen, "the Mississippi Delta begins in the lobby of the Peabody Hotel in Memphis and ends on Catfish Row in Vicksburg." Home to the richest farmland on earth, the Delta is a land and a people shaped by agriculture and ruled by the Mississippi River, a place where cotton was once king and its subjects sang the blues.

Cohen's statement may be geographically accurate, but a real description of the Delta reaches beyond mere geography. The Delta is not just a place, but a mindset. Natives of the area will tell you that you can never *really* understand the Delta culture unless you were born into it, and you'll soon find that's not an exaggeration.

Some people can't bear a moment in this hot, flat land; others would wither up and die if they had to leave it. As you travel the Delta's back roads and get acquainted with its people and with the land itself, you can decide for yourself which group you belong to.

Blues Alley

Your first Delta stop should be ***The Hollywood Restaurant*** off U.S. Highway 61 in tiny ***Robinsonville.*** Housed in an 1860s

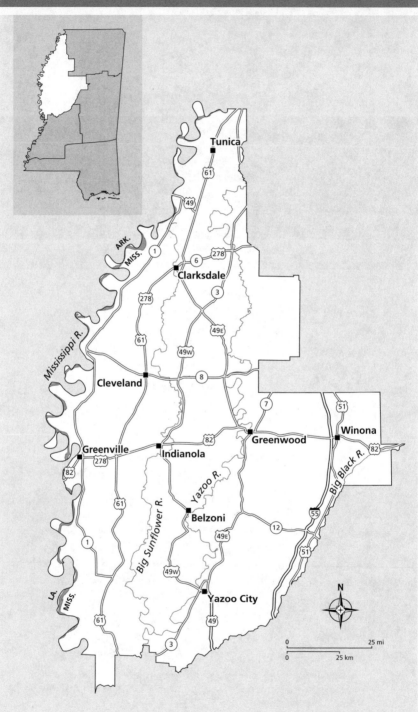

THE MISSISSIPPI RIVER DELTA

plantation commissary, The Hollywood is mentioned in John Grisham's best-selling novel *The Firm* and in Mark Cohn's Grammy-winning song "Walking in Memphis." A native of New York, Cohn frequented The Hollywood whenever he was in the mid-South, often taking the stage to sing with Muriel the piano player. Not only did Cohn write Muriel into the song, he flew her to New York to play at his wedding. The Hollywood is open for dinner Thursday–Saturday, serving up seafood, steaks, frog legs, catfish, and The Hollywood's famous fried dill pickles. The restaurant usually features live entertainment, but for the biggest names, scan the crowd—The Hollywood is a favorite of many famous musicians, including the legendary B. B. King.

Once the poorest county in the entire United States, **Tunica County** is now a booming tourist resort fueled by the nonstop action of **casino gaming.** The former agricultural villages of Tunica and Robinsonville are now the nation's third-largest gambling destination. Of course, cotton is still planted right up to the slot machines, and the towering resorts share the Delta' skyline with passing crop dusters.

Although a glitzy casino can hardly be considered an off-the-beaten path destination, several of the twenty-four-hour-a-day pleasure palaces offer some unusual exhibitions and recreational opportunities that are worth tearing yourself away from the table to experience.

Hollywood Casino (1150 Casino Strip Boulevard) is home to the biplane from Alfred Hitchcock's classic *North by Northwest,* the Harrier jet from Arnold Schwarzenegger's *True Lies,* and a 6,000-pound scale model of the ill-fated ship used in James Cameron's epic *Titanic.*

MARLO'S FAVORITE ATTRACTIONS IN THE MISSISSIPPI RIVER DELTA

McCarty Pottery,
Merigold

Doe's Eat Place,
Greenville

Cotton in bloom,
as far as the eye can see

The Shack Up Inn,
an overnight experience like no other,
Clarksdale

Glenwood Cemetery,
final resting place of the Witch of Yazoo,
Yazoo City

Cheese straws from the Mississippi Cheese Straw Factory,
Yazoo City

Kudzu sculptures,
just outside Yazoo City

Catfish Pâté,
Indianola

MARLO'S FAVORITE ANNUAL EVENTS IN THE MISSISSIPPI RIVER DELTA

BELZONI

World Catfish Festival,
April,
(662) 247–4838 or (800) 408–4838

CLARKSDALE

Sunflower River Blues Festival,
August,
(662) 627–7337

Tennessee Williams Festival,
October,
(662) 627–7337

CLEVELAND

Crosstie Arts Festival,
April,
(800) 295–7473

GREENVILLE

Mississippi Delta Blues and Heritage
Festival,
September,
(800) 467–3582

GREENWOOD

Balloon Fest,
June,
(800) 748–9064

Sky Parade,
Dates vary,
(800) 748–9064

INDIANOLA

B. B. King Homecoming,
June,
(662) 887–4454

In addition to blackjack and slots, the *Grand Casino Tunica* (Old Highway 61 North) offers the challenge of sporting clay shooting at the *Willows Sporting Clay Center,* and instruction by PGA pros at its Hale Irwin–designed *Cottonwoods Golf Course.*

The *Horseshoe Casino* (1021 Casino Center Drive) is home to the *Blues & Legends Hall of Fame Museum,* which traces the history of blues music from its Mississippi beginnings to its modern world presence. The free museum includes exhibits on blues greats John Lee Hooker, Muddy Waters, and Eric Clapton, and displays the pictures, instruments, and memorabilia of early blues performers and today's hottest blues stars. Special collections showcase women in blues, pioneer radio stations and early studios, Beale Street, and the history of the Handy Awards.

Tunica County's casinos feature live entertainment by top acts year-round. For a schedule of performances, contact the *Tunica Convention and Visitors Bureau* at (888) 4TUNICA.

Just a few minutes' drive but a world away from the hustle and glitz of the casinos lies the quiet town of *Tunica.* Here visitors can stroll the peaceful streets of the turn-of-the-twentieth-century downtown area, relax in **Rivergate Park,** or visit the restored **Tunica County Courthouse,** where the original marriage license of bluesman Robert Johnson is displayed. For an in-depth look at Tunica County pre-casinos, visit the **Tunica Museum,** where exhibits focus on agriculture, music, and the county's famous sons and daughters. Step into the past at One Museum Boulevard (off US 61, north of Paul Battle Arena) in Tunica.

Antiques buffs should also allow time for browsing the treasures at **Main Street Market Antiques** (1212 Edwards Avenue), **1251 Place** (1251 Main Street), and **Ann-Tiques** (1255 Main Street). Bargain hunters will even discover a touch of Mississippiana tucked inside the impersonal **Casino Factory Shoppes** (US 61 North and Grand Casino Parkway). The outlet mall's **Gail Pittman Outlet Store** carries bold pottery and colorful dinnerware by nationally celebrated Mississippi artist Gail Pittman.

Even before the casinos sprang up out of the cotton fields, the **Blue & White Restaurant** was a tourist attraction. The Blue & White has stood at the corner of US 61 and Mississippi Highway 4 in Tunica since 1937. Elvis Presley was once

Famous Deltans

Blues artists born in the Mississippi Delta include: Sam Chatmon, Billy Deaton, John Lee Hooker, Son House, Mississippi John Hurt, Skip James, Robert Johnson, B. B. King, Charlie Patton, Otis Spann, James "Son" Thomas, Ike Turner, Muddy Waters, Bukka White, and Sonny Boy Williamson.

The Delta was also home to a couple of country music stars. Sledge, Mississippi, was the birthplace of Charley Pride. Harold Jenkins, better known as Conway Twitty, grew up in tiny Friars Point.

The Reverend C. L. Franklin preached in Friars Point; his daughter Aretha was a member of the church choir.

Actor Morgan Freeman, known for his roles in *Driving Miss Daisy, Shawshank Redemption, The Unforgiven,* and *Nurse Betty,* grew up in Tallahatchie County and still owns a farm in Charleston. Freeman is co-owner of Madidi, an upscale restaurant, and Ground Zero, a down-and-dirty blues club, both in Clarksdale.

The late author Willie Morris immortalized his hometown of Yazoo City in his books *Good Old Boy* and *My Dog Skip.* Hollywood's version of *My Dog Skip* became an instant family classic.

Motivational speaker Zig Ziglar and the late comedian Jerry Clower also hailed from Yazoo City.

Pioneer TV producer Fred Coe was born in Alligator, Mississippi. Coe produced the 1950s live TV dramas *The Trip to Bountiful, Days of Wine and Roses,* and *Peter Pan.*

House of Blues

Many of Mississippi's most famous blues artists shared a common address—the Parchman Penitentiary. This Delta correctional facility is a former residence of such blues notables as Bukka White, Son House, and Sonny Boy Williamson. Bukka White cashed in on his three-year stay in Parchman, recording the hit "Parchman Farm Blues" and a tribute to prison uniforms, "When Can I Change My Clothes?" Although accommodations and food are free and the current residents are usually happy to welcome visitors, Parchman is not high on the list of off-the-beaten-path vacation destinations.

a frequent patron, and members of the ZZ Top band still stop by for a plate of old-fashioned country cooking whenever they play in Memphis. And country cooking it is. The Blue & White is the best place to get a quick introduction to some southern foods that even a lot of southerners might pass on. After all, it takes a special palate to appreciate turnip greens, country ham, and scrambled pork brains. The Blue & White is open for breakfast, lunch, and dinner.

Playwright Tennessee Williams spent much of his childhood in the Delta and immortalized many of the area's landmarks in his plays. In *The Glass Menagerie,* Amanda Wingfield speaks of a favorite beau who "got in a quarrel with the wild Wainwright boy. They shot it out on the floor of the Moon Lake Casino." The Moon Lake Club was a real place, a casino and dance club near the Mississippi–Arkansas state line that was one of the liveliest Delta night spots of the 1930s. In 1946, Henry Trevino purchased the property, continuing the Moon Lake tradition under the name "Henry's Place" until the 1970s. Today the old casino is a restaurant and bed-and-breakfast inn run by Trevino's descendants. Guests at **Uncle Henry's Place** enjoy gourmet seafood and Creole and Cajun dishes, then retire to rooms in the club's old casino section. Dinner is served Wednesday–Sunday and reservations are recommended, so call (662) 337-2757 for directions and a seat at the table.

Continue along US 61 South through cotton fields and farmland to **Clarksdale.** The soil around Clarksdale is black, rich, and incredibly fertile. The topsoil thickness averages 132 feet and, in some spots, stretches as deep as 350 feet. Not one square inch of this precious earth goes to waste—where other towns have medians, Clarksdale has cotton. In some sections of the city, cotton is planted right up to the front doors.

Cotton notwithstanding, Clarksdale's biggest claim to fame is as a mecca for fans of the **Mississippi Delta Blues.** The blues is a combination of mournful wails and dryly humorous lyrics that's every bit as much a way of life as a musical form. Born from the chants of slaves who worked the cotton fields in this part of the state decades before the Civil War, the blues is recognized as America's only original music. As blues great B. B. King puts it, "the blues is the truth about life, how it was lived, and how it is lived today."

Clarksdale was the first stop on the "chitlin' circuit," a route through the Delta traveled by wandering bluesmen in the 1920s and 1930s. Blues legends W. C. Handy, Charlie Patton, Muddy Waters, John Lee Hooker, Robert Johnson, and Howlin' Wolf all called Clarksdale home. Weekends found *Issaquena Avenue* packed with sharecroppers who came to town to shop, socialize, and party in rough-and-tumble nightclubs known as "juke joints."

From these humble beginnings, the blues went on to influence every other form of American music. Polished and transplanted to nightclubs in Chicago, urbanized blues became jazz, and Elvis Presley combined the blues with country music to give the world rock and roll.

The best place to begin a blues tour is the *Clarksdale Station and Blues Alley,* an old railroad depot renovated and transformed into an entertainment complex featuring shopping, dining, and live musical performances, all with a blues theme.

In this complex, #1 Blues Alley is home to the *Delta Blues Museum,* the definitive repository of the blues. In creating the museum, founder Sid Graves said, "I don't want a museum that swims in formaldehyde—I want something

A Huck Finn Adventure

The Mississippi River winds some 2,350 miles from the central United States to the Gulf of Mexico. One of the most scenic and exciting ways to explore the lower Mississippi River, which includes the entire western boundary of the state of Mississippi, is by canoe.

Clarksdale's **Quapaw Canoe Company** offers wilderness expeditions on the lower Mississippi River, its backwaters, tributaries, bayous, oxbow lakes, and flood plains. Adventurers camp on secluded sandbars, come eyeball-to-eyeball with river wildlife, and navigate swirling eddies the size of a city block, all under the leadership of an experienced river guide.

Float trips are available along any section of the river between Cairo, Illinois, and the Gulf of Mexico. Trips may last anywhere from a single day to several weeks.

A word of warning—clients must be willing to paddle and to endure nature's extremes, not the least of which is intense heat during the summer months.

For more information or to plan your Mississippi River adventure, contact Quapaw Canoe Company, (662) 627–4070, or visit the Web site at www.island63.com.

vibrant and alive." Vibrant and alive it is. Tucked among the expected guitars, harmonicas, and photographs, you'll find oddities like the folk art sculpture *Woman in Coffin* by bluesman James "Son" Thomas, who also worked as a gravedigger. An 8-foot-tall, one hundred pound, technicolor egg depicting blues scenes rests in the center of the display area. Inherited from a mock Fabergé exhibit in Memphis, the *Beale Street Blues Egg* is covered in paintings of blues artists and overlaid with bottle caps and coins collected from Beale Street.

But the most intriguing display is what's left of blues great Muddy Waters's cabin from the old Stovall Plantation. Muddy Waters (born McKinley Morgan-field) grew up in this humble cabin and worked on the plantation as a young man. In 1941 and 1942, a researcher studying the blues for a project sponsored by the Library of Congress recorded Waters's music in this cabin. The record-ings were later released as *Muddy Waters: Down on Stovall's Plantation.*

Musicians from Eric Clapton to ZZ Top have credited Muddy Waters as a primary influence on their music; The Rolling Stones even took their name from the lyrics of a Muddy Waters song. Clapton once said, "Muddy took the music of the Delta plantation, transplanted it in a Chicago nightclub, surrounded it with an electric band, and changed the course of popular music forever." In 1989, ZZ Top's Billy Gibbons took several pieces of wood from Muddy Waters's dilapidated cabin and had them fashioned into the "Muddywood guitar." The instrument toured the country as a fundraiser for the Delta Blues Museum.

For decades Waters's cabin remained on the Stovall Plantation grounds, enduring exposure to the elements and vandalism by souvenir seekers. Preser-vation came in the form of the House of Blues restaurant/nightclub chain, which "restored" the cabin to its original outer appearance, then loaded up the structure and took it on tour. Upon its return to Clarksdale, the cabin became a permanent exhibit in the Delta Blues Museum. The cabin houses a lifelike wax statue of Waters, and the Muddywood guitar is displayed near the very section of the wall from which its wood was harvested. A scrap of the news-paper used as original wallpaper is framed on the cabin wall. As the museum guide explains, "They had no money for wallpaper, insulation, or entertain-ment. The newspaper provided all three."

Posted quotations from Muddy Waters himself offer insight into this blues great's personality. "When you say blues, you know what the average guy is looking for," one reads, "half-slouching, raggedy, bottle of wine in your pocket. I wasn't that kind of blues singer. I stayed sharp. . . . They might say I can't play or can't sing, but damn it, they'll say I'm a gentleman."

The museum gift shop sells books, magazines, photos, and, of course, recordings of America's only original music. Pick up a tape or CD for the road;

you'll find the blues offer a history lesson, cultural experience, and audio tour of the Delta in every note.

Attracting fans from around the world, the Delta Blues Museum can't really be considered off the beaten path anymore. In one ten-day period, visitors from Australia, Italy, Colombia, Egypt, Russia, Portugal, Thailand, Spain, Syria, Ireland, Iceland, and England all signed the guest register. To add your name to the list, follow the many signs to #1 Blues Alley. The museum is open Monday–Saturday 9:00 A.M.–5:00 P.M., March–October; Monday–Saturday 10:00 A.M.–5:00 P.M., November–February. Admission is $6.00 for adults, $3.00 for children six–twelve, free for kids under six with an adult.

Downtown Clarksdale is filled with significant blues landmarks. Take a stroll down **Sunflower Avenue,** paying close attention to the row of shotgun houses backing up to the Sunflower River. A sign on one of these modest buildings identifies it as the **Riverside Hotel.** Originally Clarksdale's black hospital, the building became a blues landmark when Bessie Smith, the "Empress of the Blues," died there after a car wreck in 1937. The old hospital became a boarding house and hotel in 1944 and has been home to many blues greats over the past fifty years. While any blues enthusiast will enjoy a daytime visit to the Riverside Hotel, the $25 overnight accommodations are modest to say the least, and require guests to share common bathroom facilities.

Just across the street from the Riverside, you'll spot the riverboat-style building that houses **Della's Stackhouse** (232 Sunflower Avenue). This is the place to shop for rare LPs, 45s, and 78s, as well as contemporary blues CDs. Della's Stackhouse also carries vintage books, posters, and magazines; folk art; and handmade instruments fashioned by James "Super Chikan" Johnson. Drop by for a look and a listen Monday–Saturday 9:00 A.M.–6:00 P.M.

Any bluesman worth his salt once strolled and played on the stretch of road called **Issaquena Avenue.** While it's harder to catch a street performance these days, a handful of landmarks points to the area's bluesy heritage.

A guitar painted on the outside wall and a sign proclaiming NO CAMERAS OR RECORDING DEVICES hint that there was once more than hair-cutting going on at **Wade Walton's Barbershop.** A personal friend of W. C. Handy, Sonny Boy Williamson, and John Lee Hooker, the late Wade Walton was given to impromptu blues performances and gifted story-telling sessions. Patrons who spent time in Walton's chair left with not only a spiffy new look, but also a better understanding of the lifestyle called the blues. When Walton died, he took his music and his stories with him. But peeking in the windows of the now-silent shop, it's easy to imagine Walton wielding both a comb and a harmonica as his customers hummed along.

A number of the modest dwellings in this area were once home to the famous or semifamous. A marker near the barbershop on Issaquena Avenue points out the spot where W. C. Handy's house once stood. Sam Cooke spent his childhood at 2303 Seventh Street. Ike Turner's father's name is inscribed in the cornerstone at New Centennial Church, where he served as church secretary and pastor; Ike himself grew up at 304 Washington Street.

After hearing so much about it, you're probably ready for your own taste of the blues. The staff at the Delta Blues Museum can usually direct you to a *juke joint* (also spelled "jook" joint), or you can check the utility poles around town for homemade flyers announcing performances. Don't expect live music during the week; most blues artists hold day jobs and save their music for Friday and Saturday nights. There are juke joints all over the Delta, but arrangements with the artists are often last-minute and never binding. Since most of these establishments don't have telephones, the only sure way to confirm a blues performance is to show up and wait for the music to start.

A word of warning—the best blues are played in juke joints where people warn you not to go. Incidents do happen, but if you don't mess with anybody (or anybody's date), you should be safe. *Blues Station, Sarah's Kitchen, Margaret's Blue Diamond Lounge,* and *Reds* are all accustomed to welcoming tourists.

If you just can't muster up the nerve to visit a juke joint, tune in to *WROX Radio* instead. One of the country's first blues stations, WROX hired Mississippi's first black disc jockey. The late Early Wright began spinning blues (as the "Soul Man") and gospel (as "Brother Early") in Clarksdale in 1947 and continued until his retirement in 1997, just two years prior to his death at the age of 84. The University of Mississippi honored Wright's contributions to Southern culture by establishing a scholarship in his name in 1988.

"odetobillyjoe"

Visitors to rural Tallahatchie County can drive over the Tallahatchie bridge where the fictional Billy Joe McAllister jumped to his death in Bobby Gentry's sad country ballad, "Ode to Billy Joe."

WROX also claimed a pre-fame Ike Turner as both a DJ and a janitor, and legend has it a young Elvis Presley used to hang around the station in hopes of getting a chance to sing on the air. You'll find WROX, now a satellite music station, at 1450 AM on your radio dial. The former WROX studios used from 1948 to 1954 are housed in the historic *Hopson 1920 Building* at 257 Delta Avenue; plans are under way to restore the old studio space and open it as a museum.

For the best in live blues, plan a Clarksdale visit that coincides with the **Sunflower River Blues and Gospel Festival.** This free, three-day, open-air party is internationally recognized as one of the purest and bluesy-est of all festivals celebrating the art form. Be warned—the festival is held in August, and while the music is cool, the temperatures are scorching. For this year's dates, call the **Clarksdale Chamber of Commerce** at (662) 627–7337.

Just when you think there's nothing in Clarksdale *but* the blues, someone will invite you to the **Tennessee Williams Festival.** Young Tom Williams attended school in Clarksdale and spent summers visiting his grandfather, who was the pastor of **St. George's Episcopal Church** and lived in the rectory next door. The playwright's mother wrote of finding a scrap of paper upon which Williams had scrawled, "Before I was eight, my life was completely unshadowed by fear. I lived in a small Mississippi town. . . . My sister and I were gloriously happy."

Many of Clarksdale's landmarks and citizens reappeared years later in Williams's works. Now owned by Delta State University, Clarksdale's elegant **Cutrer Mansion** was originally the home of flamboyant attorney J. W. Cutrer and his equally colorful wife Blanche. The couple's legendary yard parties, masked balls, and madcap antics made quite an impression on young Tom Williams. The playwright used the Cutrers as models for characters in *A Streetcar Named Desire, Cat on a Hot Tin Roof,* and *The Glass Menagerie,* and named his most famous heroine, Blanche DuBois, after Mrs. Cutrer. The 1916 Cutrer Mansion is not open for tours, but is visible from Clark Street.

Held each October, the Tennessee Williams Festival stars Clarksdale's own citizens, who act out short scenes from his plays on their front lawns and front porches. Festivalgoers receive a map telling them which plays will be performed on which lawns at what time. The festival also includes dinner parties at the old Moon Lake Casino (now Uncle Henry's Place), seminars on Williams's work, musical entertainment, and home tours in the grand historic district between Clark and Court Streets—quite a contrast to the bluesy side of life. For this year's festival dates, call the Clarksdale Chamber of Commerce at (662) 627–7337.

Blanche Cutrer was the daughter of John Clark, founder of Clarksdale. The Clark family home where Blanche grew up is next door to the Cutrer Mansion. In fact, the Clark House originally rested on the spot where the mansion now stands. Blanche Clark Cutrer persuaded her parents to move her childhood home so that she and her husband could build their mansion on its former site. The Clark House remained in the Clark family until 2002, when Billy and Lily Strom purchased the home, lovingly restored it, and opened it as the **Belle Clark Bed and Breakfast** (211 Clark Street). For rates and reservations, call (662) 627–1280.

Williams is not the only writer to grow up in Coahoma County. Thomas Harris, author of the chilling *Red Dragon, Silence of the Lambs,* and *Hannibal,* spent his childhood in nearby **Rich.** Of course, if Harris's characters, including the infamous "Hannibal the Cannibal," are based on real people, the locals would probably rather not know about it.

Back in downtown Clarksdale, **Delta Avenue** is lined with specialty and antiques shops and locally owned boutiques well worth an hour (or two) of browsing. Try on vintage clothing at **Southern Memories,** shop for the kids at **Best Friends,** or check out the instruments at **Bluestown Music Store.**

Cat Head Delta Blues & Folk Art (225 Delta Avenue) is an example of just how addictive the blues can be. After several memorable vacations to the Delta, St. Louis residents Roger and Jennifer Stolle left their high-powered careers in Missouri, moved to Clarksdale, and opened this quirky little music and art shop.

"A year ago, I was meeting with the CEOs of major companies and taking business trips to Hong Kong," Roger said shortly after Cat Head opened. "This week, I booked a blues musician named T-Model Ford to play for our grand opening and set up a store display that included a chair made out of painted cow bones. You tell me which sounds like more fun."

Cat Head features a full selection of blues CDs, videos, DVDs, books, and collectibles, as well as an affordable, completely unique selection of southern folk art. The shop's "Sounds Around Town" chalkboard offers up-to-the-minute performance schedules for clubs and juke joints around Clarksdale, and Roger and Jennifer are always on hand to talk with visitors about the magic of the Delta. With live music often performed in the store, the overall effect is one of shopping in a juke joint. Cat Head is open Monday–Saturday 10:00 A.M.–5:00 P.M. and Sunday by appointment. You can also visit Cat Head online at www.cathead.biz.

Just across the street from Cat Head, the **Market on Delta** (257 Delta Avenue) features unique gifts and home accessories, as well as a section dubbed the **Sunflower River Trading Company.** The Trading Company offers books, prints, and T-shirts with a decidedly Delta flair, and sells **"The Path Finder,"** a brochure and map that guides visitors to unusual landmarks and destinations throughout the Delta. The Market and Trading Company are owned by Bubba O'Keefe, a successful homebuilder and entrepreneur who doubles as Clarksdale's unofficial welcoming committee. If you bump into Bubba during your visit to Clarksdale, chances are good he'll stop whatever he's doing to welcome you to town, offer you a map, and regale you with tales of everything to see and do in Clarksdale. Bubba's enthusiasm is contagious—after all, how could you not fall in love with a town whose residents are this friendly?

For a town its size, Clarksdale offers a surprising number and diversity of restaurants. A Clarksdale staple since 1924, **Abe's Bar-B-Q** is listed as one of the best pork joints in the South in the books *Roadfood* and *Goodfood*. Abe's occupies a modest building at the intersection of US 61 and US 49. A little farther south on US 61, **Chamoun's Resthaven** serves up stuffed grape leaves, kibbie, baklava, and other Lebanese and Mediterranean delicacies you wouldn't expect to find in the Mississippi Delta. Owner Bobby Tarzi has built a reputation for outstanding customer service at **Delta Amusement & Cafe**, a former "gaming house" where card games and domino matches still command almost as much attention as the plate lunches and burgers.

Just east of Clarksdale, the tiny community of **Marks** is home to the **Depot Deli**, a salad and sandwich shop housed in the historic town depot on Main Street. The decor includes the original freight scales and pot-bellied stove, as well as graffiti dating as far back as 1904. The Depot Deli is located inches from the still-active railroad tracks; hence the motto, "Step back in time and rumble."

For elegant dining and a chance at a celebrity sighting, enjoy lunch or dinner at Clarksdale's **Madidi**. Housed in a turn-of-the-twentieth-century building on Delta Avenue, the restaurant is co-owned by local attorney Bill Luckett and acclaimed actor **Morgan Freeman**. When he's not making or promoting his latest film, Freeman resides in nearby Charleston, Mississippi; the chances of bumping into him at Madidi are quite good. Even if you miss the famous actor, Madidi's upscale menu, regional art collection, and excellent atmosphere make for a memorable meal. Madidi serves fine food with a French flair Tuesday–Saturday. Call (662) 627–7770 or visit www.madidires.com for reservations.

For some lively after dinner entertainment—and another chance at a Morgan Freeman sighting—head to **Ground Zero**, the actor's blues club. Adorned with plastic tablecloths, Christmas lights, and sublime-to-ridiculous graffiti (be sure to add a word of your own), the cavernous club is a prime place to party. Ground Zero does a hopping lunch and dinner business, but is better known as *the* place to hear live music every weekend. Patrons and employees—including Ground Zero's famous owner—have been known to dance on the bar. Ground Zero is located in an old cotton warehouse at 0 Blues Alley, across the

trivia

The Ground Zero Blues Club and its owner, Morgan Freeman, were featured in the country music video *Waitin' on Joe*, written and performed by Greenville, Mississippi, native Steve Azar.

Little Known Facts about the Mississippi River Delta

In 1992, Tunica County boasted twenty hotel rooms. A dozen Las Vegas-style casinos later, the county is home to more than 6,000.

Topsoil in the Mississippi Delta is an average of 132 feet deep and, in some spots, reaches as deep as 350 feet.

The world's first franchised Holiday Inn opened its register in Clarksdale.

The Norris Bookbinding Company of Greenwood is the largest Bible binding plant in the nation.

More than 80 percent of the world's supply of farm-raised catfish comes from Mississippi.

The national 4-H Club was founded in Holmes County in 1907.

Twenty-nine ships sunk during the Civil War lie beneath the Yazoo River.

Greenwood's Grand Boulevard was once named one of America's ten most beautiful streets by the U.S. Chambers of Commerce and the Garden Clubs of America.

Just 2 miles apart, the Yazoo and Tallahatchie Rivers run parallel to each other, yet flow in opposite directions.

road from the Delta Blues Museum. For a lineup of performances, call (662) 621–9009 or visit www.groundzerobluesclub.com.

Freeman is committed to giving back to his hometown. In addition to Madidi and Ground Zero, the actor quietly supports libraries, public schools, and a number of community projects and organizations in the area. "I've been just about everywhere," Freeman says, "and there's no place better. What the state offered me, I got growing up. Now, I have something to offer the state."

Freeman has also been known to join his friend Bubba O'Keefe in welcoming visitors to Clarksdale. O'Keefe describes a recent occasion when he and Freeman approached a group on the street and invited them to the Tennessee Williams Festival. When asked if the tourists recognized Freeman, O'Keefe replies, "Yeah, but they didn't get all goosey about it."

If you're up for some unusual pre-dinner entertainment, swing by the **Hopson Commissary** on the historic **Hopson Plantation.** The country's first cotton crop produced entirely by machine—from plantin' to balin'—was grown and harvested in 1944 on twenty-eight acres owned by the Hopson Planting Company. Today the historic Hopson Commissary houses a sometime "social club" and mini-museum packed with farming memorabilia, statuary, an old post office, and a complete barbershop. A huge banner draped on one wall features a likeness of the King of Rock 'n' Roll and the proclamation, "Elvis will never leave this building." Owner James Butler, whose wife inherited the Hopson family property, collected the memorabilia for preservation from small towns all over Mississippi.

Evenings at the Commissary usually find a genial mix of locals and tourists gathered 'round the volunteer-run bar (a rescued antique soda fountain) or chatting at a handful of tables covered with red-and-white-checkered cloths. On occasion, the Commissary features live musical entertainment, often of the blues variety.

The Commissary is generally open to the public from 5:00 to 8:00 P.M. Beer and set-ups are available. If you drop by during the day, the building's exterior makes a good photo op, and if Butler or one of his friends with a key happens to be there, they'll be happy to let you in. The Commissary is open by appointment to groups, and with a little advance notice, can even arrange a nice lunch. Plans are in the works to add an antiques shop and expand the operation to daytime hours.

Make a visit to Clarksdale even more memorable with an overnight stay at the Hopson Plantation's ***Shack Up Inn.*** Butler and a handful of business partners known as "the Shackmeisters" salvaged a six-pack of authentic sharecroppers' shotgun shacks from around the countryside, relocated them to the Hopson property, added electricity and plumbing, and rent them out to overnight guests. Don't worry—while the exterior of each ramshackle shanty is authentically dilapidated, rickety, and rustic, the interiors are modern, clean, and comfy, with amenities you just won't find at the local Holiday Inn. A copper coil from a previous tenant's still has been recycled as a bathroom fixture, the circa 1970 television sets pick up only the blues channel, and your

Shack Up Inn

kitchenette might feature an old coke machine converted into a refrigerator. Landscaping on the grounds includes Christmas lights, plenty of pink flamingoes, a rusted storage tank, and a bottle tree designed to keep away evil spirits (the bottle tree prompted one guest unfamiliar with southern folklore to inquire, "What's with the vodka tree?"). Turn-down service replaces the traditional chocolates with—what else—moon pies on your pillow. And each shack comes complete with an authentically musty aroma that would be impossible to replicate. With amenities like these, who needs room service?

A stay in "Mississippi's Oldest B&B (Bed & Beer)" is an affordable experience; with rates beginning at just $50 per night, you'll have enough left over to buy a Shack Up Inn T-shirt. The Hopson Commissary and Shack Up Inn are located at the Clarksdale city limits on Highway 49 South at Hopson Road, Clarksdale. For more information on shacking up, call (662) 624–8329 or visit www.shackupinn.com.

Fans who didn't get their fill of blues lore in Clarksdale should continue down US 49 South to *Tutwiler;* where a message on the water tower proclaims the town to be "Where the Blues Was Born." Drivers are welcomed to Tutwiler by three-dimensional billboards designed to look like juke joints. Created by horticulturist Felder Rushing and acclaimed Mississippi folk artist Earl Simmons, the billboards were funded through a grant from the Mississippi Arts Commission.

The billboards direct visitors from the highway into downtown Tutwiler and **Railroad Park.** A marker where the railroad depot once stood commemorates W. C. Handy's "discovery" of the blues—the spot where the "Father of the Blues" heard a man playing guitar and singing a mournful tune about "Goin' where the Southern cross the Dog"—that's a railroad intersection in nearby Moorhead. The walls of Railroad Park next to the site are adorned with sweeping murals depicting Handy's chance meeting with the bluesman, as well as scenes from Tutwiler's history. Created by Delta artist Cristen Craven Barnard, the mural also features images of bluesman Aleck Miller, better known as Sonny Boy Williamson. Miller/Williamson is buried near Tutwiler beside the old **Whitfield M. B. Church** under a new marker erected by Trumpet Records. The grave site is easy to spot—it's the one littered with beer cans, whiskey bottles, spare change, and a dozen rusty harmonicas.

Back on US 61 South, be careful not to blink. You'll miss the Mississippi Highway 161 cutoff that leads to **Mound Bayou,** a town founded by freed slaves who once chopped cotton on Jefferson Davis's brother's plantation. The grounds of the **Mound Bayou City Hall** feature a carved wooden plaque depicting famous African Americans, including Martin Luther King Jr., Fannie Lou Hamer, and Malcolm X, but the city's most notable attraction is the **cemetery** where the town's founders were laid to rest. Too poor to afford markers, their families fashioned their own. The exquisite, hand-hewn angels and poignant inscriptions are far more impressive than anything money could buy.

A favorite stop in Mound Bayou is **Peter's Pottery.** Peter Woods and his three brothers learned the fine art of pottery from the master at McCarty Pottery in Merigold (the next town down the road). The Woods brothers left McCarty in 1998 with plans to pursue new careers, but soon realized that clay was in their blood. Together they established Peter's Pottery, the place to find animals, candlesticks, dinnerware, crosses, and vases crafted of Mississippi clay and finished with the brothers' exclusive glaze, Bayou Blue. Peter's pottery is collected worldwide; President George W. Bush is the proud owner of a Bayou Blue elephant. The brothers' work is sold at their gallery (301 Fortune Street) and in upscale gift shops statewide. To get to the gallery, turn right at the big blue industrial building across from New Salem Baptist Church, then follow the gravel road to the brown building at the end. Browse the pottery or place a custom order during regular business hours (Monday, Tuesday, and Thursday–Saturday, 10:00 A.M.–4:00 P.M.), or call (662) 741–2265.

trivia

Based on income tax returns documenting charitable donations, Mississippians are the most generous citizens in the United States.

The entire town of **Merigold** covers a mere 6 blocks but packs a lot of charm into such a small space. This Delta village (population 608) is home to a handful of quaint restaurants and specialty shops, including **McCarty Pottery.** Turn right at the post office on Mississippi Highway 161, then left on North St. Mary Street to the low cypress building surrounded by bamboo. There's no sign, but as soon as you open the door you'll know you've found the McCarty gallery and tour gardens. Lee and Pup McCarty have been making pottery for as long as anyone in Merigold remembers, but the clay for their first pieces came from a ravine near Oxford pointed out to them by novelist William Faulkner.

The McCarty collection includes dinnerware, vases, wind chimes, and candlesticks, but the McCartys are best known for their family of pottery rabbits. Each inquisitive bunny has a name, and whether you choose Lettuce, Easter, or Baby Bunny, you'll take home one of Mississippi's most popular souvenirs. Obsessed McCarty collectors can be found all over the world. Even Nikita Khrushchev had a collection of McCarty pottery, supposedly received as a gift from Armand Hammer. McCarty Pottery is open 10:00 A.M.–4:00 P.M. Tuesday–Saturday. If at all possible, try to stop by in the morning for a chat with Mr. McCarty before he retires for his afternoon nap.

The Gallery restaurant, 2 blocks from the studio, is also owned by the McCarty family and serves light lunches on dinnerware fashioned by the artists. Nearby *Crawdad's* is a popular spot for dinner, and features live music on weekends. *Po' Monkey's,* a juke joint in the best blues tradition, is open only on Thursday nights.

The next stop on US 61 is *Cleveland,* listed in Norm Crampton's *The 100 Best Small Towns in America.* W. C. Handy wrote about Cleveland in his autobiography, describing a pivotal incident at a dance held in the Cleveland Courthouse. When the audience demanded blues tunes, Handy and his orchestra were at a loss. A local trio stepped in and saved the day, performing bawdy, soulful music the likes of which Handy had never heard, but which he would later incorporate into his own songs. "My enlightenment came in Cleveland, Mississippi," Handy wrote years later. "That night, an American composer was born."

Attractions in Cleveland include the small-but-scenic campus of *Delta State University,* excellent shopping in more than thirty-five boutiques along historic *Cotton Row* and *Sharpe Avenue,* and a four-star restaurant.

Located on US 61, *KC's* specializes in "new eclectic, global cuisine" and features a superb wine cellar stocked with more than 500 selections from wineries around the world. Family-owned and operated by K. C., Dean, Don, and Wally Joe, the restaurant has been featured on the *Today* show and in dozens of culinary magazines. Chef Wally Joe was profiled on the Discovery Channel series "Great Chefs of the South," and was named one of twenty-eight "Rising Chefs of the 21st Century" by the James Beard Foundation. In 2002, KC's was inducted into the elite Fine Dining Hall of Fame, putting this Cleveland, Mississippi, restaurant in the same league as The French Laundry in California, Commander's Palace in New Orleans, and Gramercy Tavern in New York. For reservations, call (662) 843–5301.

For less discriminating palates, *Airport Grocery* (Highway 8 West) bills its burgers, barbecue, hot tamales, and other hearty fare as "out-of-this-world food at a down-to-earth place." Lunch and shopping go hand-in-hand at *A la Carte Alley* (111 South Court Street), a delightful southern bistro and gift gallery.

If you'll be staying in Cleveland overnight, book a room at *Molly's Bed and Breakfast* (214 South Bolivar Avenue), a funky little inn owned by Floyd and Molly Shaman. Floyd is a gifted sculptor, creating fascinating woodworks of every size and hue. His sculptures are scattered throughout the turn-of-the-twentieth-century house, and guests are invited to tour his studio at the back of the property. Rates begin at $70. For reservations, call Molly Shaman at (662) 843–9913.

Located on Highway 8 East between Cleveland and Ruleville, *Dockery Farms,* the most famous of the old Delta cotton plantations, is included on a long list of places as the possible birthplace of the blues. Blues great Charlie Patton called the plantation home. Patton's presence at Dockery Farms is believed to have drawn dozens of other blues musicians to the area. A barn bearing the plantation name and dates of operation is visible from the highway and is a popular photo opportunity.

On the other side of Cleveland, Highway 8 West intersects Highway 1 at *Rosedale,* a thriving port on the Mississippi River. With acres of riverfront and a 75-foot-high observation tower, *Great River Road State Park* offers spectacular views of the mighty Mississippi and enjoys the distinction of being the world's longest park. Visitors can hike a trail that winds down to the riverbank, or rent a frisbee and play the Deer Meadow Disc Golf Course. The restaurant at the park's visitor center fries up a scrumptious catfish lunch, with panoramic views of the river on the side.

Fishing is good at the park's *Perry Martin Lake,* named for an infamous moonshiner of Mississippi's Prohibition era. Perry Martin lived on a houseboat on the lake, keeping a watchful eye on the highly productive, highly illegal stills he had hidden in the woods nearby. The trails visitors roam freely today were *never* prowled after dark in Perry Martin's heyday. You won't find any of Martin's potent moonshine at Great River Road, but one of his prized stills is on display.

goingfirstclass

Jo Ann Ussery's home in Benoit can literally be described as first class—and as coach, cockpit, and cargo hold.

Upon discovering that a retired passenger jet was more affordable than a simple mobile home, Ms. Ussery had one delivered to her lakeside property, made some changes here and there, and now calls the aircraft home.

The remodeled jetliner features a kitchen, three bedrooms, and one and one-half baths. And if the Jacuzzi in the cockpit should ever flood, Ms. Ussery needn't worry. She can always use her couch cushion as a flotation device.

Continuing on Highway 1 South, the next stop is *Benoit.* Take a left at the four-way stop (yes, there's only one), go about a mile past the residential district, and take the gravel road to the right. That crumbling antebellum mansion rising out of the field is locally referred to as the *Baby Doll House.* The movie *Baby Doll* was filmed on location here in 1956. Based on a play by Tennessee Williams, *Baby Doll* was so scandalous it was condemned by the Legion of Decency. For as long as anyone around Benoit can remember, no one has lived in the Baby Doll House—at least not officially. The house is widely regarded as haunted and boasts a shadowy, convoluted past involving an escaped John Wilkes Booth. A nearby mobile home, however, is inhabited by very real residents and the property on which the Baby Doll House stands is marked by NO TRESPASSING signs. Pull up as far as the gate and get a good look at what must once have been a truly fine Delta home.

Cotton Row

This flat, fertile section of the Delta that stretches from Greenville east to Greenwood is virtually devoid of trees, but you won't need spring buds or fall foliage to tell you what season it is.

In the summertime, the heat shimmers so thickly off the highway you can actually catch it on film. Even the most resilient crops look parched without a daily drenching. Those huge, spidery pieces of machinery spanning the fields are pivot irrigation systems, designed to give each precious acre of cotton and soybeans a good soaking.

Fall sees Cotton Row at its peak, when the fields are white with "Delta Gold." When harvesting takes place in early autumn, trucks loaded with the fluffy stuff travel every Delta highway, leftover strands float lazily in the welcome breeze, and out-of-state visitors pull over to swipe a souvenir boll.

In the winter, the Delta seems determined to relive its prehistoric days as a swamp—the rain never seems to stop, the fertile soil turns to mucky gumbo, and flash floods can literally wash away the back roads.

In the spring, the whole process begins anew. And no matter how many years a particular field is worked, the land continues to reveal new treasures with every pass of the plow. The rich black earth sparkles with glass—once part of a window in a sharecropper's shack. Wild daffodils spring up where a long-ago garden once bloomed, and plows turn up shards of ancient Indian pottery, arrowheads, and even an occasional dinosaur bone or human skeleton.

Dozens of Indian artifacts are displayed at the **Winterville Indian Mounds State Park and Museum,** 5 miles north of Greenville on Highway 1. The mound builders' metropolis at Winterville includes fifteen earthen structures, one of them a massive, six-story temple mound. The mounds were built one basketful of earth at a time by the women of the tribe, while the men worked the fields and hunted for dinner. A museum on the Winterville property houses Indian artifacts recovered from all over the Delta. The museum is open Monday–Saturday 9:00 A.M.–5:00 P.M. and Sunday 1:30–5:00 P.M. Call (662) 334–4684 or visit mdah.state.ms.us.

Continue into **Greenville,** the state's largest city on the Mississippi River. Highway 1 intersects with U.S. Highway 82 here, providing an easy way to navigate the city; virtually every point of interest is located a block or two off US 82.

Your first stop should be the **River Road Queen Welcome Center,** a replica of a nineteenth-century stern-wheeler that made its debut at the 1984

New Orleans World's Fair, then returned to Greenville to greet visitors arriving in Mississippi from Arkansas. This landlocked stern-wheeler is located at the intersection of US 82 West and Reed Road, just past the US 82 and Main Street intersection. Stop to admire the miniature cotton patch planted out front, then head inside where a knowledgeable staffer will provide you with brochures and directions to Greenville attractions, hotels, and restaurants.

From the River Road Queen, head back east on US 82 to Main Street, which dead-ends at the **Mississippi River levee,** a marvel of engineering longer and taller than the Great Wall of China. Barges headed for the bustling **Port of Greenville** are visible just beyond the casinos that line the levee's edge. For a close-up view of the mighty Mississippi, stop at the observation tower at **Warfield Point Park,** nestled inside the levee off US 82, 5 miles south of Greenville. The park offers the only public riverbank campsites on the Mississippi between St. Louis and New Orleans. Call (662) 335–7275 to reserve your spot.

At the end of Main Street, 1 block east of the levee, you'll spot the **Old Number One Firehouse Museum** (230 Main Street). It's not surprising that Greenville would open a museum honoring fire fighting—in the late 1800s, the city burned to the ground not once, not twice, but on three separate occasions.

No Mistaking It

I'd like to say I stumbled upon the No Mistake Plantation by accident, but to find yourself in Satartia, the smallest incorporated town in Mississippi, you really have to be looking for something.

The town lies just off Mississippi Highway 3, 25 miles south of Yazoo City. I had directions to the No Mistake, but as it turned out I didn't need the hand-drawn map after all—the explosion of color was a dead giveaway. The antebellum plantation home was surrounded by daylilies—thousands upon thousands of daylilies, in every hue and shade imaginable.

After lunch in the tea room, the plantation's owner told me about the first mistress of No Mistake, a planter's wife who had raised a single bale of cotton every year, then used her modest earnings to build this scenic masterpiece—one garden at a time. My host concluded the tour by offering me a well-worn garden trowel and an invitation to take a living reminder of the No Mistake home.

The No Mistake Plantation has changed hands since my visit there and, sadly, no longer allows outsiders to explore its kaleidoscopic grounds. But every summer, when those generations-old daylilies burst into bloom in my own backyard, I relive that afternoon at the No Mistake Plantation—one flower at a time.

Exhibits include old fire engines, call boxes, and "fire marks"—plaques displayed only on those homes that carried fire insurance. In the old days, if firemen arrived at a burning home and didn't see the appropriate mark, they would head back to the station and leave the house to burn. Open Monday–Friday 8:00 A.M.–5:00 P.M. and weekends 1:00–6:00 P.M., the Firehouse Museum is a favorite with kids, who can dress in fire-fighting garb, pull a real fire alarm, and pretend to douse the flames with a working hose.

Grown-ups with a literary bent will find the ***Greenville Writers Exhibit*** at the William Alexander Percy Memorial Library (341 Main Street) of interest. According to the local chamber of commerce, Greenville boasts more published writers per capita than any other town in the nation. The list of distinguished authors includes Ellen Douglas, Walker Percy, Hodding Carter, and Civil War historian Shelby Foote, who gained national notoriety as a featured commentator in Ken Burns's epic PBS series, *The Civil War*. The Greenville Writers Exhibit includes photographs, original manuscripts, and displays celebrating Greenville's rich literary heritage.

Dinnertime in Greenville calls for a trip to ***Doe's Eat Place,*** where you'll find the biggest, best steaks in Mississippi, and quite possibly in all of America. In fact, *Men's Journal* proclaimed Doe's porterhouse steak "the best thing to eat in America," period. With maps to the restaurant distributed in every convenience store and hotel lobby in Greenville, Doe's can't really be considered off the beaten path, but its stubborn refusal to conform to any level of restaurant normalcy is what puts Doe's on everyone's "must see" list.

For starters, the restaurant is housed in a dilapidated 1903 grocery-store-turned-honky-tonk-turned-tamale-stand-turned-restaurant that looks as though it should be condemned, if not by the building commission, then at least by the local health department. Patrons enter through the kitchen, where the owner ("Little Doe," son of restaurant founder "Big Doe") will turn to you with a hefty steak in each hand and say, "Aunt Florence will seat you." Aunt Florence will indeed lead you to a rickety table, where a friendly waitress will soon appear with a bowl of anchovies or a sample of Doe's famous hot tamales. While you wait for the main course, you can eavesdrop on the conversations of other diners in the cramped little room, who range from Doe's regulars chatting with the staff to first-time patrons wondering if the restrooms might actually be outside somewhere.

Be warned—dinner at Doe's could put you in a coma. The smallest steak on the menu weighs in at a whopping two pounds and comes with French-fried potatoes and fresh bread. The food is nothing short of delicious, and though the atmosphere seems a little rustic at first, it soon becomes quite comfortable. Doe's is open only for dinner Monday–Saturday.

The restaurant is located on **Nelson Street,** which is also home to some down-and-dirty blues clubs. Although it's true that some of these establishments have a reputation for vice and violence, visitors who stick to the blues and stay out of the street life aren't likely to run into trouble. A particularly popular club is **Perry's Flowing Fountain** (816 Nelson Street), where the headline act was once a young married couple named Ike and Tina Turner.

A safe bet for excellent entertainment is the **Walnut Street Entertainment and Restaurant District.** Home to a lively mix of nightspots and eateries, Walnut Street has emerged as Greenville's most popular entertainment area.

For a daylong dose of the blues, follow the crowds to a forty-acre patch in the Delta outside Greenville on the third Saturday in September. Once you've attended the **Mississippi Delta Blues and Heritage Festival,** nothing but a live performance will ever do again. The festival brings the biggest names in blues for an all-day blowout—the Woodstock of the blues world. Bring a lawn chair or blanket and an ice chest and be warned—late September in Mississippi is still hot and humid. For this year's lineup of performers, call (662) 335–3523 or (800) 467–3582.

Nearby **Stoneville** is home to the largest USDA research facility in the nation. The **Silicon Valley of Agriculture** isn't open for public tours, but an ever-growing lobby display explains how common household items like disposable diapers and aerosol cans were developed through USDA research. Take home a cotton bale of your own (in miniature, of course) from **Little Bales of Cotton,** a downtown Stoneville shop specializing in cotton souvenirs.

From Greenville, take US 82 East toward Greenwood, or backtrack to State Highway 1 and pick up a few more attractions farther south.

Located 5 miles off Highway 1 South on Mississippi Highway 12, **LeRoy Percy State Park** is home to the only **hot spring** in Mississippi, but it's not the place for a leisurely soak—the ninety-four-degree water has already been claimed by the local alligator population. You can enjoy a not-too-up-close-and-personal visit with the scaly reptiles (rumored to enjoy marshmallows) from a raised boardwalk above their hot artesian water home. A nature trail through the park offers a look at the Delta of old—a steamy jungle of a place overrun by Spanish moss and cypress trees.

You can camp overnight or stay in a cabin at LeRoy Percy, or return to Highway 1 and continue south a short distance to **Chatham.** This small community on picturesque **Lake Washington** is home to **Linden-on-the-Lake,** a palatial bed-and-breakfast inn originally constructed around 1900. Rates begin at $75; call (662) 839–2181.

Highway 1 intersects with US 61 South at **Rolling Fork,** birthplace of blues great Muddy Waters. A bend in the road near Rolling Fork is home to

The Birth of the Teddy Bear

One of the world's most popular toys was born in tiny Onward, Mississippi, as the result of a presidential pardon.

In 1902, President Theodore Roosevelt participated in a black bear hunt in the Onward area. The hunt was led by former slave, Confederate soldier, and skilled hunting guide Holt Collier. When a 235-pound bear attacked one of Collier's prized hunting dogs, the guide clubbed and lassoed the bear, tied it to a tree, and invited the president to shoot it. Roosevelt refused to kill the tethered animal, claiming it would not be sportsmanlike. A cartoonist with the *Washington Post* captured this noble gesture on paper, and the story of "Teddy's Bear" quickly spread nationwide.

Soon after, a savvy New York merchant named Morris Michton made toy history by creating a cuddly toy christened "the Teddy Bear." Michton went on to found the Ideal Toy Company, starting the entire business with revenues generated by the original Teddy Bear.

Guide Holt Collier went on to become known as the greatest bear hunter in the South. A 2002 book by Mississippi author Minor Buchanan titled *Holt Collier: His Life* recounts Collier's many adventures, including the famous Teddy Bear Hunt.

In an interesting footnote (pawnote?) to the story, the 2002 Mississippi legislature passed a bill naming the Teddy Bear the official state toy of Mississippi.

a growing collection (or herd) of wire-sculpted dinosaurs fashioned by a local resident.

Rolling Fork is also home to **Mount Helena,** a private home built in 1896 by Helen and George Harris. Constructed atop an Indian mound—the only rise in the pancake-flat land for miles—the Colonial Revival–style mansion is clearly visible from US 61. Mount Helena is lovely in its own right, but the house is most famous because its original mistress, Helen Johnstone Harris, is widely believed to be the ghostly Bride of Annandale (see sidebar in "The Heartland" chapter).

Your next stop on US 61 is **Onward,** the birthplace of the Teddy Bear. The **Onward Store** displays photographs from President Theodore Roosevelt's famous bear hunt and sells souvenir teddy bears and T-shirts from the spot where this favorite childhood toy originated. The country grocery even markets its own, limited edition "Onward Teddy Rough Rider Roosevelt Bears," which are handmade by a seamstress in Greenville. The Onward Store is open 7:30 A.M.–7:30 P.M., seven days a week.

Even if you've ventured as far south as Onward, it's just a short backtrack up US 61 to the northeastern section of the Delta. Heading north back toward

Greenville, you'll pass through tiny towns boasting the most creative names in the state—tongue-twisting monikers like Anguilla, Nitta Yuma, and Panther Burn.

US 61 North and US 82 intersect just outside Greenville near **Leland.** As you head east on US 82, keep a sharp eye out for talking frogs, fashion-conscious pigs, and perennial roommates Bert and Ernie. This Delta town is home to the **Birthplace of the Frog,** a museum honoring Leland native Jim Henson, the creator of the beloved Muppets. You'll find original Muppets and Muppet memorabilia at this fanciful exhibit on South Deer Creek Drive, 1.5 miles west of the intersection of US 82 and US 61. Fans will delight in learning the inspiration behind their favorite Muppets; for example, Kermit the Frog is affectionately named after Henson's boyhood best friend. Hobnob with the stars of *The Muppet Movie* and *The Muppets Take Manhattan* Monday–Saturday 10:00 A.M.–4:00 P.M., 2:00–5:00 P.M. on Sunday. There's no admission fee, but Kermit and the gang do appreciate donations. Be sure to add your name to the guest register, which already lists Muppet fans from Australia, England, and Japan.

A worthwhile stop for browsing is family-operated *Jiminey Creek.* Owner Sandra Pieralisi and her daughters, Jennifer Pieralisi and Lara Martin, offer a variety of gifts and collectibles, including candles, bath products, pet gifts, picture frames, bird feeders, cards, and children's clothes and toys.

Jennifer Pieralisi is a gifted potter who works on-site. Influenced by Japanese functional ware, Jennifer's hand-glazed stoneware is beautiful enough to display as a treasure, yet durable enough for everyday use. Several of Jennifer's creations are displayed in Jiminey Creek; she also takes custom orders.

Other gifts with a local flair include Muddy Waters Coffee, Walter Anderson prints, and pictorial coffee-table books by Mississippi wildlife photographer Stephen Kirkpatrick (yes, he's my husband). Jiminey Creek is located at 105 North Broad Street. Call (662) 686–7600 or visit www.jimineycreek.com.

Like most Delta communities, Leland's music of choice is the blues. The first in a series of planned downtown murals, **Blues Highway** depicts some seventeen blues greats, all from Washington County. Artists from across the state joined forces to create the colorful tribute.

The Leland Historic Foundation manages the Leland Blues Project, a series of concerts and projects celebrating the town's important contribution to the blues. The campaign includes the annual **Highway 61 Blues Festival** in downtown Leland and fundraising efforts for the creation of a **Leland Blues Museum.** Blues legend B. B. King purchased the museum's first commemorative brick.

Speaking of B. B. King, your next stop on US 82 East is **Indianola,** B. B.'s birthplace. King began his musical career singing gospel, but as he explains, "Gospel songs got me encouragement. Blues tunes got me a tip and a beer. Do

I really need to say anything else?" A mural of B. B. King and his guitar "Lucille" adorns a brick wall at the corner of Front Street and Second Street in downtown Indianola. The town also features a park and a street named after its most famous homeboy, who returns to entertain at the Annual *B. B. King Homecoming,* a down-home blues concert held the Friday after Memorial Day. Indianola is a far cry from Hollywood, but you will find King's handprints, footprints, and autograph in the sidewalk at the corner of Second and Church Streets.

For a memorable dining experience, don't miss the *Crown Restaurant and Antique Mall,* the birthplace of catfish pâté. Open for lunch only, the restaurant offers an upscale menu starring owner Evelyn Roughton's world-famous catfish recipes. You'll have a choice of several entrees, one of which is always an exotic concoction like catfish thermadore, shrimp-stuffed catfish, or black-butter catfish. You'll also be required to sample Evelyn's award-winning catfish pâtés.

The original Smoked Catfish Pâté won Evelyn "Best Hors d'oeuvre" honors in the 1990 Fancy Food Show held in New York City. Her follow-up delicacy, a creamy blend of catfish and capers dubbed "Mississippi Mousse," captured second place in the "Best Seafood, Meat, and Pâté" category at the 2000 show.

The Buried Treasure and the Headless Horseman

Schlater, Mississippi is a tiny town full of big tales. If the legends are true, this modest agricultural community is home to both buried treasure and a headless horseman.

The tale of the buried treasure dates back to the Civil War. When the county treasurer was warned of approaching Union soldiers, he gathered up all of the county's gold, silver, and currency, stuffed them into his saddlebags, and whisked the riches away to a "secret hiding place." He returned—saddlebags empty—just in time to see the Union troops gallop into town. The treasurer planned to return the money after the war, but died before he could retrieve it, taking the secret location of his hiding place to the grave. Despite the best efforts of professional treasure hunters, local kids, and even Teddy Roosevelt, the treasure has never been found.

Schlater's headless horseman is the ghost of Red Elm, an Indian brave who fell in love with a married woman named Mrs. Janes. Ignoring her repeated rebuffs, Red Elm pursued Mrs. Janes relentlessly—even, it seems, after her husband decapitated him. Shortly after Red Elm's murder, Mrs. Janes herself died of typhoid fever; the headless ghost made its first appearance wailing near her grave. If you visit Schlater, you'll find Mrs. Janes's grave in *McNutt Cemetery*—under two red elm trees that have grown together as one.

Purchase a tub or two of the scrumptious pâté to serve to your friends back home—but don't tell them what they're eating until *after* they've licked the bowl clean.

Evelyn and her husband Tony opened the antiques mall first, then added the restaurant in 1976. Antiquing has since taken a back seat to the food, but all of the seventeenth-, eighteenth-, and nineteenth-century English antique furnishings in the Crown are for sale. If you really like the table you eat off or the chair you sit in, you can take it with you.

Lunch includes a catfish entree, sampling of the pâté, and your choice of any or all of the Crown's collection of homemade pies. You can buy a tub of the pâté or any of the pie mixes at the restaurant, or take home one of the Crown's mail order catalogs.

Lunch is served 11:00 A.M.–2:00 P.M. Monday–Saturday. Visit the Crown at 112 Front Street in downtown Indianola, or call (662) 887–4522 or (800) 833–7731 to order a catalog.

The *Gin Mill Mall* (109 Pershing Avenue) showcases fine furniture hand-crafted by owner Tom Bingham. Many of Bingham's pieces are crafted of historically significant wood. Fallen trees, old houses slated for demolition, even sunken ships have all served as raw material for Bingham's masterful creations. Each table, chair, clock, or wardrobe comes with a "birth certificate" that lets its owner know the origin and age of the wood. The Gin Mill Mall also hosts a full calendar of art exhibitions, book signings, and art talks and demonstrations, usually involving a festive wine and cheese reception. For information on upcoming events at the Gin Mill Mall, call (662) 887–3209.

On your way out of Indianola, stop by the *Indianola Pecan House* on the left side of US 82 just west of the 82–49 intersection and pick up a snack for the road. The Pecan House offers gourmet nuts, candies, spices, desserts, and dressings (be sure to try the Vidalia onion jelly) and usually has a tableful of samples that's worth a stop in itself. You can also pick up one-of-a-kind Delta souvenirs, ranging from catfish neckties to Civil War sculptures. The Pecan House also does a thriving mail-order business; call (800) 541–6252 for a catalog packed with goodies.

From Indianola continue on 82 East and follow the signs to Florewood US 82 East and follow the signs to *Florewood River Plantation State Park.* The one-hundred-acre park offers living history interpretations of life on an 1850s cotton plantation. More realistic than the perpetual parties and hoop skirts of *Gone With the Wind,* Florewood focuses on the endless details of daily life and includes costumed interpreters working in the "big house," commissary, foreman's quarters, and more than a dozen outbuildings. The Civil War siege of Fort

Pemberton is replayed at Florewood the third weekend in March, when costumed Union and Confederate reenactors bring long-resolved conflicts to vivid life. Florewood also hosts a plantation Christmas candlelight tour the first weekend in December.

Admission is $2.00 per vehicle. Florewood is closed on Monday and offers limited tours December–February. Call (662) 455–3821 or (800) 748–9064 for more information and dates and times of special events.

Just as you come into *Greenwood,* you'll spot signs pointing you toward the *Cottonlandia Museum* (US 82 West). The $4.00 admission buys a look at several rooms of artifacts dating all the way back to the Ice Age. Exhibits include Indian pottery, 10,000-year-old mastodon bones, historic trade beads, a swamp diorama, an April 15, 1865, news clipping with the headline, "President Dead," and pieces of the Union gunboat *Star of the West* recovered from the waters near Greenwood.

The *Greenwood Blues Heritage Museum and Gallery* (214 Howard Street) is a tribute to Greenwood's role in the history and development of the

Viking Range Corporation

When a client enamored with the culinary arts asked Greenwood homebuilder Fred Carl to include a restaurant-quality range in her new home, Carl encountered one barrier.

No such range existed.

It seemed the high heat and massive proportions associated with professional cooking equipment required more insulation and space than a residential kitchen could handle.

Realizing the potential for a commercial-type range designed for the home, Carl sketched a preliminary design on the back of an order form. This rudimentary blueprint led to the founding of Viking Range Corporation and the creation of a whole new category of kitchen appliances.

Unveiled in 1987, Viking's original stainless steel cooking machine swept impassioned cooks, discriminating homeowners, and interior designers off their collective feet. Other manufacturers have since imitated the Viking style, but Viking Range remains the industry leader.

Today the company offers more than fifteen high-end appliances, each marked by striking commercial design, maximum power, and unrivaled engineering. The Viking plant in Greenwood ships ranges, dishwashers, refrigerators, and gas grills to more than sixty countries worldwide.

Every order is a salute to Fred Carl's spirit of innovation, and to the Greenwood, Mississippi company that has become synonymous with the epicurean lifestyle.

The Lady in Red

One of the strangest mysteries in Mississippi history began on April 24, 1969, when a backhoe digging on the Egypt Plantation unearthed the Lady in Red.

At a depth of just three feet, the backhoe struck a fitted, cast-iron coffin with a glass lid. Inside was the perfectly preserved body of a petite young woman. She was clad in an expensive red velvet dress with a frilly lace collar. Her small hands were encased in white gloves, her dainty feet in stylish black boots. She had been dead for more than a century.

The workers who unearthed the lady described her as "miraculously preserved, with long auburn hair and the beautiful skin of a young woman."

Her body had been preserved in alcohol, an unusual funeral practice of the early 1800s. Based upon the embalming technique and style of her clothing, the Lady in Red died in the late 1830s.

No one ever came forward to claim the lady and no record of her burial was ever found. With no clue as to her identity, the owner of Egypt Plantation had the lady interred at Odd Fellows Cemetery in nearby Lexington, where she remains today. The marker on her grave reads simply, "Lady in Red . . . Found on Egypt Plantation . . . 1835–1969."

blues, with a special emphasis on the music, life, and controversial demise and burial of bluesman Robert Johnson.

Greenwood has always seen itself as a genteel town of cultured Delta folk; this concern with propriety and appearances helped make **Lusco's** (722 Carrolton Avenue) one of the most popular dining establishments of the Prohibition era. Restaurateur Charles Lusco built private, partitioned rooms that allowed his guests to imbibe without fear of being observed. Even today, guests at Lusco's enjoy delicious seafood and steaks in private cubicles, summoning discreet waiters with the touch of a buzzer. Of course, the rules concerning alcohol are a little more relaxed today—the restaurant serves beer and wine coolers and allows guests to bring their own wine and liquor. But don't overindulge—remembering which cubicle is yours after a trip to the restroom can require all of your wits. Reservations are recommended; call (662) 453-5365.

Greenwood hosts two popular summer festivals worth braving the heat for. June brings the **Balloon Fest,** a weekend of balloon rides and entertainment highlighted by the mass ascension of nearly one hundred colorful hot-air balloons.

Sky Parade features hot-air balloons, stunt flying, and live entertainment, and is famous for stunning military air shows guaranteed to give you goose bumps. If the words "Blue Angels" make your heart beat faster, this festival is for you. Dates for Sky Parade vary. For specific dates and entertainment schedules for all Greenwood festivals, contact the **Greenwood Convention and Visitors Bureau** at (800) 748–9064.

Do not, repeat, *do not* leave Greenwood without a stop at **The Mississippi Gift Company.** Owned by Greenwood residents Tim and Cindy Tyler, The Mississippi Gift Company is the only retail store in the entire state that carries only products made in Mississippi. The Mississippi Gift Company offers more than 350 food and gift items, including gourmet snacks, sauces, and Mississippi-shaped chocolates; artwork; books (including titles by me and by my husband); note cards; pottery; candles; and cotton, catfish, and magnolia-themed souvenirs. The Mississippi Gift Company specializes in gift baskets, and they'll gladly ship a Mississippi souvenir to your friends back home. Visit The Mississippi Gift Company's retail store at 300 Howard Street in historic downtown Greenwood, or shop on the Web at www.MSGIFTS.com, or request a free catalog packed with goodies by calling (800) 467–7763 or (662) 455–6961.

If you're in the area in the spring, continue east of Greenwood on US 82 to charming **Carrollton,** where the stately mansions and cozy cottages built by Carroll County's original settlers still stand. Visitors will also discover a collection of antebellum churches (one built with funds raised through a chain letter), and a town square that looks more like a movie set than anything from the real world.

Follow the fragrance of cider, spice, and roses across Big Sand Creek to **North Carrollton** and the **Carriage House Candle Company.** Christye Stanton studied the art of candlemaking with the Amish of Pennsylvania Dutch Country, then began making and selling her own candles in her Carrollton home. As Christye tells it, "I didn't cook anything in my kitchen for two years except candles." When demand for her aromatic products outgrew her space, Christye moved her shop to a century-old mercantile building on North Carrollton's historic Main Street.

The Carriage House is truly a family affair. Christye is joined in the shop by her three equally creative sisters—Terri Dillon, who makes pottery in the on-site studio full time, and Sandra Edwards and Connie Smith, who make gift baskets in the shop on weekends. The sisters' father, Lee Collins, contributes handmade birdhouses, as well as delivering his daughters' lunch to the shop every day—a lunch packed, of course, by their mother. The most recent addition to the Carriage House staff is Christye Stanton's husband, Durward, who gave up his job in the corporate world to serve as the shop's wholesale sales rep.

Christmas with Sandy

Every December, visitors from around Mississippi travel to Carrollton to celebrate Christmas with Sandy Haley. The strange thing about this holiday tradition? Sandy has been dead for more than thirty years.

Angry because her parents wouldn't let her go out one night, fifteen-year-old Sandy swallowed the poison her father used to combat pests on the family farm. What was meant to be a dramatic gesture instead was fatal. Sandy died on June 24, 1966, and was buried in the Haley family plot across the street from Hickory Grove Baptist Church.

Every Christmas since, Sandy's mother, Mayzell Haley, has decorated her daughter's grave with hundreds of lights, countless figurines, stars, and angels, a fully trimmed Christmas tree, and Santa's sleigh, complete with eight tiny reindeer. The display has its own electric meter, attached to a utility pole installed by Mississippi Power Company just for Sandy's grave. A timer turns the lights on at 4:55 P.M. and off at 11:00 P.M.

Sandy's mother describes the Christmas display as a way of easing sorrow with celebration. Sandy's visitors, many of whom have signed a guest book at the cemetery fence, describe it as "touching," "tragic," and "bizarre."

But while opinions may vary, one thing is certain. Though she's been dead for more than three decades, Sandy Haley will always have company for Christmas.

Family traditions also weigh heavily in the Carriage House's product lines. Christye Stanton's original candle scent, "grandmother's rose," is actually based on a chemical analysis of her grandmother's prized tea rose bush. The "mimosa" candle and pottery pattern recall the family tradition of an annual Easter portrait under the mimosa tree. "Daisy's coconut delight," "apple dumpling," "sugar cookie," and "blueberry cobbler" are all based on family recipes.

You'll find the Carriage House Candle Company at 104 East Main Street. Call (662) 237–6001.

Northwest Carroll County was once the stomping ground of blues great Mississippi John Hurt. Hurt's granddaughter, Mary Frances Wright, has plans to turn Hurt's modest shotgun house in the minuscule Valley community into the ***Hurt Museum.***

"I want to have the things inside my grandfather really loved, like peanuts, soft hats, and sweet potato pies," Ms. Wright explains. "I want to have it look as closely as possible to the way it looked when my grandfather lived and played there."

Wright had the Hurt house moved about 3 miles from its original location to a creek bottom off Valley/Avalon Road. The new location is near the Delta hamlet of Avalon, made famous in Hurt's "Avalon Blues." At the time of this writing, the house was still undergoing renovation and was not yet open for tours. Hurt, who died in 1966, is buried just west of downtown Valley, 1 mile down St. James Church Road.

Once you've explored the eastern edge of the Delta in Carroll County, backtrack about 25 miles on US 82 West to Mississippi Highway 7 South. The *Itta Bena* area is home to two of the three churchyards rumored to be the *final resting place of blues great Robert Johnson.*

As a rule, bluesmen lived a rough life, often dividing their time between playing the blues, romancing other men's wives, and engaging in "cuttin's" and "shootin's." Johnson was no exception. He was living in Greenwood when he was poisoned by a jealous lover (or a lover's jealous husband, the story isn't clear which) at a local juke joint and died a horrible death at age twenty-seven—a fitting end, some said, for the man who sold his soul to the Devil for the ability to play the blues. In spite of this wicked pact and his

Robert Johnson's Deal with the Devil

"I went down to the crossroad,
fell down on my knees.
Asked the Lord above, 'Have mercy,
Save poor Bob, if you please.' "

The lyrics to Robert Johnson's "Cross Road Blues" may ask for mercy from the Lord, but according to legend, Johnson actually got his talent from the Devil.

As the story goes, Johnson met with the Devil at the crossroads of US 61 and U.S. Highway 49 on a dark summer night, and agreed to sell his soul for the ability to play the blues.

Most Delta residents scoffed at the notion of the Devil giving music lessons, but Son House, Willie Brown, and other noted bluesmen of the day were amazed by how quickly Johnson learned to play the guitar.

No other resident of Clarksdale has ever claimed to see the Devil hanging around in the area, but standing at a Delta crossroads on a hot, black summer night, it's easy to imagine a dark figure in the dusty road, waiting for the next aspiring musician.

wicked ways, Johnson was buried in a churchyard—or at least, it's believed he was buried in *some* churchyard, *some*where. Conflicting stories place Johnson's grave in either the **Payne Chapel M. B. Churchyard** at **Quito,** the **Mount Zion M. B. Church** just north of **Morgan City,** or the **Little Zion M. B. Church** north of Greenwood.

One of Johnson's ex-girlfriends claimed to have witnessed his burial in an unmarked grave at the Quito location. She further stated that Johnson was in Hell and wouldn't appreciate flowers, much less a tombstone. Nevertheless, a Georgia rock band contributed a marker bearing Johnson's name and the inscription RESTING IN THE BLUES.

The Mt. Zion site features an elaborate, four-sided obelisk engraved with the words, HIS MUSIC STRUCK A CHORD THAT CONTINUES TO RESONATE. HIS BLUES ADDRESSED GENERATIONS HE WOULD NEVER KNOW AND MADE POETRY OF HIS VISIONS AND FEARS. To get to the Mt. Zion church, take a left at the sign on Highway 7 that says MATTHEW'S BRAKE NATIONAL WILDLIFE REFUGE. Mt. Zion is the white frame church on the left.

In recent years, an eyewitness came forward to swear she watched as her own husband buried Johnson at the Little Zion location. That gravesite, too, now bears a marker honoring the King of the Delta Blues.

Although Johnson's actual resting place may forever remain a mystery, all three gravesites draw their share of whiskey bottles, rusty harmonicas, and well-worn guitar picks, left by blues fans from around the world.

Catfish Corridor

The Catfish Corridor reaches from Belzoni through Yazoo City and south to the Delta's end at the kudzu-covered hills near Vicksburg. South of Greenwood, King Cotton's dominance has been challenged by a new crop. Here the green-and-white fields give way to **catfish farms**—acre after acre of square ponds where Mississippi's newest cash crop thrives. Eighty percent of the world's farm-raised catfish comes from this area of Mississippi.

Continue on state Highway 7 South to **Belzoni** and **Humphreys County,** the **World Catfish Capital.** With more than 120 catfish farms covering more than 40,000 acres, catfish is the number-one crop in the county. At 6,000 catfish per acre, the county's fishy residents far outnumber its human population.

The **Catfish Capitol Visitors Center** honors the bewhiskered crop with exhibits tracing the industry from pond to plate. The Catfish Capitol can even arrange a catfish farm tour for you; just call (800) 408–4838 and give them a little advance notice. To get to the visitors center, take Highway 7 to US 49, take a left onto Jackson Street, then take the next road to the right. The Catfish Capitol

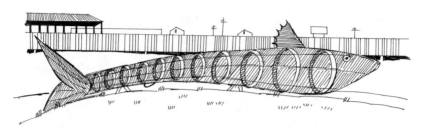

Catfish Fountain at Catfish Capitol

is hard to miss—look for the 40-foot catfish in the pond out front. If a look at the exhibits leaves you longing for a taste, head up US 49 West about 5 miles to **Isola** and **Peter Bo's** restaurant. Peter Bo's will fry up an order of catfish anytime of the day or night, breakfast included.

Things in Belzoni get really, *really* fishy the first Saturday in April, when the entire county turns out for the **World Catfish Festival.** Activities include live entertainment, the crowning of Miss Catfish, the world's largest fish fry (2,500 pounds, plus hush puppies), and a catfish-eating contest that's not for the squeamish.

For more information on catfish and the Catfish Capitol, visit www.catfish capitolonline.com or call (662) 247–4838.

Of course, there's more to Belzoni than just catfish. The most famous artist to come from the Delta is the late Ethel Wright Mohamed, whose work hangs in only two places—a Belzoni exhibit known as **Mama's Dream World** and the Smithsonian Institution in Washington, D.C. Dubbed "the Grandma Moses of stitchery," Mrs. Mohamed used intricate needlepoint pictures to tell her stories of life in the Delta. Mrs. Mohamed captured her children, her housekeeper, even the family pets in needlepoint, referring to them all as "my funny little people." Other than a few pieces donated to charity and the work displayed in the Smithsonian, all of her creations remain in Belzoni; Mrs. Mohamed never sold a single stitch. Call (662) 247–3633 to arrange an appointment to tour Mama's Dream World. Chances are good your guide will be the artist's own daughter, Carol Mohamed Ivy, who is featured in the stitchery.

Before you leave Belzoni, take a break from the road at **Wister Gardens,** a fourteen-acre park on the northern outskirts of town. Be sure to snap a picture of the statue of Johnny Appleseed, presented to Wister Henry, the garden's founder, by the Men's Garden Club of America.

Back on US 49, catfish ponds continue to dominate the stretch of road south of Belzoni. Most of the ponds are at eye level, but an occasional rise in the road offers a glimpse across surface after shimmering surface. Keep an eye out for the blatant poachers known as cormorants—large black birds that swoop down into the ponds to catch an easy dinner.

After those long, flat roads stretching to the horizon, the hill that signals the entrance to **Yazoo County** looks more like a small mountain. The county bills itself as the spot "where the Delta meets the hills," and indeed, one side of the county touches the flat edge of the Delta while the other rolls gently into the loess bluffs.

For a unique dining, shopping, and conservation experience, stop by the **Hines Broadlake Grocery** on US 49 just west of Yazoo City. Daily lunch specials featuring Eva Hines's country cooking bring in hungry farmers from all over the Delta. Every fall, Thursday at Hines is fried pigskin day and Friday is one giant barbecue. The grocery is located across the road from the Hines's working farm, where Eva and her husband John raise their own cattle and hogs. The grocery half of the business sells their homegrown beef and pork—every last bit of it. You'll find freezers stocked with pigs' feet, tongues, tails, snouts, and other parts city folk have probably never dreamed of ingesting. Eva is usually happy to let first-time guests sample some of the more unusual delicacies, including hog's head cheese, which she describes as "everything that's left."

If you were able to handle the hog's head, you might even be ready to graduate to chitlins (also known as chitterlings), another delicacy whose source of origin is seldom discussed. Pick up an order at the **All My Children** fast food restaurant just a mile or two down the road in **Yazoo City.**

In addition to a Delta side and a Hill side, Yazoo City boasts a dark side. The tale of the **Witch of Yazoo** has been kept alive not only by local residents, but by late author **Willie Morris,** a Yazoo City native who repeated the spooky story in his books of childhood reminiscences, *Good Old Boy* and *My Dog Skip*. When Morris died in 1999, he was buried in Glenwood Cemetery, thirteen paces from the witch's grave.

The witch's tale is repeated every spring during the annual **Yazoo Festival,** which includes fire sales in Yazoo City shops, twilight tours of Glenwood Cemetery, a competitive scavenger hunt, musical entertainment, arts and crafts, and a street dance. The witch's name is sure to come up again at the **Remembering Willie** celebration, when friends and admirers of the beloved author gather to reminisce, laugh, and express admiration for a brilliant writer, loyal friend, and lifelong prankster. For this year's festival dates, call the **Yazoo County Convention and Visitors Bureau** at (662) 746–1815 or (800) 381–0662, or visit www.yazoo.org.

Make your first stop in town the **Yazoo Visitors Center,** located in the **Triangle Cultural Center.** Take US 49 to Broadway Street, go down the steep hill, then take a right at the first traffic light.

The Witch of Yazoo

In the late 1800s, Yazoo City was home to a self-proclaimed witch, a crazy old woman who lured fishermen to their deaths in her home on the banks of the Yazoo River.

Eventually, a group of vigilantes chased the old woman into a nearby swamp, where she met her death in a pool of quicksand. Just before her "ghastly, pockmarked" head was sucked below the surface, she vowed to return from the grave and burn the entire town on the morning of May 25, 1904. The old woman's body was pulled from the quicksand and buried in Glenwood Cemetery, the plot surrounded by a thick iron chain, each link 15 inches long.

You guessed it. On May 25, 1904, all of downtown Yazoo City was indeed destroyed by fire, and visitors to the old woman's grave found a link missing from the chain.

You'll find the century-old chain and a new marker inscribed, "the Witch of Yazoo" near the fountain in the center of the old section of the cemetery at the intersection of Lintonia and Webster Streets. Visit the witch and give the chain a tug yourself—if you dare.

Housed in the old Main Street School built in 1905, the Cultural Center houses a collection of small-but-interesting museums. The *Jerry Clower Exhibit* honors the late country comedian and former Yazoo City resident (say "haw!"). The "Jimmy Carter Slept Here" display showcases a roomful of furniture from a local home where the former President once passed the night (rumor has it the china he ate off of is locked away in a safe deposit box). On the third floor you'll discover a small historic museum with exhibits from prehistoric days through modern times. Plans are under way to add a "Famous Yazooans" room. The visitors center and exhibit rooms are open Monday–Friday 8:00 A.M.–5:00 P.M.

Be sure to ask the friendly staff for a walking tour guide to the *Yazoo City Historic District.* The homes included aren't open for tour, but a stroll along wisteria-lined streets offers a look at charming examples of Victorian, Queen Anne, Gothic, Italianate, and Greek Revival architecture. Staff at the visitors center can also give you directions to homes of significance you won't find listed in brochures, like the childhood homes of author Willie Morris and motivational speaker Zig Ziglar and the house where President Jimmy Carter once spent the night.

Housed in a restored turn-of-the-twentieth-century mansion, the *Oakes African-American Cultural Center* (312 South Monroe Street), displays photographs, folk art, sculpture, and other exhibits celebrating African-American history in Yazoo County. The mansion was once the home of Augustus J. Oakes, a prominent Yazoo City resident who founded Oakes Academy, a private school for African-American children, in 1884. Oakes is buried in Glenwood Cemetery.

For a Yazoo City adventure that's not just *off* the beaten path, but way, way *above* it, give **Zoo City Skydivers** a call. For around $200 you can take a morning lesson, then jump out of a perfectly good airplane the same afternoon. You'll even get a video to show all your friends. Brave souls can reach Zoo City Skydivers at (662) 746–3483.

If all that action stimulates your appetite, or if you just need a snack for the road, pick up a tin of **Mississippi Cheese Straws,** baked locally at the **Mississippi Cheese Straw Factory** and sold in shops all over Mississippi. You'll also find a wide selection of goodies at **Gilbert's Gourmet Gifts,** a specialty foods shop located in the back of **Gilbert's Lumber Yard.** Gilbert's also offers unique souvenirs, including the popular kudzu candle. Further shopping opportunities await at the **Cheshire Cat, Essco's,** and **Cindi's,** but if it's antiques you're looking for, the locals recommend a trip to the nearest pawn shop, explaining that "some people just don't realize what they have."

As you head out of town, you'll notice a profusion of green vines covering everything—*everything*—in sight. This rampant vegetation is **kudzu,** described by writer Lewis Grizzard as "the vine that ate the South." You'll find thriving displays of kudzu all over Mississippi, but the tenacious vine is especially prolific in the area between Yazoo City and Vicksburg. Once hailed as the remedy for the erosion of valuable farmland, kudzu became a nuisance, then an example of nature gone wild, when its growth could not be contained. The stuff grows an average of 6 inches per day, so fast you can almost watch it spread. The thick vine eagerly swallows up telephone poles, trees, buildings—virtually anything in its path. Don't stand in one place too long!

Wrap up your visit to the Delta by heading east on Mississippi Highway 16, then north up I–55 to **Vaughn,** where you'll spot an exit directing you to the **Casey Jones Railroad Museum State Park.**

This museum of Mississippi railroad memorabilia is housed in an old depot less than a mile from the site of the crash that killed engineer Casey Jones. The museum is open Monday, Tuesday, Thursday, and Friday 8:00 A.M.–4:00 P.M., and Wednesday and Saturday 8:00 A.M.–noon. Admission is $1.00 for adults and 50 cents for children.

An old barn on Possum Bend Road is home to **Harkins Woodworks,** where Greg Harkins makes rocking chairs and primitive furniture by hand using techniques passed down from the mid-1800s. Harkins's famous chairs have graced the homes of Presidents Bill Clinton, Ronald Reagan, George Bush, and Jimmy Carter, as well as those of Pope John Paul II, Paul Harvey, Bob

The Legend of Casey Jones

Shortly after midnight on April 30, 1900, the train Cannonball left Memphis, Tennessee, with Jonathan Luther Casey Jones at the throttle of engine #382. Trying to make up time on his run to Canton, Jones barreled through a stop signal only to spot a freight train stalled on the track ahead. Realizing a crash was inevitable, Jones ordered his fireman to jump clear, but stayed on board himself to try and brake the train. Casey's heroic effort cost him his life.

The tale of Casey Jones and the ill-fated Cannonball might have ended that night if not for the musical skills of an engine wiper named Wallace Sanders, who composed "The Ballad of Casey Jones" as a tribute to his friend. The song became a hit, and Casey Jones became a legend.

As for engine #382, it was repaired and put back in service on the same route. Just three years later, the 382 crashed again, killing the train's fireman and critically injuring its engineer. All told, the doomed 382 took five lives before it was finally retired from service in 1935.

Hope, and George Burns. Place your own order on your way through Vaughn, then leave a shipping address and be patient—Harkins spends about thirty hours on each chair, even handpicking the tree he starts with. Harkins has turned down offers to automate and mass produce, preferring to stick with the exquisite craftsmanship that makes each chair a signed, dated, one-of-a-kind work of art. Call (601) 362–4233 for directions to Harkins's shop.

The famed chair maker also offers an unusual dinner option. When Harkins learned that *St. Anne's,* a lovely old church built by his great-great-great grandfather in the 1800s, was slated for demolition, he invested his own money to move the church building to his property near Benton, Mississippi. On Friday nights from October to June, Harkins serves dinner by reservation in the old church building. Patrons choose from steak, seafood, or chicken, all accompanied by Harkins's homemade tamales and homespun stories, many of which relate to the history of St. Anne's. Be warned—this is not your typical, restaurant-type experience. Although the food is quite good, the service is unhurried and relaxed; you'll have plenty of time to explore and photograph the old church and to listen to a song or two performed by Greg and other assorted Harkins family members. Go for an unusual evening in the Mississippi countryside and with camaraderie as your goal, you'll not be disappointed. Dinner at St. Anne's is $30 per person, BYOB, and all proceeds go toward the continued renovation and upkeep of St. Anne's. Call (601) 594–3879 for dinner reservations and directions to the church.

Places to Stay in the Mississippi River Delta

The following is a partial listing of the many hotels, motels, and bed-and-breakfast inns in the area not mentioned in the text.

Lincoln Ltd. is a full-time reservation service for bed-and-breakfast inns statewide. For reservations in any area of Mississippi, call (601) 482–5483 or (800) 633–6477.

GREENWOOD

The Alluvian Hotel
318 Howard Street,
(866) 600–5201

Rivers' Inn
(bed-and-breakfast)
1109 River Road,
(662) 453–5432

INDIANOLA

Holiday Inn Express
601 Highway 82 West,
(662) 887–7477

ROBINSONVILLE

Horseshoe Casino and Hotel
1021 Casino Center Drive,
(662) 357–5500

Sam's Town Hotel and Gambling Hall
1477 Casino Strip Resorts Boulevard,
(662) 363–0711

YAZOO CITY

Parker-Roark House
(bed-and-breakfast)
528 East Broadway,
(662) 746–5276

Places to Eat in the Mississippi River Delta

The following is a partial listing of the many restaurants in the area not mentioned in the text.

CLARKSDALE

Turner's (plate lunches)
330 Issaquena Avenue,
(662) 627–2884

ALSO WORTH SEEING

DURANT

Holmes County State Park

GREENVILLE

Bayou Caddy's Jubilee Casino

Las Vegas Casino

The Light House Point Casino

TUNICA

Bally's Saloon and Gambling Hall Hotel

Bluesville

Casino Factory Shoppes

Fitzgerald's Casino

Gold Strike Casino and Hotel

Grand Casino

Harrah's Tunica Casino and Hotel

Hollywood Casino Hotel and RV Park

Horseshoe Casino and Hotel

Isle of Capri Casino

Sam's Town Hotel and Gambling Hall

Sheraton Casino

CLEVELAND

Sharpe Street Station
(steaks, seafood, appetizers;
live entertainment on
weekends)
201A Sharpe Street,
(662) 846–0000

GREENVILLE

Shapley's in the Delta
(steaks, seafood)
205 Central Avenue,
(662) 334–6655

GREENWOOD

The Cotton Patch
(breakfast, short orders,
sandwiches)
US 82 Bypass,
(662) 453–4155

Crystal Grill
(home-cooked meals,
steaks, seafood)
423 Carrollton Avenue,
(662) 453–6530

Webster's
(steaks, seafood)
216 West Claiborne,
(662) 455–1215

Yianni's (steaks, seafood)
506 Yalobusha,
(662) 455–6789

INVERNESS

Hometown Restaurant
(steaks, burgers,
sandwiches)
704 East Grand Avenue,
(662) 265–5753

ROSEDALE

White Front Cafe
(hot tamales)
902 Main Street,
(662) 759–3842

YAZOO CITY

Main Event Cafe
(sandwiches, salads,
appetizers)
310 South Main Street,
(662) 746–4171

The Heartland

The Heartland stretches from Jackson, Mississippi's capital city and geographic center, through several rural communities south of the "big city" limits, then west to the historic towns that line the bluffs of the mighty Mississippi River.

As explorers of this area of the state soon discover, the Heartland manages to be urban and rural, Old South and New, and cosmopolitan yet down-home friendly—all at the same time.

The Jackson Metro Area

Ask out-of-state visitors to name a city in Mississippi and they'll usually pick Jackson, recalled from that often-recited list of state capitals learned in elementary school. But adventures in the Jackson Metro Area aren't limited to the capital city. Many of the region's genuine pleasures lie in the spirited college towns, quaint country villages, and folksy town squares just outside the city limits.

A tour of the Metro Area begins just off Interstate 55 South in *Canton,* where the focal point is the antebellum *Madison County Courthouse.*

Make your first stop in this charming southern hamlet the *Canton Convention and Visitors Bureau,* housed in the

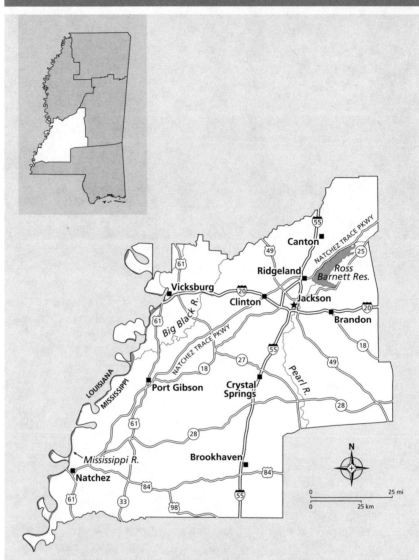

Canton

55

49

Natchez Trace Pkwy

25

Ridgeland

Ross
Barnett Res.

Vicksburg

61

20

Clinton

Jackson

Big Black R.

61

Natchez Trace Pkwy

Brandon

20

18

55

27

49

18

Louisiana

Mississippi

Port Gibson

Crystal
Springs

Pearl R.

28

61

28

Mississippi R.

Brookhaven

84

Natchez

84

61

33

98

55

N

0   25 mi
0   25 km

lovely old **Trolio Hotel** on the west side of the Canton Courthouse Square. The friendly bureau staff will provide brochures and help you plan a day exploring the town. If you stop by the Trolio on the second Tuesday of the month, you'll be treated to a quilting demonstration by the Allison's Wells School of Arts & Crafts quilters. The third Saturday of "even" months (February, April, June, August, October, and December), the Trolio hosts the Magnolia Woodturners. The Convention and Visitors Bureau is open Monday–Friday 9:00 A.M.–5:00 P.M., and Saturday 10:00 A.M.–2:00 P.M.

Frequent visits by Hollywood have earned Canton a reputation as the Movie Capital of Mississippi. *A Time to Kill* (based on the novel by Mississippi author John Grisham), *My Dog Skip* (based on the book by the late Mississippi author Willie Morris), *The Ponder Heart* (based on the novel by the late Mississippi author Eudora Welty), *The Rising Place,* and *Oh Brother, Where Art Thou?* (believe it or not, *not* based on books by Mississippi authors) were all filmed entirely in Canton. Scenes from the films *Mississippi Burning, The Chamber,* and *The Ghosts of Mississippi* were also shot within the city limits.

The **Canton Movie Museum,** (141 North Union Street), also referred to locally as "the Museum at Wohner's Corner," showcases props and sets from several of the films. Visitors can pay a call to Jake Brigance's law offices or the coffee shop from *A Time to Kill,* take a seat in the beauty salon from *The Ponder Heart,* or risk a peek at the spooky crypt from *My Dog Skip.* The museum also includes a Willie Morris tribute section featuring a replica of the late

MARLO'S FAVORITE ATTRACTIONS IN THE HEARTLAND

Quaint downtown Madison (my home)	Old Court House Museum, Vicksburg
The Natchez Trace Parkway as it runs alongside the Ross Barnett Reservoir, Ridgeland	Sunday mornings in the churches of Port Gibson
The Old Capitol Museum, Jackson	Windsor Ruins, Port Gibson
Vicksburg National Military Park, Vicksburg	Antebellum homes and bed-and-breakfast inns, Natchez
Mississippi River Bridge, Vicksburg	Cocktail hour at Natchez Under-the-Hill, Natchez

author's writing desk, complete with notes transcribed word-for-word from his own. To tour the museum, call or stop by the Canton Convention and Visitors Bureau. Call (601) 859–1307 or (800) 844–3369.

In 2000, Canton received a federal grant to develop a film production complex, which could include a larger museum as well as state-of-the-art production facilities. Who knows—someday the Canton Square may rank right up there with Rodeo Drive as a hot spot for star sightings.

Even before Canton hit the silver screen, the town was famous as the home of the *Canton Flea Market.* Held twice yearly, this juried economic extravaganza attracts 1,100 vendors from twenty-nine states and thousands of shoppers from around the country. Wares include fine art, paintings, pottery, jewelry, crafts, antiques, and plants displayed around the Courthouse Square, in the old jailhouse, and on the grounds of Grace Episcopal Church, Sacred Heart Catholic Church, and other area churches. Come prepared to fight the traffic and pay a premium price for a good parking spot, and don't forget your flashlight—the best deals are made before dawn. The Canton Flea Market is held the second Thursdays of May and October. Call (800) 844–3369 for more information, including details on shuttle bus packages featuring highly coveted and well-worth-it restroom privileges.

If you prefer shopping as a leisure activity instead of an extreme sport, visit the Canton Square on one of the 363 other days of the year. You'll find two antiques malls and a number of gift shops and specialty boutiques, and can browse sans the crowds.

Worthwhile shopping stops include *Sulm's* (3338 North Liberty), a great source for upscale gifts and accessories, unique women's clothing, and jewelry; the *Market Gallery* (3332 North Liberty), where you'll find artwork by Canton Flea Market vendors year-round; *Fletcher's Flowers and Gifts* (119 North Union Street), which offers surprises for every member of the family, including Fido and Fluffy; and *The Mill Store* (620 East Peace Street) and *Whatever Works* (189 East Peace Street), where the merchandise is endless and shopping takes on the feeling of a treasure hunt.

If you're in a redecorating mode, be sure to stop by *The Linen Shop* (3346 North Liberty Street). The shop sells designer fabrics at affordable prices, sometimes by the pound. The Linen Shop is a favorite haunt of Jackson resident Laurie Hickson-Smith, one of a team of designers featured on The Learning Channel's wildly popular do-it-to-your-neighbor's-house-yourself show, *Trading Spaces.*

The Canton Square is also a great spot for dining. Owned by Greg Harkins of Harkins Woodworks (see previous chapter), *Harkins Family Bakery* (118

West Center Street) serves up sensational hot tamales as well as lunch specials and baked goods. ***Davidson's Corner Market*** (108 Center Street) serves lunch Monday–Friday, and dinner Thursday–Saturday, with live music on Friday and Saturday nights. Connected to the restaurant, ***Davidson's Kitchen and Gourmet Shop*** sells fancy condiments, coffees, and sweets to share with the folks back home.

Dining in Canton isn't limited to the Square. Housed in an antebellum cottage in the historic depot district, ***Christine's Back Porch*** (123 Depot Street) is the place for pure southern fare, including sweet tea to die for. The lunch menu is best described as whatever Christine decides to cook that day.

The rationale behind Canton's slogan, "the city of lights" becomes abundantly clear each December, when the town launches its month-long ***Victorian Christmas Festival.*** From Thanksgiving to New Year's, downtown Canton is ablaze with more than 200,000 white lights. The celebration includes the annual opening of the ***Christmas Animation Museum,*** a child-pleasing display of 125 moving figures set in vignettes depicting the town's history. An old-fashioned carousel and horse-and-buggy rides round out the winter wonderland atmosphere.

From Canton it's just a short drive south past the horse stables on U.S. Highway 51 to ***Madison,*** one of Mississippi's premier residential communities. *Southern Living* magazine hails Madison as the place to find "fun shops and casual dining . . . with boutiques, galleries, and restaurants that are drawing a lot of attention." Madison's tiny downtown district is a favorite haunt of antiques buffs, who are sure to find treasures in the shops that circle the ***Historic Madison Depot Station*** on Main Street off US 51 (Main Street is also Mississippi Highway 463). For a handcrafted souvenir, stop by ***Pickenpaugh Pottery,*** located just off Main Street near the depot area. The Pickenpaugh pottery shop is also the Pickenpaugh residence; visitors to Pickenpaugh will usually find a landscaping project in progress that's every bit as unique as the pottery.

Other shops worth an afternoon's browsing include ***Persnickety*** (2078 Main Street), an elegant-yet-funky establishment packed with distinctive, upscale home accessories, fine china, pottery, candles, and gifts found nowhere else in Mississippi; ***Bearly Made, Inc.*** (2086 Main Streeet), where kids design and assemble their own, one-of-a-kind teddy bears; and ***The Inside Story*** (2081 Main Street) a reliable source of unusual picture frames, jewelry, clothing, and gifts.

A casual dining option within walking distance of Madison's shops is the ***Strawberry Café*** (180 Main Street) for sandwiches and lunch plates. Barbecue lovers should head toward the I–55 interchange at Madison (the only interstate interchange in Mississippi adorned with red bricks) and *The Haute Pig* (1856 Main Street), a down-home good barbecue joint with an upscale moniker.

From downtown Madison, cross I–55 and travel along Mississippi Highway 463 to the *Chapel of the Cross.* The tranquility that envelops this tree-shaded churchyard and antebellum chapel is reason enough for a visit, but if you're in the mood for a mystery, drop by around twilight. You might be lucky enough to bump into the *Bride of Annandale*—the chapel's resident ghost.

This area of rural Madison County was the setting of a kidnapping plot gone awry in Mississippi author Greg Iles's best-selling novel, *24 Hours.*

Mississippi Highway 463 intersects Mississippi Highway 22 just northeast of *Flora* and the only petrified forest in the eastern United States. The *Mississippi Petrified Forest* was designated a National Natural Landmark by the National Park Service in 1966. According to geologists, the giant trees embedded in the earth here are some thirty-six to thirty-eight million years old. A well-marked trail through the wooded park can be easily explored in half an hour. The path ends in the earth science museum and gift shop, where visitors may purchase sparkling crystals, chunks of petrified wood, fossils, and other geological souvenirs. The Petrified Forest is open 9:00 A.M.–6:00 P.M. April–Labor Day, and 9:00 A.M.–5:00 P.M. the remainder of the year. Admission is $5.00 for adults and $4.00 for children and seniors. Call (601) 879–8189.

From Flora it's just a short drive along U.S. Highway 49 South to tiny *Pocahantas.* A small sign points out the POCAHANTAS TRADING DISTRICT, but if you're headed for *Big D's Bar-be-cue,* it's just as easy to follow your nose.

Chapel of the Cross

The Bride of Annandale

Annandale was a huge Madison County plantation built in the 1840s. The plantation owner's daughter, Helen Johnstone, fell in love with the dashing Henry Vick, and their wedding was planned for May 21, 1859, at the Chapel of the Cross. But mere days before the nuptials, Henry was killed in a duel. He was buried at midnight in the churchyard behind the chapel, and the devastated Helen wore her wedding gown to the funeral. Helen eventually married, but never forgot her first love. The last words uttered from her deathbed were, "He's coming back for me."

Visitors to the Chapel of the Cross often report sightings of a sad woman clad all in white, sitting on a bench near Henry Vick's grave. If you go, don't wait for Helen past twilight. It's illegal to prowl the cemetery after dark, and as a number of unfortunate ghost-hunters can verify, it's a law that's strictly enforced.

Barbecued pork ranks right up there with grits and catfish on the list of Mississippi delicacies, and Big D's is the perfect spot to stop for a sample (don't forget the napkins).

Continue on US 49 South from Pocahantas into Jackson, or double back on Mississippi 463, then follow U.S. Highway 51 south of Madison to *Ridgeland.*

Ceramics enthusiasts should make time to visit the *Gail Pittman Studio and Factory Outlet* (290 South Perkins; 601–856–7120 or 601–856–5646). Artist Gail Pittman began "playing around" with ceramics at her kitchen table in 1977. Today, the Gail Pittman collection includes more than 140 products ranging from dinnerware to home accessories to wall coverings, available in more than forty original, colorful patterns. Gail Pittman pieces are prized by fans, collectors, and brides-to-be nationwide and make distinctive gifts. The factory outlet shop at the studio sells "seconds" only, Monday–Saturday, 9:00 A.M.–4:00 P.M. First-quality Pittman pieces are sold in shops and galleries statewide. An extensive Gail Pittman selection is available nearby at *The Everyday Gourmet* (1625 East County Line Road; 601–977–0864), where Pittman made her first commercial sale.

Ridgeland is also home to the shop and studio of Vicki Carroll, another talented potter offering hand-painted dinnerware and accessories. The *VC Original Studio and Seconds Shop* (601–853–7413) is open Monday–Friday 8:00 A.M.–5:00 P.M. at 209 West Ridgeland Avenue.

Other off-the-beaten-path shopping opportunities in Ridgeland include the *Log Village,* a charming area of folksy shops, and the *Antique Mall of the South,* which promises "no crafts or flea market items." Both are located on US 51.

MARLO'S FAVORITE ANNUAL EVENTS IN THE HEARTLAND

CANTON

Canton Flea Market,
May and October,
(888) 868–7720

Mississippi Championship Hot-Air Balloon Festival,
July,
(800) 844–3369

JACKSON

Crossroads Film Festival,
April,
(601) 366–3829

Mal's St. Paddy's Day Parade,
March, (601) 355–7685

Jubilee! JAM,
June,
(601) 960–2008

Mistletoe Marketplace,
November,
(601) 948–2357

NATCHEZ

Spring and Fall Pilgrimages,
mid-March to mid-April;
month of October,
(800) 647–6742

Angels on the Bluff,
October,
(800) 647–6724

Great Mississippi River Balloon Race,
October,
(800) 647–6724

VICKSBURG

Civil War Reenactments,
April, June, and July,
(800) 221–3536

The entrance to the northern section of the scenic *Natchez Trace Parkway* is in Ridgeland directly off US 51. A short jaunt along the Trace leads to the *Mississippi Crafts Center,* housed in a log cabin complete with rocking chairs on the front porch and a cheerful fire burning inside. The crafts center displays and sells one-of-a-kind masterpieces made by the members of the *Craftsmen's Guild of Mississippi,* including basketry, pottery, woodwork, and jewelry. The crafts center also stages frequent live demonstrations—visitors may arrive to find artisans whittling, weaving, carving, or quilting on the front porch.

Annual events at the Crafts Center include autumn's *Pioneer and Indian Heritage Festival,* a celebration of the state's frontier past, and June's *Children's Crafts Sampler,* when talented guild members offer hands-on instruction to children.

The Madison–Ridgeland stretch of the Natchez Trace Parkway borders the 33,000-acre *Ross Barnett Reservoir.* Continue north along the Trace from

Ridgeland and you'll arrive at the ***Reservoir Overlook,*** a grassy plateau that offers a lovely view of the water and provides the perfect setting for a picnic. The "rez" is a hot spot for power boating, skiing, sailing (watch out for those jet skis!), camping, and fishing.

When the sun goes down, activity moves to the many restaurants and nightclubs that dot the shoreline in the ***Main Harbor Marina*** area just off Spillway Road. Stop by ***Cock of the Walk*** (141 Madison Landing Circle) for a taste of Mississippi farm-raised catfish served by waiters clad in flamboyant riverboat garb. Dinner is served on tin plates in a casual atmosphere that's perfect for families traveling with kids. But stay alert—you don't want to get hit by the flying cornbread.

With its wide selection of hotel chains and restaurants, Ridgeland promotes itself as one of Mississippi's best places to sleep and eat. The city is indeed home to more excellent restaurants, laid-back bistros, casual dining chains, and fast food eateries than can be listed, but there are a couple that warrant a special mention.

Sample the artistically prepared seafood at ***Little Tokyo II,*** located at the end of County Line Road in the Promenade Shopping Center. Skilled sushi chef Tomio Demura opened the original Little Tokyo, Mississippi's first authentic sushi bar, in Jackson in 1987. Establishing a sushi restaurant in the land of fried catfish was a bold gamble that paid off. Encouraged by the phenomenal success of the original, Demura opened Little Tokyo II in 1996, trusting the management of the second sushi bar to his capable and friendly wife, Fumiko Demura. Within a few years, the sushi craze hit the Jackson area full force. Adventurous diners now choose from among five sushi restaurants, but in this sushi addict's opinion, the original is still the best. For authentic Japanese cuisine, artful presentation, flawless service, and fish so fresh it's almost swimming, stop by Little Tokyo II (876 Avery Boulevard). If you can't make it to the Ridgeland location, try the original Little Tokyo in Lefleur's Gallery Shopping Center in Jackson.

An elegant choice for fine dining is ***The Parker House*** (104 South East Madison Drive). Steve and Barbara Parker opened the original Parker House in Ridgeland's Centre Park shopping center in 1994. By 1998, the popular restaurant was experiencing growing pains. When the Parkers mentioned their hunt for a new location to regular patrons Ernie and Jean Adcock, the Adcocks offered a novel solution—why not move the restaurant into their spacious home? In less than a week, the deal was done. The Adcocks built a smaller home, their roomy former residence was remodeled, and in 1999, The Parker House reopened at its new location in Ridgeland's Olde Towne district. With its welcoming fireplaces, intimate piano bar, elegant antiques, rich tapestries, and fine art, the restaurant retains the feeling of dining in an elegant private home. The beautifully landscaped property boasts towering oak, pecan, and willow trees, and a swimming pool accented by a decorative fountain and soft lighting—the ideal setting for dining al fresco. Add a menu as inviting as the atmosphere, and it's little wonder The Parker House was awarded the Wine Spectator Award of Excellence 2002 and was named the 2001 Restaurant of the Year by the Mississippi Restaurant Association. For reservations at The Parker House, call (601) 856–0043 or visit www.theparkerhouse.com.

From the reservoir area, take Spillway Road (which turns into Lake Harbor Drive as it crosses the reservoir back into Ridgeland) to Old Canton Road, then head south into **Jackson.** You'll know you've left Ridgeland and entered Mississippi's capital city when you cross County Line Road, a major thoroughfare lined with retail shops and restaurants. Located at the intersection of I–55 and I–20, Jackson is hardly off the beaten path, but even this busy city nicknamed the "crossroads of the South" offers a few undiscovered treasures.

Follow County Line Road west to the small but significant campus of **Tougaloo College** (500 West County Line Road). Located on the old Boddie Plantation, Tougaloo is a historically black, private liberal arts college founded in 1869. Tougaloo played a vital role in the civil rights movement of the 1960s. Researchers and history buffs will appreciate the Lillian Pierce Benbow Room of special collections in the Coleman Library, where thousands of documents, tapes, photographs, and other artifacts tell the compelling story of the struggle for equal rights.

The civil rights movement also helped create one of the most impressive art collections in Mississippi. In the early 1960s, a student from Brown University visiting Tougaloo College described the limited opportunities for black students in Mississippi to study art to his sister, Dore Ashton, a former art critic for the *New York Times*. Ashton organized a group of artists, critics, and collectors who put together the permanent **Tougaloo Art Collection,** the first contemporary art collection in the state. Ashton's group also established a fund for future purchases. Today the Tougaloo Collection includes more than 1,000 paintings, sculptures, and wood carvings valued at between $3 and $5 million. The collection is housed in the college's Coleman Library. Call (601) 977–7839 for viewing hours.

From County Line Road, pick up I–55 South and head toward downtown. The Frontage Road runs along either side of I–55 near the Northside Drive and Meadowbrook exits. Located on the eastern side of I–55, upscale **Highland Village** offers a number of clothing stores, home accessory shops, and galleries worth an afternoon's exploration.

Highland Village is also home to one of Mississippi's most celebrated restaurants, ***Bravo! Italian Restaurant and Bar.*** Co-owned by high school buddies Dan Blumenthal and Jeff Good, this exceptional restaurant serves innovative Italian cuisine and fine wines. Bravo! is a four-time winner of the Wine Spectator Award of Excellence and was named Jackson's Restaurant of the Year four years in a row. The restaurant hosts popular cooking classes and wine tastings, as well as weekly specials. Drop by for a discounted glass of your favorite vino on Wine Down Wednesday, or indulge in a special bottle on Vintage Saturday. For a look at upcoming events at Bravo! visit www.bravobuzz.com.

That striking Art Deco building on the western side of I–55 at Meadowbrook is ***Banner Hall,*** home to one of Mississippi's premier independent bookstores. Boasting a cozy, friendly atmosphere and a knowledgeable staff of bookworms, ***Lemuria*** is the place to pick up the latest bestseller or a classic literary masterpiece, often signed by the author. The walls are decked with photos of famous writers who've held readings or signings in this popular gathering

Lights, Camera, Action!

In the last decade, Mississippi has become a hot spot for Hollywood.

The Firm, The Client, A Time to Kill, The Chamber (all based on best-selling novels by Mississippi author John Grisham), *My Dog Skip, Ghosts of Mississippi, The Ponder Heart,* and *Oh Brother, Where Art Thou?* were among the many movies made in Mississippi.

Several of these films were shot in and around Jackson, where celebrity sightings became commonplace. Sandra Bullock, Chris O'Donnell, Alec Baldwin, James Woods, and director Rob Reiner were all spotted in local restaurants. Faye Dunaway had her portrait painted by a Jackson artist, Gene Hackman played golf at a Madison country club, and Keifer Sutherland took a turn on the drums at a local nightspot.

Delighted to meet a genuine "Sister Act," Whoopi Goldberg entertained a group of nuns from St. Dominic Hospital in her rented Madison County home. Crowds jammed a local ballfield to watch George Clooney play catch in a pair of overalls (sans shirt), and I must confess to calling all of my friends from a local gym when Samuel L. Jackson and Matthew McConaughey showed up for a workout.

Not content with just watching, thousands of Mississippians flocked to open casting calls for roles as extras. Several of my friends and business associates vied for parts, and a few actually made it to the silver screen.

As for me, I admit to waiting in line for two hours in hopes of making the cut for *A Time to Kill.* Alas, the word from Hollywood was, "keep your day job."

spot for bibliophiles. Call (601) 366–7619 or visit www.lemuriabooks.com to check on your favorite title or inquire about authors' appearances.

Be warned—the tempting aroma of fresh-baked bread emanating from Banner Hall's first floor **Broad Street Bakery** (the sister restaurant of award-winning Bravo!) is impossible to resist. If you really want to concentrate on browsing in the bookstore, give in to the temptation and enjoy a hearty, made-to-order sandwich before heading upstairs.

Back on I–55, continue south to the Lakeland Drive exit, then head west to **Woodland Hills** and the **Fondren District,** two older Jackson areas marked by specialty shops, galleries, and a rich sense of history and character that's impossible to duplicate in a modern mall or strip shopping center.

trivia

Upon its completion in 1925, the ten-story Lamar Life Building (317 East Capitol Street) was hailed as Jackson's first skyscraper.

Dating to the 1890s, the eclectic area near the intersection of North State Street and Old Canton Road was Jackson's first suburb; residents traveled back and forth to downtown via streetcar. Today, the Fondren District is a shining example of neighborhood revitalization. Interesting stops here include the **Treehouse Boutique** (3000 North State Street), featuring unusual gifts and ladies' apparel; the **Everyday Gardener** (2905 Old Canton Road), a paradise for green thumbs; **Interiors Market** (Woodland Hills Shopping Center), where more than thirty antiques, accessory, and gift shops share display space under a single roof; and **Brown's Fine Art and Framing** (630 Fondren Place) and **Bryant Galleries** (4755 Old Canton Road), upscale galleries showcasing original paintings and sculpture.

Take a shopping break at **Brent's Drugs and Soda Fountain** (655 Duling Avenue), a Jackson tradition featuring cherry cokes, milkshakes, and burgers at the counter since the 1940s.

Two of Jackson's most popular museums are found just off Lakeland Drive on the eastern side of I–55. Just five minutes from downtown, the **Mississippi Museum of Natural Science** seems worlds away from city life. The museum complex is nestled in a wooded, 300-acre site featuring 2.5 miles of winding nature trails, a woodland pond, and a forest area that serves as a natural habitat for native birds, animals, and plants. Inside the 73,000-square-foot facility, vast windows and a huge central skylight provide a visual link to the outdoors. Exhibits showcasing Mississippi's natural heritage include a white-tailed deer exhibit, a "wall of fossils" display, and a 100,000-gallon, twenty-tank aquarium system swimming with 200 species of native fish, reptiles, and amphibians.

"The Swamp," a 1,700-square-foot greenhouse and 20,000-gallon aquarium, is home to alligators and turtles. A 200-seat auditorium screens natural science films and hosts speakers and special events.

The Museum of Natural Science is located in **LeFleur's Bluff State Park** at Lakeland Drive and Riverside Drive just past the Lakeland Drive exit on I–55. The museum is open Monday–Friday 8:00 A.M.–5:00 P.M., Saturday 9:00 A.M.–5:00 P.M., and Sunday 1:00–5:00 P.M. Admission is $4.00 for adults and $2.00 for children. For information on changing exhibits and special programs, call (601) 354–7303.

Another distinctly Mississippi museum awaits just down Lakeland Drive. The **Jim Buck Ross Agriculture and Forestry Museum** includes living history re-creations of life on an 1860s farm (watch out for those chickens!) and in a 1920s small town, as well as a 40,000-square-foot exhibition hall featuring talking, snoring (yes, snoring) mannequins so lifelike they've been known to make unsuspecting visitors jump. The museum and grounds are open 9:00 A.M.–5:00 P.M. Monday–Saturday, and 1:00–5:00 P.M. Sunday. Admission is $4.00 for adults, $3.00 for seniors, $2.00 for children ages six to eighteen, and 50 cents for children under six.

The Ag Museum is also home to the **Chimneyville Crafts Gallery,** which displays and sells native, traditional, and contemporary works by the members of the Craftsmen's Guild of Mississippi. Artisans are often on hand at the gallery, demonstrating their pottery, painting, carving, and weaving techniques. Keep in mind, the work shown and sold here is *art,* and is priced accordingly. But for those in search of a one-of-a-kind Mississippi gift or collectible, this is the place.

With your newfound treasure carefully wrapped, get back on I–55 South and head toward downtown Jackson. Take the Fortification Street exit, head right to North Jefferson Street, then turn left to tour **The Oaks** (823 North Jefferson Street), the oldest house in the capital city. Built in 1846, the house served as General William Tecumseh Sherman's headquarters during the Civil War. Period furnishings include the sofa from a young Abraham Lincoln's Illinois law office.

Back on Fortification Street, you may be surprised to spot a white picket fence smack on the corner of one of Jackson's busiest intersections. The fence surrounds the 1857 **Manship House** (420 East Fortification Street), home of Jackson's Civil War–era mayor, Charles Henry Manship. In addition to his civic involvement, Manship was an early practitioner of ornamental painting, specializing in the same type of "faux finish" work popular in homes today. Manship transformed the inexpensive lumber used to trim the home's interior into rich wood grains and fine marble. The stenciled floors in the nearby Mississippi

Governor's Mansion are also believed to be Manship's work. Both The Oaks and the Manship House are closed on Monday; the Manship House is also closed on Sunday.

Head just a couple of blocks south of Fortification Street and you'll find yourself in the heart of downtown Jackson. The city was originally laid out following Thomas Jefferson's checkerboard plan, which alternated squares of urban development with public squares or "greens." The result is a downtown district in which trees outnumber utility poles, and it's actually possible to hear birds singing above the traffic. Mississippi's version of a "bustling metropolis" is green and smog-free, with high-tech business conducted in buildings that witnessed the Civil War and sociable natives always ready to extend a gracious southern welcome.

From the historic to the ultramodern, attractions in Jackson share a cultural flair. In addition to antebellum *City Hall* and the *"New" Capitol* building (dedicated in 1903), the handful of city blocks that make up downtown are home to no fewer than a dozen historic buildings and museums, all within easy walking distance.

In the 1860s, Union troops reduced the town to a smoking ruin, earning Jackson the dismal nickname "Chimneyville." More than 130 years later, the handful of antebellum structures that survived the Civil War are still among the city's most impressive. The home of Mississippi's governors since 1842, the proud Greek Revival–style *Governor's Mansion* at 300 East Capitol Street served as a hospital during the war and was the scene of General Sherman's victory dinner following the fall of Vicksburg. When the state legislature recommended destroying the deteriorating mansion in the early 1900s, public outcry saved the building. Rescued by cries of "Will Mississippi destroy that which even Sherman would not burn?" the mansion was instead renovated to its former glory, opened for public tours, and designated a National Historic Landmark. Free tours are conducted on the half-hour Tuesday–Friday 9:30–11:00 A.M.

Capitol Street dead ends at the *Old Capitol,* a favorite landmark of Mississippians and home of the *State Historical Museum.* This restored architectural marvel houses exhibits chronicling Mississippi history from the days of the Indians to the Civil War to the Civil Rights movement, but the real attraction is the building itself—a magnificent Greek Revival statehouse built in 1833. Much of Mississippi's past is preserved in the corridors of this proud old building. It was here that the Ordinance of Secession was passed in 1861 in a hall "crowded to the point of suffocation with visitors who beckoned the state to secession." Jefferson Davis spoke here on more than one occasion, and the governor was arrested on the staircase at the war's end. There's no admission charge to visit this grand old museum, an affiliate of the Smithsonian Institution, which is open weekdays 8:00 A.M.–5:00 P.M., Saturday 9:30 A.M.–4:30 P.M., and Sunday 12:30–4:30 P.M.

Housed in the first school for African-American children in Mississippi, the **Smith Robertson Museum and Cultural Center** (528 Bloom Street, 1 block off High Street) celebrates the state's African-American history and heritage. The museum is named for Smith Robertson, a former slave who became a successful businessman, respected community leader, and eventually served as a Jackson alderman. Acclaimed novelist Richard Wright, author of *Native Son* and *Black Boy,* was a student at Smith Robertson from 1923 to 1925. The school was closed in 1971 during public school desegregation. In 1984 the building was reopened as a museum to interpret the history of African-American Mississippians. Exhibits document the contributions of African Americans to education, politics, business, and the arts in Mississippi. Smith Robertson schedules regular folk art demonstrations and workshops and operates a gift shop featuring locally crafted African-American artworks. The museum is open weekdays 9:00 A.M.–5:00 P.M., Saturday 9:00 A.M.–noon, and Sunday 2:00–5:00 P.M. Admission is $1.00 for adults and 50 cents for children.

The **Farish Street Historic District** just west of downtown was an important African-American residential and business district of the late nineteenth century. Prior to desegregation, Farish Street was the center of the African-American professional and trade community. Bounded by Amite, Fortification, Lamar, and Mill Streets, this 125-acre area features more than 600 listings in the National Register of Historic Places. A drive through the district offers a look at Creole, Queen Anne, shotgun, and bungalow-style cottages constructed by the premier African-American contractors of the day.

Visitors particularly interested in African-American heritage may want to take a side trip to northwest Jackson to see the ***former home of Civil Rights activist and NAACP field secretary Medgar Evers***. Evers and his wife, Myrlie, bought this modest home with a GI mortgage in 1957. Shortly after midnight on June 12, 1963, Medgar Evers was shot in the driveway as he returned home from a meeting at a nearby church, his arms full of "Jim Crow Must Go" T-shirts. (See sidebar, "Justice for Medgar Evers, next page). Myrlie Evers donated the house (located at 2332 Margaret Walker Alexander Drive) to Tougaloo College, which is preserving it as a historic and cultural site. The humble house itself is far from awe-inspiring. But along with the modest neighborhood surrounding it, the Medgar Evers home stands as a symbol of the simple longing for freedom and opportunity that inspired the civil rights movement, and the ultimate sacrifice made by a leader for the cause. For an

Justice for Medgar Evers

On June 12, 1963, Medgar Evers, a field secretary for the NAACP, was shot and killed by a sniper in his own driveway. A white supremacist named Byron De La Beckwith was tried twice for the murder in 1964. Both trials ended in hung juries.

In 1989, the Hinds County District Attorney's office reopened the case when new evidence revealed that the now-defunct state Sovereignty Commission, created in 1956 to preserve segregation, aided Beckwith's defense by screening potential jurors.

Hinds County Assistant District Attorney Bobby DeLaughter prosecuted Beckwith, now seventy years old, in 1994 for the third time. Thirty-one years after the murder, Beckwith was found guilty.

The reopening and retrying of the Beckwith case was the subject of the 1996 feature film *Ghosts of Mississippi,* which starred Alec Baldwin as Bobby DeLaughter, James Woods as Beckwith, and Whoopi Goldberg as Evers's widow, Myrlie Evers-Williams. Evers's sons, Darrell and Vann, played themselves in the movie; his daughter Reena was played by Yolanda King, daughter of the late Martin Luther King Jr. The film was shot on location in Jackson.

Describing the scene in which the guilty verdict is finally returned, the late Darrell Evers said, "It was like reliving the entire thing. . . . I always wondered if I'd be able to cry in that scene. It was no problem."

appointment to visit the Medgar Evers home, call the Coleman Library at (601) 977–7710 or (601) 977–7839.

The street on which Evers's home is located, **Margaret Walker Alexander Drive,** was named for another famous African American, the late author of the novel *Jubilee,* often referred to as the African-American version of *Gone With the Wind.*

The city of Jackson dedicated both the library in Evers's neighborhood and the street on which it stands to his memory. Neighborhood residents raised funds and erected a life-size, bronze *statue of Evers* in front of the Medgar Evers Boulevard Library at 4215 Medgar Evers Boulevard.

The Evers home and library and more than fifty other sites related to African-American heritage are included in the **Jackson Civil Rights Movement Driving Tour brochure,** a free guide available from the Jackson Convention and Visitors Bureau. The booklet includes descriptions of and directions to public buildings, businesses, residences, and churches where history was made. Highlights include the Mississippi state fairgrounds, where demonstrators were held behind hogwire fences when local jail cells reached capacity; the former site of Woolworth's, where a peaceful sit-in turned into one of the most violent confrontations of the movement; Collins Funeral home, where 4,000 mourners gathered to pay tribute to slain hero Medgar Evers; and the former home of white civil rights movement supporter Jane Schutt, who transformed a cross burned on her front lawn in December 1963 into a beautiful and enduring Christmas decoration. Marked with blue and yellow tour signs, sites are located in downtown Jackson, the Medgar Evers historic district, and on or near the campuses of Jackson State University and Tougaloo College. To order a copy of the guide, call (800) 354–7695 or visit www.visitjackson.com.

After you've completed your tour of downtown, cross back to the north side of Fortification Street and drive through the lovely old residential area known as **Belhaven.** Towering trees, generations-old southern gardens, and an eclectic collection of architectural styles are the hallmarks of this gracious old neighborhood. Belhaven's most famous resident was the late Pulitzer Prize–winning author **Eudora Welty.** The creator of *The Ponder Heart, The Optimist's Daughter, The Robber Bridegroom,* and other classic southern tales spent most of her life in the Tudor-style house at 1119 Pinehurst Street. A young Eudora and her parents moved into the house in 1923; other than a few years in New York and time spent traveling, Miss Welty resided and wrote in the house until her death in 2001 at the age of ninety-two.

Eudora Welty's literary career spanned six decades, beginning in 1936 with the publication of her first short story, "Death of a Traveling Salesman." Her novel *The Optimist's Daughter* captured the Pulitzer Prize in 1973. Miss Welty was also the winner of the Guggenheim Award, the O. Henry Award, the National Book Award, the William Dean Howell Medal from the American Academy of Arts and Letters, and countless other awards for her writing. She was given honorary degrees from both Harvard and Yale Universities and received France's highest civilian honor, The French Legion of Honor (1996).

Although she achieved international fame, Miss Welty will always be intrinsically linked to Jackson, her hometown and the city she immortalized in so many pages. As a child, Eudora Welty often roller-skated through the marbled halls of the State Capitol on her way to the downtown library. She was usually

trivia

Author Eudora Welty's birthplace at 741 North Congress Street is located directly across the street from the childhood home of novelist Richard Wright. Only in Mississippi, the state known for its literary heritage, will you find the childhood homes of two Pulitzer Prize–winning authors across the street from one another.

greeted at the door by a frowning librarian, who would send little Eudora back home to put on her petticoat, a lecture on library etiquette still ringing in her ears. In an ironic twist, the main branch of the Jackson Public Library system is now known as the Eudora Welty Library. In later years, the famous author was a strong benefactor of performing and cultural arts in Jackson. "Miss Eudora" could still be spotted shopping at the Jitney 14, a local Belhaven grocery store, until shortly before her death.

In a gesture typical of her well-known generosity, Miss Welty deeded her Pinehurst Street home to the Mississippi Department of Archives and History. The Eudora Welty Foundation—whose board members include John Grisham, MaryAnn Mobley, Mary Chapin Carpenter, and other celebrities—was established to maintain the property as a museum. While the garden is now open, the **Eudora Welty House** is scheduled to open to the public in 2006.

A popular tradition in the neighborhood is the **Greater Belhaven Market,** an open-air affair featuring fresh fruits and veggies, home-cooked treats, arts and crafts, and seasonal items ranging from cut flowers to pumpkins to Christmas trees. The market is staged in the vacant lot behind McDonald's at the corner of Fortification and North State Streets. It's open rain or shine Saturdays from 9:00 A.M. to 1:00 P.M., March through December.

Downtown Jackson offers a couple of down-home diners straight out of the 1940s. Operating under the motto, "It's the food that counts," **The Elite** (141 East Capitol) has been pleasing the palates of discerning diners for more than a century. Just down the street, **The Mayflower** (123 West Capitol), also in business for decades, has perfected the art of homemade roll baking.

The Jackson restaurant scene also includes dozens of casual and formal establishments serving everything from barbecue to sushi, Chinese to Indian, white tablecloth to paper plate. Choices are citywide and too many to list; for a few recommendations, see the end of this chapter.

If you're interested in good food *and* the Jackson nightlife, your next stop is **Hal 'n Mal's** (200 South Commerce Street). Operated by brothers Hal and Malcolm White, this downtown restaurant, bar, and microbrewery serves up some of the best food and hottest entertainment in Jackson. Local politicians, entertainers, and movers-and-shakers gather at Hal 'n Mal's for a cup of gumbo or an ostrich sandwich; the fictional Adam Cayhill and Hez Kerry planned their legal strategies over a plate of red beans and rice here in John Grisham's *The Chamber.* Malcolm White describes the nightclub as a "ladder club—we get the big acts on their way up, then we get 'em again on their way down."

The colorful White also stages one of Jackson's wackiest annual events, the **Mal's St. Paddy's Day Parade.** Part pub crawl, part Mardi Gras, and 100 percent green, the parade rolls through downtown Jackson on the Saturday closest to St. Patrick's Day. Past parade themes have included "Irish I Was a Movie Star," "Irish I was a Catfish," and "Elvis was Irish." The daylong, free festivities include a fun run, children's parade, and street dance featuring several bands, but in recent years the parade highlight has been the appearance of the nationally famous Sweet Potato Queens.

Greenery aside, perhaps the most impressive cultural event hosted by Mississippi is the ***International Ballet Competition,*** which visits the United States every four years. Jackson is the only U.S. host city for the IBC, which assembles the world's most talented dancers in competition for the gold medal. The 2002 event brought more than one hundred competitors from twenty-four countries, as well as ticket holders from seven foreign countries and thirty-eight states. The IBC returns to Jackson in 2006.

The Sweet Potato Queens

It began as a harmless hijinks during the Mal's St. Paddy's Day Parade, a once-a-year chance for a group of successful professional women to don tall red wigs and short chartreuse dresses, pad their bras and their backsides, climb aboard a float, and flaunt their way through downtown Jackson chucking sweet potatoes at the crowd.

But with the publication of "Boss Queen" Jill Connor Browne's 1999 smash bestseller *The Sweet Potato Queens' Book of Love,* this group of fun-loving women became a national phenomenon. The book thrust the Sweet Potato Queens and the St. Paddy's Day Parade into the spotlight, and touched off "Queen" hysteria nationwide. *The Sweet Potato Queens' Book of Love* quickly sold more than 625,000 copies. When Browne published her follow-up tomes, *God Save the Sweet Potato Queens* and *The Sweet Potato Queens' Big-Ass Cookbook and Financial Planner,* the madness only increased.

Mid-March now finds packs of women journeying to Jackson, wearing everything from tiaras to tutus and traveling under names like the Birmingham Butterfly Queens, the Missouri Ozark Raspberry Princesses, and the Tennessee Trailer Trash Queens. Television news crews camp out at Jackson International Airport the day before the parade, interviewing scores of women who've traveled from as far as New York City to pay homage to the Sweet Potato Queens. Hotels are booked to overflowing, restaurants are packed with strangely clad women, and no fruit or vegetable is safe.

To see the original Sweet Potato Queens in action, make plans to attend the next Mal's St. Paddy's Day Parade in Jackson. But be warned: The hotel room next to you is likely to be populated by Turnip Green Queens, Florida Navel Orange Queens, or Pink Flamingo Queens.

Overnight visitors to the capital city will find luxurious bed and breakfast accommodations in the heart of downtown. The 1888 *Millsaps Buie House* (628 North State Street) has been in the same family for four generations. Call (601) 709–3315 or (800) 784–0221 or visit www.millsapsbuiehouse.com. Located within steps of the building for which it was named, the *Old Capitol Inn* (226 North State Street) is an elegant bed-and-breakfast housed in the old YMCA building. Call (601) 359–9000 or (888) 359–9001, or visit www.oldcapitolinn.com.

Nearby Belhaven is home to the *Fairview Inn* (734 Fairview Street), a grand Colonial Revival mansion named the 2003 North America & Caribbean Most Outstanding Inn by Conde Nast. Call (601) 948–3429 or (888) 948–1908 or visit www.fairviewinn.com. Another choice near downtown is the *Poindexter Park Inn* (803 Deer Park Street), a turn-of-the-twentieth-century restored home that also provides guests with a self-guided tour of local blues sites. Call (601) 944–1392.

Just west of Jackson off I–20, the college town of *Clinton* features an historic "Olde Towne" district marked by bricked streets and specialty shops. Stop by the *Gravity Gallery Coffeehouse & Café* (202 West Leake Street) for a home-cooked breakfast or scrumptious sandwich, a hot cuppa Joe, and a look at the funky artwork covering every inch of wall space. Gravity also features live music "as often as possible," and hosts a Saturday breakfast (9:00–11:00 A.M.) featuring live jazz and sinful beignets.

More original artwork is displayed across the street at the *Wyatt Waters Gallery* (306 Jefferson Street). Phenomenally talented watercolorist and all-around nice guy, Wyatt Waters is one of Mississippi's most admired and collected fine artists. Waters paints on location and can often be spotted around the Jackson area behind his easel, palette in hand. If you can't make it to Waters's Clinton gallery, you can view his paintings and books at www.wyattwaters.com.

Founded in 1826, Clinton's *Mississippi College* (200 South Capitol Street) is one of the oldest in the nation and was the first college in the United States to graduate a woman. The *Provine Chapel* on campus served as a combination hospital and horse stable during the Civil War.

Located on thirty-two acres of wooded land near the Olde Towne district, the *Clinton Nature Center* features hundreds of labeled trees and shrubs, a peaceful 2-mile nature trail, and a butterfly garden. The Nature Center property encompasses portions of the original Natchez Trace, largely unchanged since the first explorers set foot there more than three centuries ago. The Nature Center is located at 617 Dunton Road in Clinton. Call (601) 926–1104 or visit www.clintonnaturecenter.org.

Fans of Elvis should follow I–20 east of Jackson to the city of *Pearl* and the store *King's English.* Owned by a pair of die-hard fans, the shop is devoted entirely to Elvis memorabilia and merchandise. Shelves are stocked with Elvis watches, Elvis T-shirts, Elvis beach towels, Elvis coffee mugs, Elvis cookbooks, Elvis sunglasses, Elvis mouse pads, and—well, you get the Elvis picture. King's English can even hook you up with an Elvis impersonator. You'll find King's English at 2405 U.S. Highway 80 East, in Pearl's Bright's Shopping Center.

Tiny **Byram,** located just south of Jackson on I–55, made history in Japan when the town's **swinging bridge** was featured on the popular Japanese television program *Bridges of the World.* One of only four suspension bridges left in Mississippi, the 360-foot, graffiti-plastered, wooden plank bridge was built in 1905 by Mississippi engineers who dubbed it the "mini-Brooklyn Bridge." The bridge is open to pedestrian traffic only, offering a pleasant stroll across the Pearl River.

Farmland and Festivals

Follow the signs from I–55 South to US 49 South, where the cityscape quickly gives way to rural Mississippi. Communities just outside the Metro Area are known for their festivals, which usually honor a favorite local crop, and for their folk art, pieces of which are perceived as cultural masterpieces or dressed-up junk, depending on who you ask and how much it costs.

For a fresh taste of life on the farm, stop by **Spell's Blueberry/Pumpkin Farm** in **Richland.** Depending on the season, you can sample fresh, juicy berries or choose your own version of the Great Pumpkin. A witch frequents the farm around Halloween, to the delight of children who are encouraged to leave the pumpkin patch with the biggest specimen they can roll.

Eskimos and catfish probably have nothing in common except **Jerry's Catfish House,** an igloo-shaped restaurant located right on the highway in **Florence.** Jerry's claim to fame is an all-you-can-eat deal on Mississippi's favorite bewhiskered treat that has crowds lining up for dinner before the doors open at 5:00 P.M. If you're into "junking," the **Magnolia Flea Market** on US 49, 5 miles south of Florence, assembles twenty or so dealers peddling antiques, furniture, collectibles, toys, Oriental rugs, and other assorted stuff. Search for treasures any time from 10:00 A.M.–5:00 P.M. Wednesday–Saturday, or 1:00–5:00 P.M. Sunday.

The igloo and flea market are just up the road from the tiny community of **Star,** where country music sensation Faith Hill hit her first high note in the church choir. Star is also home

trivia

Country music superstar and Cover Girl model Faith Hill grew up in Star, Mississippi, and was briefly enrolled at nearby Hinds Community College.

to one of nature's oddities. Ask a native for directions to the **Rockhouse,** a shallow cave in a wooded hillside. The Rockhouse isn't particularly impressive unless you know the story behind its origin. It seems the sandstone in the area is high in salt; the white-tailed deer that live in the woods around Star actually *licked* the cave into existence.

Continuing south on US 49, you'll spot signs directing you to **The Piney Woods School.** This Christian boarding school for disadvantaged African-American students has attracted national attention for its old-fashioned teaching philosophy and phenomenal success.

The school was founded in 1909 by Dr. Laurence Jones, who came to Mississippi with nothing but a Bible, $1.65 in change, and a dream of a school where a "head, heart, and hands" education would be available for poor, rural black children. Dr. Jones taught his first classes under a cedar tree and was nearly lynched by a group of men who thought he was preaching against whites. After talking with Dr. Jones, the men were so inspired that they not only put away their rope, but donated $50 to the school. The tree is still standing, marked by a plaque reading, A LOG, A DREAM, A VISION, A RESTLESS URGE, A YOUNG MAN, LAURENCE C. JONES. Nearby is the log cabin that served as Piney Woods' first schoolroom by day and as Dr. Jones's quarters and a sheep shed by night.

In 1954, Dr. Jones was a guest on Ralph Edwards's television show, *This Is Your Life.* Edwards asked every viewer who was impressed with Piney Woods to send in $1.00. This call raised more than $700,000, and was the beginning of the school's endowment program.

Dr. Jones's dream is now a national model that's been featured in numerous publications and on more than one segment of *60 Minutes.* More than 90 percent of Piney Woods graduates go on to college, many on scholarships. Visitors are welcome to tour the fifty-acre campus and the surrounding 1,950 acres of farmland, lakes, and pine woods and to view exhibits chronicling the school's inspiring history. Dr. Jones is buried on the Piney Woods campus, under a cedar tree near the spot where he taught his first lesson.

The catchy country tune "Watermelon Crawl" was surely inspired by a visit to nearby **Mize.** The population of this small Smith County community nearly doubles in July, when locals and out-of-towners alike cool off at the Mize **Watermelon Festival.** This daylong celebration includes a flea market, seed-spitting contest, greased watermelon races, watermelon-eating contest, and the obligatory crowning of the Watermelon Queen. The Watermelon Festival is held the third Saturday in July unless the month has five Saturdays; then the festival moves to the fourth Saturday. To get your juicy slice, take US 49 South to Mississippi Highway 28, then follow the signs a few miles east to Mize.

If you travel west of US 49 on Highway 28, you'll find yourself in ***Hazle-hurst***, the setting for Beth Henley's Pulitzer Prize–winning play *Crimes of the Heart.* The dark comedy was later made into a movie starring Jessica Lange, Sissy Spacek, and Diane Keaton.

Hazlehurst's ***Signature Works,*** a manufacturer of housewares and paper products, is the nation's largest employer of the blind and visually impaired. The company's grounds feature Mississippi's only ***Garden for the Blind.*** While beautiful to look at, the garden can also be enjoyed by the visually impaired. All of the plants were chosen for their distinctive aromas or unusual textures. A bubbling fountain provides a melodic backdrop, and fixed pathways are outlined with handrails for easy navigation. The effort to create the garden was spearheaded by Margaret McLemore, a Hazlehurst resident who visited a similar garden while traveling in England.

Take I–55 20 miles south of Hazlehurst to ***Brookhaven,*** proclaimed by one of the first electric street signs in Mississippi as A HOMESEEKER'S PARADISE.

According to an account from the period, when the two-story sign was originally switched on in 1915, "all sound stopped. It was as if the people were awe-stricken." The sign continued to amaze and astound visitors until 1943, when it was donated to the war effort. Fifty-three years later, the sign was re-erected at its original location at the intersection of West Cherokee Street and South Whitworth Avenue in downtown Brookhaven, where it continues to welcome homeseekers today.

Brookhaven showcases several of its graceful turn-of-the-twentieth-century and contemporary homes, churches, and examples of commercial architecture with an annual ***Spring Home and Garden Tour*** the Saturday after Easter. In conjunction with the tour, ***Rosehill Cemetery*** hosts ***"Brookhaven Biographies,"*** a walk through Brookhaven's history led by Rosehill's "residents" as portrayed by members of Brookhaven High School's award-winning forensic team. Both events are sponsored by the ***Brookhaven–Lincoln County Chamber of Commerce.*** Call (601) 833–1411 or (800) 613–4667.

trivia

Bob Pittman, founder of MTV, is a native of Brookhaven.

Two of Brookhaven's private homes also feature unique mini-museums. Take your cheatin' heart to the residence of Benton Case (410 South Whitworth Avenue), where you can see and hear the ***Hank Williams Sr. Collection.*** Case's fascination with the late country superstar began in 1947 when Case, a country music performer himself, heard his first Hank Williams song, "Never Again." He's been an avid fan ever since. Case's collection includes all of Hank

Williams's 45 and 78 LP records (in mint condition), posters, photographs, T-shirts, and a hand-cranked phonograph and battery-powered radio.

A member of the Hank Williams Sr. National Society and Fan Club, Case is more than happy to share his wealth of knowledge and his appreciation for Williams with other fans. As Case explains it, "Hank Williams' music will live on because there will always be a cheatin' heart, someone so lonesome they could cry, or someone who can't help it if they're still in love with you." To schedule an appointment to see the collection, call Benton Case at (601) 833–5138.

trivia

The $30 million Mississippi School of the Arts is located in Brookhaven on the former campus of antebellum Whitworth College. Talented junior and senior high school students come to Brookhaven to study dance, music, theater, visual arts, and creative writing.

A mini-museum of another culture is found in the home of Reverend William Matthews. The *Uzbek Museum* features crafts, paintings, clothing, and cultural artifacts collected by Reverend Matthews during his years of teaching at the University of Bukhara in Uzbekistan, a former republic of the Soviet Union. The Matthews home is located at 1443 Monticello Street NE. Call (601) 833–8435 for an appointment to view the collection.

Another beautiful artifact from a faraway land hangs in the sanctuary of the *First Baptist Church* on Monticello Street. The magnificent *tapestry of Christ* praying in the Garden of Gethsemene, a generous 22 feet by 24 feet long, was handwoven in a small village in Beijing, China. Local Mississippi artist Asem Zeini created an oil painting to use as a guide. Church members then hand-carried the painting to China.

Initially, the Chinese artisans were reluctant to undertake the project because of its size. But upon learning that the man in the painting was a spiritual leader and the tapestry would hang in a place of worship, they expressed honor at being chosen to create the work.

According to the weavers, the tapestry is the largest ever made in their area. The finished piece contains one hundred hand-tied knots per square inch, for a total of 7.6 million. As many as eighteen weavers worked on the piece at a time, laboring for more than two years. The finished tapestry was hung in the sanctuary in 1996, with the hope that all those who view it will see not dyed wool and knots, but a loving, caring Savior. To view the tapestry, contact Connie Hodges at (601) 833–5118.

Artwork of a different sort waits at *The Posey Place,* a third-generation soap-making company and gift shop. Follow the invigorating scent of peppermint, the rich aroma of vanilla, or the soothing fragrance of lavender to this squeaky-clean shop located at 124 West Cherokee Street in Brookhaven.

Nearby **Bogue Chitto,** Mississippi, is home to two talented artists working in different mediums. Stop by **Gone to Pot** to observe or participate in pottery-firing workshops coordinated by artist Merrie Boerner. Boerner loads her "groundhog" wood-firing kiln (an unusual kiln that's one of only three in Mississippi) with up to 400 pieces of pottery provided by workshop participants. Flames lap through the stacked pots, giving the pieces a unique color called flashing. Ash from the burning wood deposits on the pots and becomes a glaze. Boerner's workshops attract participants from around the country, who not only practice their art, but also cook and camp together for the duration of the four-day seminars. Local residents and pottery collectors also come to the firings to share the food, claim a treasure during the kiln unloading, and shop at Boerner's studio. For more information on workshops or to view Boerner's work, call (601) 833–5631 or e-mail boerner@tislink.com.

Bogue Chitto is also home to **The Happy Sack,** where artists Jan and Bob Godbold create collectible angels, functional windows and door inserts, and decorative hanging pieces of stained glass. The Godbolds' shop is housed in a 50-foot train boxcar at 3053 Willow Lane Southeast. Call (601) 734–2539.

Back in Brookhaven, Bob and Tollie Jones combine nature and fine dining at **Gnome Delights,** where a picnic lunch includes a presentation on edible flowers, floral arranging, or other topics related to the culinary or gardening arts. Potted herbs and plants are also available for purchase. Dinner is served at Gnome Delights on Friday and Saturday. Call (601) 833–0425 for reservations (required) and directions to Gnome Delights and **Dr. Bob's Yard and Garden Shop.**

Area artists of all ages handpainted the tables at **Knibble's Gourmet Deli** (106½ South Whitworth), where the sandwiches and salads are as creative as the tables they're served on. Other local specialties include the flat hot dogs at **Bob's Sandwich Shop** (208 East Cherokee) and the fried chicken and country-style veggies at the **Round Table** (314 West Cherokee), where guests serve themselves from a revolving lazy Susan in the middle of each table.

Dessert calls for a double—okay, make it a triple—scoop from **Clear Branch Farms Homemade Ice Cream.** Operating under the scripture, "Oh taste and see that the Lord is good" (Psalm 34:8), this family-owned and -operated business has given Brookhaven the scoop for more than a century. Whether you choose plain ol' vanilla or one of twenty-plus more adventurous flavors, you're sure to agree it's a little taste of heaven. You'll find Clear Branch Farms at 412 West Monticello Street in Brookhaven.

Located on South First Street, *The Coffee Pot* no longer serves food or coffee, but it's worth driving by to snap a photo of the larger-than-life coffee pot perched atop the roof—a caffeine addict's dream come true. The building was constructed in the 1920s, and has been referred to as the first fast-food restaurant in the South. In the 1930s, The Coffee Pot staged one of fast food's earliest promotions when a pianist played on the roof for twenty-four hours straight.

If your plans call for an overnight stay in Brookhaven, make reservations at the *Four Cedars Country Inn.* This Acadian-style cabin made entirely of rough-sawed southern pine offers a fully equipped, modern kitchen, rustic hand-crafted furniture, and a stunning view of the sunset from the front porch's double swing. This is one spot where rain is welcome—its rhythmic pitter-patter on the tin roof guarantees a soothing slumber. For reservations and directions, call (601) 835–2694.

trivia

In a state that sees very little ice, it may come as a surprise that hockey is the largest pro sport. Teams take to the ice in Jackson, Biloxi, and Tupelo.

If you're in the Brookhaven area on the last Saturday in June, head back north about 35 miles to *Crystal Springs,* home of the annual *Tomato Festival.* The celebration recalls Crystal Springs's history as the "Tomatopolis of the World" with live entertainment, a flea market, children's activities, and, of course, tomatoes. Fried green tomatoes, tomato sandwiches, stuffed tomatoes, salsa—even tomato gravy ladled over hot tomato biscuits. Ketchup, anyone?

Tomatoes may or may not be on the menu at *Camp Windhover,* a wooded retreat just east of Crystal Springs. Primarily a summer arts camp for children, Camp Windhover also offers themed weekend retreats for adults interested in photography, ceramics, painting, food and wine, and other creative pursuits. For about $100, including housing, meals, and art fees, you, too, can be a happy camper. For more information or a list of scheduled retreats, visit www.campwindhover.com or call (601) 892–3282.

From Crystal Springs, continue on I–55 North toward I–20 and the towns and cities that fell in the path of the Civil War assault on Vicksburg. General Ulysses S. Grant's campaign for the "Gibraltar of the Confederacy" left a swath of destruction through this area of the state. But what seemed an unfortunate location in the 1860s is now a business advantage; the cities and towns that suffered Civil War destruction now welcome thousands of Yankees and Rebels drawn to the area for its rich Civil War history.

One of many skirmishes took place in *Raymond,* a small community located on Mississippi Highway 18. Despite the careful plans of the ladies of the community, the Battle of Raymond was no picnic. When the Rebels marched out to meet the Yanks on May 12, 1863, they were counting on a quick victory. Tables at the **Hinds County Courthouse** and **St. Mark's Episcopal Church** were laden with food in anticipation of a celebratory, post-battle feast.

But the 2,500 Union troops the Rebs were expecting turned out to be 12,000. The ensuing battle was fierce, bloody, and for the South, disastrous. The retreating Confederates fled past the buffet, although legend has it that a few *Yankees* did stop for a snack before returning to the Rebel rout. The gaily decorated tables intended for cheerful feasting and toasting instead became the scene of ghastly field surgeries and amputations; century-old bloodstains still mar the church floors.

The courthouse and the church, both located on West Main Street, are among the many landmarks listed in a driving tour guide to Raymond available at www.raymondms.com. Other sites listed include **Waverly,** which served as temporary headquarters of General Ulysses S. Grant during the Vicksburg campaign; the **Confederate Cemetery,** where many of the soldiers killed in the battle were buried; and the **Dupree House and Mamie's Cottage,** an historic property and bed-and-breakfast inn. Another Web site, www.battleofray mond.org, offers extensive information about and first-hand accounts of the Battle of Raymond, as well as updates on the current effort to establish a marked Raymond Battlefield Park.

Journey from the Civil War era to medieval times with a visit to Raymond's enchanting **McGee's Castle.** Built by owner "Knight" Dale McGee, the spectacular castle and grounds (complete with moat) seem lifted directly from the court of King Arthur. The castle is known locally for its dazzling Christmas driving tour. Five dollars a car buys a look at Santa and Mrs. Claus, a life-size nativity scene, and the castle towers and turrets adorned with thousands of Christmas lights. McGee's Castle also hosts weddings and parties year-round and offers magical bed-and-breakfast accommodations. An overnight stay begins at about $125 and comes complete with dreams of knights and dragons, stones and sorcerers, and the chivalry of the mythical Camelot. You'll find McGee's Castle on Pine Hill Drive just off Main Street. For a map, directions, and information about events at the castle, call (601) 857–8997 or visit www .mcgeescastle.com.

You'll discover yet another era at **Little Big Store,** a specialty shop located in the historic **Raymond Depot Building** at 201 East Main Street. Little Big Store specializes in rare and out-of-print records. Spend a day browsing among the real vinyl albums and nostalgia-inspiring 45s, or call (601) 857–8579 to inquire about your favorite oldies.

Continue south on Highway 18 approximately 20 miles to **Utica** and the **Museum of the Southern Jewish Experience.** Located on the grounds of the Henry S. Jacobs Camp for Living Judaism, the museum chronicles the history of the Jews in the American South from before the Civil War to the civil rights movement and beyond. Exhibits include religious artifacts, a photographic portrayal of the South as seen through Jewish eyes by renowned photographer Bill Arron, and a video presentation celebrating the journey of the Jewish people from nineteenth-century Europe to the modern American South. The museum is open by appointment. Admission is $5.00 for adults, $4.00 for students. Call (601) 362–6357 for more information.

From Utica head north to I–20 West and **Edwards,** site of the **Battle of Champion Hill.** The May 16, 1863, Confederate loss at Champion Hill led to the fall of Vicksburg, which ultimately cost the Confederacy the Civil War. A noted military historian emphasized the importance of the battle to the war's outcome, writing that "the drums of Champion Hill sounded the doom of Richmond." The 1852 **Coker House** near the battle site was used as a hospital by both Union and Confederate forces. More than 6,200 wounded and dead soldiers littered the grounds of the Coker House; a "limb pit" in the yard hides scores of amputated arms and legs. In the 140-plus years since the battle, time has wreaked more damage on the house than cannon fire. Plans to restore the deteriorating structure are currently in the works. The only other structure remaining on the battlefield is the **Hiawatha House,** a privately owned cottage where mortally wounded Confederate Brigadier General Lloyd Tilghman died during the battle. According to legend, the walls and floor still bear Tilghman's bloodstains. The battle for Champion Hill is reenacted from time to time; call the Mississippi Division of Tourism at (800) 927–6378 for the next battle date.

Edwards is also the home of the "world famous" **Cactus Plantation.** Follow the giant billboards (a la "See Rock City") and you absolutely cannot miss this prickly attraction. Sights at the Cactus Plantation include a farmhouse listed on the National Register of Historic Places, lazy Shetland ponies dozing in the sunshine, assorted chickens, and more than 3,000 varieties of colorful cacti, including one particularly interesting specimen dressed in southern gentleman's attire. Known as "the Cactus Colonel," this peculiar creature is displayed under the caption, "My cactus is finger-sticking good." The plantation also sells and displays several varieties of bromeliads, daylilies, and tropicals. Be sure to visit the "gift shop," a makeshift market displaying everything from Civil War–era wine bottles to flower pots to minié balls. The Cactus Plantation is open Monday–Saturday 9:00 A.M.–5:00 P.M. and Sunday 1:00–5:00 P.M. Call (601) 852–2705.

The River Cities

A tour of the River Cities begins in Vicksburg, home of the Vicksburg National Military Park, and ends in Natchez, where you'll find the highest concentration of antebellum mansions in the United States.

This section of the state features at least one historic bed-and-breakfast mansion, Civil War monument, or well-preserved battlefield every 10-miles. Reminders of the antebellum South and the War Between the States dominate not only the landscape, but the very mindset of the people here, reminding visitors that soil once fought and died for is never again an ordinary plot of ground.

From Bovina, follow I–20 West toward the Mississippi River, through steep loess bluffs, gently rolling hills, and ever-encroaching kudzu to the Civil War time capsule that is *Vicksburg.*

President Abraham Lincoln called this river city "the key . . . let us get Vicksburg and all that country is ours. The war can never be brought to a close until that key is in our pocket." A victory at Vicksburg would sever Texas, Arkansas, and Louisiana from the Confederacy and give the Union complete control of the Mississippi River. For over a year, Vicksburg seemed impregnable as Union forces made several fruitless attempts by land and water to capture the city.

When direct charges failed, Grant decided to starve the city into submission. For forty-seven days and nights, the Union forces engaged in "the grand sport of tossing giant shells into Vicksburg." Accompanied by their slaves and taking their furniture and possessions, the frightened citizens sought shelter from the constant rain of shells in caves dug into the hillsides. (Six of these shelters remain hidden in the bluffs surrounding Vicksburg, but the caves aren't easily accessible, and the locals advise against any spelunking.)

Soldiers and citizens suffered alike as the siege wore on. The summer heat was terrible, water supplies dwindled, and mule meat became a delicacy. As the long, sweltering days passed, the distance between the lines shrank, until aggressors and defenders were virtually eyeball-to-eyeball. During lulls in the shelling, Union and Confederate soldiers exchanged jokes and

"giddyup, jeffdavis!"

Throughout the Civil War, General U. S. Grant rode a horse named "Cincinnatis." In his memoirs, however, the northern general owned up to stealing a horse from Confederate President Jefferson Davis's Brierfield plantation near Vicksburg.

What did the Union general christen the stolen mount?

"Jeff Davis," of course.

stories along with coffee and tobacco, and two brothers from Missouri who were fighting on opposite sides were reunited.

On July 3, with his army and the civilian population starving, General John C. Pemberton met with Grant to discuss the terms of surrender. When Grant demanded "unconditional surrender," Pemberton replied, "Sir, it is unnecessary that you and I hold any further conversation. We will go to fighting again at once. I can assure you, you will bury many more of your men before you will enter Vicksburg." Grant relented, offering parole to the city's defenders. On July 4, 1863, the Confederate flag over the courthouse was lowered, and the Stars and Stripes flew once again in Vicksburg. It would be more than one hundred years before the city again observed the Fourth of July.

The Confederates defending the city were outraged by the surrender. Many of the southern soldiers destroyed their rifles, scattered their ammunition on the ground, and tore their battle standards into shreds. In a remarkable show of respect for the defenders, the occupying Union forces refrained from taunting the vanquished. According to one witness, the Federal troops instead entered the war-torn city with a "hearty cheer for the gallant defenders of Vicksburg," and offers of food were extended with the sentiment, "Here, brave Reb, I know you are starved nearly to death."

With the fall of Vicksburg, the Union regained control of the Mississippi River from Cairo, Illinois, to the Gulf of Mexico. Upon hearing of the surrender, President Abraham Lincoln wrote, "the Father of Waters again goes unvexed to the sea."

The final days of siege and battle are replayed endlessly on the green expanses and rolling hills of the **Vicksburg National Military Park,** where 1,800 acres of fortifications and earthworks lined with monuments tell the dramatic story of the defense and fall of the "Gibraltar of the Confederacy." The Confederate and Union lines are identified, and markers trace the progress of the Union soldiers as they pushed uphill under fire in the thick heat of the Mississippi summer. Generals made of stone lead the charge, bronze horses eternally race into battle, and moss-covered cannons guard the city against a final attack.

Nearly all of the twenty-eight states that sent soldiers to Vicksburg erected markers, statues, and monuments in the park, the largest of which is the **Illinois Memorial,** an imposing dome-topped structure inscribed with the names of every Illinois soldier present at Vicksburg. Forty-seven stone steps leading into the monument represent the forty-seven days of siege. Of the thousands of names listed inside, two are of particular interest. Fred Grant, the general's twelve-year-old son, is listed as his aide. Also listed is Albert D. Cashire, who served throughout the Vicksburg campaign. When Cashire was hospitalized years later, he was discovered to be a *she*—an immigrant named Jennie Hodgers, who had masqueraded as a man for nearly half a century.

Also displayed at the Military Park is the USS *Cairo,* a Union ironclad sunk by the Confederacy and raised after a hundred years underwater. Remarkably intact artifacts recovered from aboard ship, including a running watch, dishes, photos, and clothing, are displayed in an adjoining museum. The National Military Park is located at 3201 Clay Street; for information on guided tours, tapes, and events, call (601) 636–0583. The Military Park is open seven days a week from 8:00 A.M.–5:00 P.M. Admission is $5.00 per car; for $30.00, a personal guide will ride along with you.

trivia

The late actress Beah Richards was a resident of Vicksburg. Richards's final performances included a role in Oprah Winfrey's *Beloved* and an Emmy-winning guest performance on TV's *The Practice.*

Visitors often remark that Vicksburg is still fighting the Civil War, and at least twice a year, they're absolutely right. The city's Civil War story is reenacted in May and again in July during the **Vicksburg Civil War Siege Reenactment.** The *Memorial Day Reenactment* includes Union and Confederate tent camps, truce periods during which soldiers barter for coffee and information and attend church services, and bloody assaults on the Confederate lines. Smaller in terms of the number of participants but equally stirring is the *Fourth of July Reenactment,* which concludes when Union troops take control of the city, lower the Confederate flag, and raise the Stars and Stripes over the courthouse—usually to the jeers and taunts of the towns-people, who seem to forget this is not *really* 1863.

The reenactors themselves are a serious bunch, often refusing to acknowledge they're playing a part. Their clothing, campsites, ammunition, even their conversation with spectators, is authentic to the 1860s. Many of the reenactors who make the annual trek to Vicksburg travel thousands of miles to participate in the campaign—much as their ancestors did nearly a century and a half ago. And whether they're motivated by sympathy for the conquered or the romance of fighting for a lost cause, the majority of reenactors prefer to fight for the Confederacy—even the Yankees.

Relive the siege any time of year through *The Vanishing Glory,* a thirty-minute, wide-screen production that relies on the eyewitness accounts, letters, and diaries of citizens and soldiers to tell the Vicksburg story. Show times are every hour on the hour from 10:00 A.M.–5:00 P.M. at the theater at 717 Clay Street. Admission is $5.50 for adults and $3.50 for students.

A number of Vicksburg's **antebellum mansions** survived the siege and are open for tours; about a dozen operate as bed-and-breakfast inns. Many of the homes played significant roles in the war and still bear the scars of battle. A Union cannonball tore through the front door at **Cedar Grove** and is still embedded in the parlor wall. Cedar Grove was built in 1840 as the home of John and Elizabeth Klein. Mrs. Klein was a relative of the much-loathed Union General William Tecumseh Sherman. Soon after the shelling began in Vicksburg, General Sherman personally escorted the Klein family to safety, and Union forces occupied the house until the end of the siege. Grant himself is said to have slept in the master bedroom.

But even though Cedar Grove bore the scars of shelling, the residents of Vicksburg never forgave the Kleins for their affiliation with the hated Yankee general. When the Kleins's sixteen-year-old son Willie was accidentally shot to death on the back stairs, townspeople reportedly told Elizabeth Klein she had placed a curse on the child by naming him after the despised Sherman.

Yankee affiliations aside, Cedar Grove stands as a testimony to the glory days of the Old South. In addition to bed-and-breakfast accommodations and daily home tours, Cedar Grove offers romantic gourmet dining by candlelight, a cocktail hour in the five-acre formal gardens or in the **Mansion Bar,** and sweeping views of the Mississippi River from the rooftop gardens. Cedar Grove may even harbor a ghost. Mr. Klein was fond of smoking a pipe in the gentlemen's parlor each evening, and guests and staff alike have reported the distinct odor of pipe tobacco lingering in the empty room at twilight.

With rooms available in the mansion, carriage house, and pool-side garden cottages, Cedar Grove is the largest bed-and-breakfast in Mississippi. The highly recommended **Andre's Restaurant** is open for dinner at 6:00 P.M. daily. For rates and reservations, call (800) 862–1300, or visit www.cedargroveinn.com.

A bomb squad was called to **McRaven** in the 1950s to remove a live Civil War shell from a wall. Built in three separate sections, McRaven combines the distinct architectural styles of the Frontier (1797), Empire (1836), and Greek Revival (1849) periods. John Bobb, the master of McRaven, was shot and killed by Union troops in the garden and may be one of several ghosts who reportedly call McRaven home. The house is among Mississippi's most haunted— lights turn on and off by themselves, footsteps echo in empty stairwells, the piano stool moves of its own accord, and current owner Leyland French claims the *previous* owner often follows him around the house. When asked if he minds living alone in such a place, French smiles and says, "Who's alone?" McRaven welcomes ghost hunters nine months out of the year but is closed December–February. Living history demonstrations are held in the home on the Fourth of July weekend, Labor Day weekend, and Memorial Day weekend.

The **Duff Green Mansion** served as a Civil War hospital, with Confederate soldiers treated in the basement to shield them from the shells and the

unfortunate Union wounded quartered on the roof. The mistress of the plantation, Mary Green, gave birth to a son in a cave during the Vicksburg siege and
christened him William Siege Green. Overnight guests at **Anchuca** can sleep
in the same bed where Jefferson Davis, President of the Confederacy, often
passed the night. And if you're traveling with Rover, you'll want to stay at the
Cherry Street Cottage, where well-behaved pets are welcome.

Several additional homes welcome visitors during the annual **Spring and
Fall Pilgrimages.** For a complete list of the many historic tour homes and
bed-and-breakfast inns and this year's Vicksburg Pilgrimage dates, stop by the
welcome center located near the scenic **Mississippi River Bridge,** call the
Vicksburg Convention and Visitors Bureau at (800) 221–3536, or visit www
.vicksburgcvb.org.

Prominently situated atop a hill on Cherry Street, the 1858 Vicksburg courthouse was a favorite target for Union shells until all of the Federal prisoners in
Vicksburg were moved into the courtroom—a ploy credited with saving the
building. The **Old Court House** is now one of the state's best historical museums, filled to the rafters with an extensive collection of Civil War letters, soldiers' diaries, period clothing, and other artifacts related to Vicksburg history.
Exhibits include the tie worn by Confederate President Jefferson Davis upon
his inauguration, a never-surrendered Confederate flag, and a minié ball that
supposedly impregnated a local woman when it passed through a soldier's
"private parts" before striking her own. Nicknamed "Vicksburg's Attic," the Old
Court House is literally packed with artifacts—some items are even suspended
from the ceiling. Tours are self guided, but if curator Gordon Cotton is in, ask
him to tell you a story or two. Cotton knows more of the local lore and legend
than anyone in Mississippi and has an endless repertoire of tales that bring
Vicksburg's long-ago history to vivid life. The Old Court House Museum is
located at 1008 Cherry Street, in the heart of historic downtown. The museum
is open Monday–Saturday 8:30 A.M.–5:00 P.M. and Sunday 1:30–5:00 P.M.

Several historic homes and the **Vicksburg Garden District** are located
on Washington Avenue, which also runs into a quaint area of shops and small
museums. The **Biedenharn Museum of Coca-Cola® Memorabilia** (1107
Washington Street) is housed in the building where Coca-Cola was first bottled
in 1894. The museum chronicles the history of the world's most popular soft
drink and serves up "the real thing" in floats from the old-fashioned soda fountain. **Yesterday's Children Antique Doll and Toy Museum** (1104 Washington Street) displays more than a thousand playthings, and the **Gray and Blue
Naval Museum** (1102 Washington Street) houses the world's largest collection
of Civil War gunboat models. **The Corner Drug Store** (1123 Washington
Street) includes a collection of Civil War medical equipment and cure-alls and

Lakemont's Perfumed Lady

When William Lake was killed in a duel in 1861, his wife was watching through a spyglass from the second floor of their Vicksburg home. Today the home, still known as Lakemont, is thought to be haunted by Lake's widow.

The present owners claim to hear the rustle of petticoats and smell the overpowering scent of sweet, old-fashioned perfume. The presence is strongest during the month of October—the same month in which William Lake died.

more than one bullet scarred with the teeth marks of unfortunate patients forced to undergo surgery without the benefit of anesthesia.

The **Attic Gallery** (1101 Washington Street) lives up to its name, bursting with an eclectic collection of pottery, paintings, carvings, and other local and regional art. "Attic" is an apt description of the gallery. The place is packed with colorful artwork, and if you hunt, poke, and rummage long enough, you're sure to find something that seems painted, sculpted, or thrown just for you. Owner Leslie Silver has operated this Vicksburg treasure trove for more than thirty years and is one of Mississippi's foremost experts on folk art. The Attic Gallery displays a wealth of this "outsider" work, including some surviving pieces by folk artist Earl Simmons, whose marvelous Bovina, Mississippi, home and gallery were destroyed by fire in 2002.

Interesting architectural pieces, including old clawfoot bathtubs, doors, windows, and stained glass, share space with southern art, jewelry, and collectibles at **Art & Soul of the South** (1300 Washington Street).

Vicksburg's slogan is "History and Much, Much More," and true to its word, the city does offer more than Civil War attractions. The **Jacqueline House African American Museum** (1325 Main Street) celebrates the city's African-American history and culture. Hours are 9:00 A.M.–12:00 P.M. and 2:00–5:00 P.M. Monday–Saturday. **The Heritage Center** (1414 Washington Street), an art gallery and bookstore with an African-American emphasis, also offers exhibits and cultural programs.

Boo the villain, cheer the hero, and throw peanuts at the entire cast of **Gold in the Hills,** a live performance originally staged in 1934 and listed in the *Guinness Book of World Records* as the longest-running old-fashioned melodrama. Players take the stage during March, April, and July at the **Parkside Playhouse** (101 Iowa Street). Call (601) 636–0471 for ticket information and showtimes.

For an experience that's not only off the beaten path but more than a little off-the-wall, swing by ***Margaret's Grocery, Market, and Bible Class*** on U.S. Highway 61 a few miles north of the center of Vicksburg. A sign proclaiming ALL IS WELCOME, JEWS AND GENTILES atop a huge tower of red, white, and blue masonry sprinkled with Bible verses and cryptic phrases is the first hint that Margaret's offers more than bread and milk. In fact, the groceries are hard to spot inside, overshadowed by reproductions of the Ark of the Covenant and the Ten Commandments, a glass doorknob referred to as "the all-seeing eye," and other unique artifacts, most of which are decorated with tiny mirrors, costume jewelry, and Mardi Gras beads.

The elaborate archways, pillars, and towers of brick are the work of ninety-plus-year-old Reverend H. D. Dennis, Margaret's husband. The Reverend promised Margaret if she married him, he'd turn her store into a palace, and he was true to his word. The Lego-like construction project hasn't stopped yet; the Reverend is still adding on to the elaborate structure, which serves as a combination residence, grocery store, and house of worship. "God is the greatest architect," Dennis says. "I'm only his assistant."

The teetering structures stretch more than 100 feet along US 61, attracting stares, waves, honks, and more than a few tourists curious enough to venture inside. Margaret and the Reverend welcome visitors, but don't stop unless you have time to listen to one of the Reverend's fiery sermons, which usually includes a dire warning about the "boats," the floating casinos that line the river in front of Vicksburg. Margaret herself is also on hand, quick to point out that they don't charge admission, but welcome "free donations." Margaret's Grocery is more than a bit eccentric, but visitors will leave with a warm feeling, assured that "they can do right if they really want to," and knowing the Reverend will pray for their safe journey.

Continue south on US 61 to the all-but-extinct town of ***Grand Gulf.*** Once one of the busiest ports between New Orleans and St. Louis, Grand Gulf endured a series of disasters that eventually wiped out the town. Grand Gulf stoically survived citywide fires, a yellow fever epidemic, and a devastating tornado before the Mississippi River changed its course, gobbling up fifty-five city blocks in the late 1850s. What little was left of the once-thriving city was burned by the Union army during the Civil War.

Though you'll still find it on the map, Grand Gulf is so small it doesn't even warrant a zip code. This isolated hamlet's sole claim to fame is its rich nineteenth-century history, preserved in the ***Grand Gulf Military Monument Park.*** The 400-acre park includes Fort Wade, where heavily armed Confederates repelled Grant's initial landing attempt; the ***Grand Gulf Cemetery,*** where black Union troops who occupied the town are buried and the headstones offer a synopsis of Grand Gulf's tragic history; well-preserved earthworks built by the Grand Gulf defenders; and several restored buildings moved to the park from other sites in Mississippi, including the Sacred Heart Catholic Church, which was moved from the ghost town of Rodney. The park museum—named one of the best small museums in the nation by *Reader's Digest*—contains hundreds of Civil War artifacts, including soldiers' letters and diaries, guns, and bloodstained uniforms. An outbuilding houses a collection of carriages and wagons, including a rare Civil War ambulance and a one-man submarine used to smuggle whiskey during Prohibition. The Mississippi River is visible for miles from the park's observation tower, and it's easy to imagine Grant's troops assembling for the attack.

The park also includes nature trails and facilities for tent and RV camping. Admission is charged only for the museum and RV camping. Grand Gulf Military Monument Park is located 10 miles northwest of Port Gibson and US 61 on Grand Gulf Road. The office is open daily 8:00 A.M.–5:00 P.M. and the park is open until dusk. Call (601) 437–5911.

Nearby **Port Gibson** is probably the only town in the South that uses a quote from the much-loathed General Grant as its slogan. In a rare departure from his scorched-earth policy, General Grant declared Port Gibson "too beautiful to burn" and left the town's picturesque collection of homes and churches unscathed. Port Gibson was the first town in Mississippi designated a National Historic District.

Most of the ***antebellum homes and churches*** that so enchanted the general are located directly on US 61 South, which turns into Church Street in Port Gibson. Drive as far as the visitors center located at the south end of the street, where a helpful volunteer will provide you with maps, brochures, and background information on the homes and churches, then leave your car parked at the visitors center and enjoy a walking tour of Church Street.

Port Gibson's most striking structure is the ***First Presbyterian Church,*** its steeple topped by a 10-foot gold hand pointing heavenward. The church was built in 1859 under the dynamic leadership of the Reverend Zebulon Butler. Butler himself labored with the workers and craftsmen during the church's construction, but he died just before the building was completed. Ironically, the first service held in the new church was his funeral. The original hand atop the steeple was fashioned of wood—to the delight of area woodpeckers, who showed little respect for this holy symbol. The present metal hand topping the church has become Port Gibson's most famous landmark. Notable features inside the church include the original slave gallery and the chandeliers from the steamboat *Robert E. Lee;* each chandelier features a figure of General Lee on horseback.

Just down the street is *St. Joseph's Catholic Church,* where an eerie trick of the light and stained glass makes the very air inside the church seem blue at any hour of the day. Exquisite panels carved of walnut depict religious symbols, including the Ten Commandments and the Lamb of God, and enhance the solemn atmosphere of reverence that permeates this 1849 house of worship. Church Street is also home to the oldest synagogue in Mississippi, *Temple Gemiluth Chessed.*

Most of the historic homes along Church Street are open for tours only during Port Gibson's annual *Spring Pilgrimage* weekend, but *Oak Square Plantation* (601–437–4350 or 800–729–0240) accommodates visitors and overnight guests year-round. Bed-and-breakfast accommodations are also available at *Bernheimer House* (601–437–2843 or 800–735–3407), a 1901 Queen Anne–style home. For this year's pilgrimage dates, call the *Port Gibson-Claiborne County Chamber of Commerce* at (601) 437–4351.

Civil War buffs will want to stop by *Wintergreen Cemetery,* where Confederate General Earl Van Dorn is buried facing his beloved South and a section known as "Soldier's Row" is the final resting place for Union and Confederate soldiers. True Blue-and-Gray buffs can pick up a map of *General Grant's March Route* through the county, available at the visitors center on Church Street. Sections of the route have been left undisturbed for more than 140 years; the dirt road and steep ravines navigated by Grant's 20,000 troops remain largely untouched. The road is impassable during inclement weather, and explorers are advised to check in with the Port Gibson-Claiborne County Chamber of Commerce before setting out. Guided tours of Grant's march route are offered during the *Main Street Heritage Festival,* which also includes a 5K run, arts-and-crafts show, and venison cook-off. For this year's dates, call (601) 437–4500.

The local Port Gibson arts agency known as the *Mississippi Cultural Crossroads* was formed to promote local arts and culture and to preserve and celebrate the African-American art form of quilting. Work by the Crossroads Quilters is displayed in galleries across the South. Colorful patchworks and vivid murals line the walls of the Cultural Crossroads' headquarters at 507 Market Street in downtown Port Gibson. Open weekdays 8:00 A.M.–5:00 P.M., the *Quilt Gallery* displays works of every size, color, and pattern, all made locally and all for sale. Of particular interest are "memory quilts," which depict scenes from the quilter's own life. Other folk art forms include "pants quilts," made from sturdy strips of work trousers, and "string quilts," which prove a good quilter can make something pretty out of almost nothing. Cultural Crossroads sponsors *Pieces and String,* an annual quilting exhibition and contest held the last full weekend in March. For more information, contact the Cultural Crossroads at (601) 437–8905.

African-American history of a later era is preserved in the exhibit *No Easy Journey,* a permanent collection of photographs and artifacts commemorating the Civil Rights movement in Claiborne County. Haunting images of African-Americans facing billy clubs and guns, picketing local businesses, and marching the streets of a 1960s Port Gibson in search of equal rights remind visitors of the turbulent era and celebrate the progress that has been made over the past forty years. Housed in the Claiborne County administration building, this free exhibit is open Monday–Friday 8:00 A.M.–5:00 P.M.

No visit to the Port Gibson area is complete without a side trip to the *Windsor Ruins.* A dusty road winding through the quiet countryside leads to the crumbling remains of what was the largest antebellum mansion in Mississippi. Mark Twain wrote about the palatial Windsor in *Life on the Mississippi River,* noting that "the mansion high above the bluffs was visible for miles in every direction." Following the Battle of Port Gibson, Union troops claimed the house as a hospital, and the eloquent pleas of the mistress of Windsor saved the mansion from destruction at their hands on three separate occasions.

Windsor survived the war only to burn to the ground at the hands of a careless smoker in 1890. Twenty-three towering Corinthian columns are all that remain of the once-opulent mansion, and a sketch drawn by a Union soldier in May of 1863 is the only known image of the house in its heyday. The dramatic ruins have been featured in a number of movies, including *Raintree County,* which starred Elizabeth Taylor and Montgomery Clift. A map indicating the shortest route to the Windsor Ruins is available from the visitors center

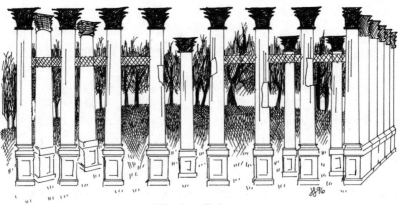

Windsor Ruins

Travels with Frosty

One of the best research tools I've discovered for travel writing isn't a guide book, an Internet listing, or even a well-marked map.

It's my dog, Frosty.

An American Eskimo Spitz, Frosty is forty pounds of fluffy white fur, intelligent brown eyes, and adventurous spirit. The Eskimo Spitz is a striking dog and a rather uncommon breed for Mississippi—traits that turned out to be invaluable during the researching of *Mississippi Off the Beaten Path*.

When I drove into small towns with Frosty hanging out the window, we caused quite a stir. People invariably wanted to pet him, offered him water, and, as an afterthought, talked to me, too.

I was made privy to local legends, received detailed directions to out-of-the-way attractions, and soaked up the local color, all from people who shared freely with me while petting my dog. I gathered critical information not because I was a skilled field researcher, but because I was Frosty's traveling companion.

As for Frosty himself, I'd like to believe he put up with all the attention as a favor to me and out of dedication to the project, not simply because he enjoyed being doted on by strangers all over Mississippi.

Since he worked so hard on this book, it's only fair that I tell you Frosty's favorite spot in *Mississippi Off the Beaten Path*. It was the Windsor Ruins, paws down. It seems those twenty-three towering, Corinthian columns have a lot more doggy appeal than an ordinary fire hydrant.

on Church Street, or you can take US 61 South, then follow the signs to Mississippi 552 West and the ruins.

Heading back to US 61 on Mississippi 552, you'll pass **Alcorn State University.** Founded in 1871, Alcorn was the nation's first land-grant college for African Americans. Alcorn's **Oakland Chapel** features the iron staircase that once led to the front doors of the Windsor mansion.

Just south of the intersection of Mississippi 552 and US 61 in **Lorman** is the **Old Country Store,** which first opened its doors to shoppers in 1875. Today, the Old Country Store houses **Mr. D's Old Country Store Restaurant and Gift Shop.** Stop by between 10:00 A.M. and 10:00 P.M. for a sandwich, burger, or barbecued ribs, or sample a little of everything from the buffet.

Just across US 61 from the Old Country Store is the turnoff to **Rosswood Plantation,** yet another of Mississippi's elegant antebellum bed-and-breakfasts. Nestled on a one-hundred-acre Christmas tree farm, the 1857 mansion was built by David Shroder, the same architect who designed Windsor. Visitors may peruse the diary of Dr. Walter Ross Wade, Rosswood's original owner. His journal recounts the adventures of life on the plantation before and during the Civil War, including descriptions of parties and balls reminiscent of the opening scenes of *Gone With the Wind*. Rosswood is open for tours March–October 8:30 A.M.–5:00 P.M. Monday–Saturday, and 12:30–5:00 P.M. Sunday. Admission is $10. Overnight rates begin at $140. Call (800) 533–5889 for reservations.

trivia

Actor Michael Clarke Duncan attended college at Alcorn State University in Lorman. His heartbreaking performance in *The Green Mile* earned Duncan an Oscar nomination.

For an adventure way, way, way off the beaten path, take the first road to the right on the south side of the Old Country Store and head for the *Rodney Ghost Town.*

Incorporated in 1828, Rodney was known for its high level of culture and business activity. The Mississippi River flowed past Rodney, rendering the town a bustling center of commerce and distribution. In its heyday, Rodney was home to two banks, two newspapers, thirty-five stores, a large hotel, an opera house, and several saloons. By 1860, with a population approaching 4,000, Rodney was one of Mississippi's most prosperous towns.

Then the Civil War depleted Rodney's wealth, and the town was nearly wiped out by a series of disastrous fires. But it was Mother Nature who dealt the final blow. Around 1869 the Mississippi River changed its course, leaving Rodney high and dry. The population dwindled over the coming decades, and in 1930, Mississippi Governor Theodore Bilbo issued an executive proclamation abolishing the town.

Union gunboats shelled Rodney during the Civil War, and a cannonball is still embedded in the facade of the 1829 *Rodney Presbyterian Church,* the deserted town's most prominent building. Thick grass carpets the brick steps in front of the church, spreading all the way to the front doors. A separate entrance at the side of the building opens to a narrow flight of super-steep stairs leading to the old slave gallery. The ancient town cemetery is hidden behind the church up a steep hill, its overgrown grave sites surrounded by an ornate wrought-iron fence. A second old church, a Masonic lodge, and an old store are the only buildings still standing, and cotton grows in the old riverbed.

Getting to Rodney is easy—as long as you don't get lost. Be warned: The route alternates between total gravel and one-step-up-from-gravel asphalt, and will give your shock absorbers a workout they'll never forget. The country roads you'll follow probably have names, but the complete absence of any signage renders them irrelevant.

From the intersection of US 61 South and Mississippi Highway 552, head northwest on 552. At just under 4 miles, you'll see an unmarked asphalt road on your left. Take that left, then travel less than 1 mile to the first right turn. Follow this road 1 mile, then take a right (the asphalt option as opposed to the gravel option) at the fork in the road. This road runs into Rodney about 7 miles and several jarring bumps later.

When the lonely feel of the ghost town begins to seem a bit unnerving, head back down that bumpy road to US 61 South. When you reach the intersection of US 61 and the **Natchez Trace Parkway,** you can take the Trace or continue on US 61 to **Fayette.** Either route will eventually lead you to Mississippi Highway 553 and **Springfield Plantation.**

Springfield boasts a legacy of intrigue and romance few historic homes can rival. In the spring of 1791, Andrew Jackson and Rachel Robards were married in the parlor of this beautiful mansion, touching off a scandal that would haunt the Jacksons for the rest of their lives. At the time of their marriage, both bride and groom mistakenly believed Rachel and her first husband had been granted a divorce. When word of their invalid marriage spread, political opponents began a vicious smear campaign, accusing Jackson of "sleeping under the blanket with another man's wife."

Like many homes with a romantic past, Springfield is rumored to be haunted. The strains of long-ago melodies are said to echo through the home's west wing, where a ballroom once occupied the second floor. Who knows—perhaps the restless spirits of the famous newlyweds still share a wedding day dance. Springfield Plantation is open year-round 9:30 A.M. until sunset Monday–Saturday and 10:30 A.M. until sunset Sunday. Hours vary November–March. Call (601) 786–3802 for specific hours and admission fees.

fromslavesto foundersofanation

In 1834, Captain Issac Ross, a plantation owner in Lorman, freed his slaves and arranged for their passage back to their homeland on the west coast of Africa. There, these freed slaves founded the nation of Liberia.

Years later, their descendants returned to Lorman and placed a commemorative stone at the captain's gravesite honoring his kindness and celebrating the magnanimous gesture that led not only to the freeing of their ancestors, but to the founding of their country.

Highway 553 makes a scenic loop west of the Natchez Trace that includes the historic **Church Hill** community, home to a number of working plantations, historic homes, and churches. The area's 1830 **Cedars Plantation** was once owned by actor George Hamilton.

For a look at accommodations of a more rustic sort, rejoin the Natchez Trace from Highway 553 and head south to the **Mount Locust Inn,** a 1700s version of Howard Johnson's. Restored to its original 1780 appearance (complete with split rail fences and coonskin caps on the bedposts), Mount Locust offers a glimpse of the "luxury" accommodations of the day. Between 1785 and 1830, more than fifty of these frontier inns or "stands" existed along the Old Natchez Trace. For approximately 25 cents, weary travelers enjoyed a supper of "mush and milk" and the privilege of sleeping in a room packed with saddles, baggage, and other wayfarers. Located approximately a day's walk apart, these establishments offered not only a meal and a place to rest, but a spot of civilization in the vast wilderness surrounding the Trace. Mount Locust is the only inn left standing. The former sites of other frontier stands are marked along the parkway.

trivia

Mount Locust Inn is the scene of a grisly discovery in Mississippi author Nevada Barr's bestseller *Hunting Season.*

The next stop on the Trace is even older. Built around A.D. 1400 by ancestors of the Creek, Choctaw, and Natchez Indians, **Emerald Mound** is the second-largest Indian mound in the United States. The ceremonial earthen structure covers some eight acres, measures 770 feet by 435 feet at its base, and stands 35 feet high. Emerald Mound was a center of Indian civic, ceremonial, and religious rituals from 1300 to 1699.

The Natchez Trace ends at US 61, which runs into the heart of Natchez. But first you'll drive through the old territorial capital of **Washington,** once known as the "Versailles of the Mississippi Territory."

Turn right off US 61 at the sign pointing to historic **Jefferson College.** The first educational institution chartered in the Mississippi Territory, Jefferson College conducted its first classes in 1811. A young Jefferson Davis was a student here, and according to local lore, naturalist John James Audubon instructed drawing classes on campus, Andrew Jackson was entertained here following the Battle of New Orleans, and United States Vice President Aaron Burr was arraigned for treason under the campus's giant "Burr Oaks."

The college closed with the outbreak of the Civil War, reopening in 1866 as a preparatory school. Classes were conducted here until the 1960s, when the buildings were restored to their 1800s appearance and the campus became a museum. If the college looks familiar, you may have seen it on television. Historic Jefferson College played West Point in the miniseries *North and South* and also appeared in *The Horse Soldiers* starring John Wayne and in Disney's *Huck Finn.* The grounds are open from sunup to sundown and the buildings are open 9:00 A.M.–5:00 P.M. Monday–Saturday and 1:00–5:00 P.M. Sunday.

Continue on US 61 South to history-rich **Natchez,** the oldest settlement on the Mississippi River. Make your first stop the **Natchez Visitors Reception Center** at the end of Canal Street overlooking the famed Father of Waters. This spacious facility houses the Natchez Convention and Visitors Bureau, the Natchez arm of the National Park Service, and a state-operated Mississippi Welcome Center. *The Natchez Story,* a short film on the history of the area, airs every half hour (admission to the film is $2.00 for adults, $1.00 for children under eighteen, and $1.50 for seniors). The visitors center also houses interesting exhibits, a gift shop, and an excellent bookstore devoted to local and regional history, but its strongest asset is a knowledgeable, friendly staff eager to introduce you to the rich heritage of Natchez. The visitors reception center is open Monday–Saturday 8:00 A.M.–5:00 P.M. (open until 6:00 P.M. March through October) and Sunday 9:00 A.M.–4:00 P.M.

This corner of southwest Mississippi was the quiet domain of the Natchez Indians until 1716, when French settlers established Fort Rosalie on the bluffs overlooking the Mississippi River. French, British, and Spanish flags each took turns flying over the settlement until 1797, when Andrew Ellicott raised the first American flag over Natchez, signaling the beginning of U.S. governance.

Despite its rich European history, Natchez is best known as a bastion of the antebellum South. Prior to the Civil War, more than half the millionaires in America lived in Natchez, erecting palatial mansions with fortunes built on cotton. Natchez surrendered to Union forces early in the conflict; the city was spared the burning and destruction suffered by much of the South.

All told, Natchez boasts an incredible 500 surviving antebellum structures, including breathtaking homes, ornate churches, and public buildings where history was made.

The grand southern tradition of the pilgrimage was born in Natchez way back in 1932. A late freeze wiped out the blooms scheduled for a weekend garden tour, so the members of Natchez's garden clubs opened their antebellum homes for visitors instead. Many of these ladies were hesitant to participate in such a bold venture. Times had been tight in Natchez in the sixty years following the Civil War, they argued. Didn't the homes need remodeling first? Of course, it was the very fact that the homes *hadn't* been changed since the prewar days that made them such an attraction. This impromptu tour was such a fabulous success that in 1932 the ladies scheduled the first *official* Spring Pilgrimage, and the rest is tourism history.

During **Spring and Fall Pilgrimages** approximately thirty of Natchez's grand old buildings are open for tours. While most Mississippi pilgrimages are held over a week or weekend, the Natchez extravaganza lasts a full month, running from mid-March to mid-April and again in October. No experience on

The Ghost of King's Tavern

For a dining experience that's literally out of this world, stop by King's Tavern (619 Jefferson Street in Natchez), a steak and seafood house operating in the oldest building in the Natchez Territory. The fare at King's Tavern is quite delicious, but the restaurant's real attraction is Madeline, its resident ghost.

The exact origin of King's Tavern is lost to history, but the building was probably constructed somewhere around 1760. The first mail to the region was carried down the Natchez Trace by Indian runners and left in a small post office on the tavern's first floor. Bullet holes in the heavy doors speak of bandits who once stalked travelers along the Trace, the claw prints of bear and cougar are still visible in the floors, and in the 1930s three skeletons (accompanied by a jeweled dagger) were unearthed in the tavern walls.

A young serving girl named Madeline—rumored to be the mistress of the tavern owner—worked in the midst of all this adventure. Apparently Madeline found King's Tavern so exciting, she just couldn't bear to leave—even 200 years after her death. Restaurant employees and patrons speak of lights switching on and off by themselves, footsteps that ring through the vacant upper floor, and water dripping n certain spots while everything else is dry. Apparently Madeline still tries to keep her customers happy—she operates the old dumbwaiter from time to time.

King's Tavern is open for dinner 5:00–10:00 P.M. and serves lunch during the pilgrimage. If you go, ask for a seat at one of Madeline's tables.

earth is as thoroughly southern. Costumed hostesses recite each magnificent home's history, punctuated by lots of curtseying, plenty of "y'alls," and frequent sips of that quintessential southern cocktail, the mint julep. Visitors marvel at perfectly preserved Aubusson carpets, hand-blocked Zuber and Delicourt wallpaper, marble fireplace mantels, silver-plated door knobs and bronze chandeliers, priceless paintings and sculptures, and heirloom imported china. Horse and carriage rigs clip-clop through downtown, once again the preferred mode of transportation. Magnificent displays of antique roses, camellias, Japanese and saucer magnolias, dogwood trees, jasmine, daffodils, and azaleas remind guests that this spring spectacular began as a garden tour.

After so many years in the pilgrimage business, Natchez has home tours down to a science. Each morning or afternoon tour package buys admittance to three houses for $21; you'll need to stay several days in order to see all of the homes.

The festivities aren't limited to the home tours. During the spring pilgrimage, the most popular evening entertainment is the **Confederate Pageant,** a live performance featuring nearly 300 locals in period dress recalling the glory days of the Old South. Completely and unapologetically biased, the pageant is guaranteed to bring tears of pride to southern eyes and pangs of guilt to Yankee consciences.

Another side of the Old South is portrayed in the **Southern Road to Freedom,** a stirring musical celebration of the African-American experience in Natchez. Finally, Natchez pokes fun at its own traditions in **Southern Exposure,** a lighthearted satire of the pilgrimage itself performed at the Natchez Little Theatre. Pilgrims who visit during the fall can take in a vaudeville-style performance of the **Mississippi Medicine Show** or enjoy the music of *Amos Polk's Voices of Spiritual Hope.*

Several of Natchez's mansions are also open during the *Christmas in Natchez* celebration, which features homes decorated in Victorian Yuletide finery, costumed hostesses, and candlelight tours and receptions.

For pilgrimage dates, details on individual or group tours, reservations for bed-and-breakfast stays, and information and tickets to evening entertainment, call *Natchez Pilgrimage Tours* at (800) 647–6742 or visit www.natchez pilgrimage.com.

About fifteen magnificent antebellum homes are open year-round, many of which double as bed-and-breakfasts. Each home has its own tale to tell, which may include unusual architecture, Civil War adventures, or a ghost story.

The Roxie Gold Hole

If a visit to Natchez leaves you longing for a mansion of your own, take a side trip 20 miles east of town down U.S. Highway 84 to the Roxie Gold Hole, a small pond dug one shovelful at a time by treasure hunters.

According to local legend, a gang of Natchez Trace bandits buried a treasure chest 7 feet wide and 3 feet deep in a sinkhole near Roxie. Treasure hunters dragged shovels around the woods in Roxie for years before finally unearthing a corner of what appeared to be the genuine treasure chest. The problem? All that gold was very heavy. Each time the hunters jarred the chest, it sank a little deeper into the sinkhole. Finally, in 1959, an enterprising group of diggers had the good sense to secure the chest with a thick chain, then brought in heavy equipment to hoist the treasure from its hiding place. Alas, the treasure still slipped away, and eventually people gave up the idea of ever retrieving it.

To the casual observer, the Roxie Gold Hole looks like nothing more than a small pond. But if you know what to look for, you'll soon spot a thick, taut cable, still firmly secured to a pine tree on one end and to something very, very heavy that lies underwater at the other.

Several of the mansions served as quarters for Union soldiers during the Civil War, and occasionally tales still surface of family treasure hidden behind paintings, buried on the grounds, or dropped down the cistern. Many of the homes have appeared in movies and several were featured in the popular television miniseries *North and South*. The tour homes are located all over town, and admission prices and hours vary; stop by Natchez Pilgrimage Tours (located at the corner of Canal and State Streets in the Old Depot Building) for tickets, maps, and up-to-the-minute information before embarking on a tour.

Tour homes of particular interest include **Rosalie,** which served as Union headquarters during the occupation; **Stanton Hall,** where the ghost of Colonel Stanton is said to greet guests with a hearty, "Good morning," and his ghostly children scamper the halls, accompanied by their long-dead cocker spaniel; **Linden,** used as the model for Tara's grand entrance in *Gone With the Wind;* **The Briars,** site of Jefferson Davis and Varina Howell's 1845 wedding ceremony; and **Magnolia Hall,** which features a pilgrimage costume museum and is rumored to be haunted by a former owner desperate to communicate a message beginning with the letter *M*. Established in 1988, the **Natchez National Historical Park** includes **Melrose,** the elegant 1845 urban estate of a wealthy cotton planter. Tours are conducted by docents who love these old houses and know them well. As they recount each home's fascinating story, history long past and people long dead come alive.

Perhaps the most haunting tour home is **Longwood,** the unrealized dream of Dr. Haller Nutt. The largest octagonal house in North America, Longwood was to be the wealthy Louisiana planter's town home—a six-story, thirty-two-room, 30,000-square-foot showplace. No expense was to be spared in the construction, furnishings, or workmanship; Dr. Nutt even arranged for the most skilled northern craftsmen to travel to Natchez to build his splendid palace. By early 1861, the exterior and basement of the home were completed. Then the Civil War swept through the South. The northern carpenters dropped their tools and returned home to join the fight, leaving Longwood unfinished. The war ruined Nutt financially, and he died in 1864, his glorious vision a mere shell. The craftsmen never returned to Longwood, and the mansion came to be known in Natchez as "Nutt's Folly."

Now the property of the Pilgrimage Garden Club of Natchez, Longwood remains exactly as it appeared in 1861; the chisels and hammers are still where the workmen dropped them, and the paintbrushes are still in the original cans. Visitors wander through the oddly shaped, furnished rooms in the basement, then gaze up through level after level of scaffolding surrounding empty space. With such a tragic history, it's no surprise that Dr. Nutt's ghost is still felt around Longwood, perhaps waiting for someone to complete his ill-fated masterpiece.

And if a Longwood tour guide should happen to stumble or recite an incorrect statistic during a tour, Dr. Nutt is sure to express his displeasure by making the lights blink.

Many of the famous Natchez residents you'll hear about during the home tours are buried in the **Natchez City Cemetery.** Situated on a bluff overlooking the river, the ninety-five-acre cemetery features dozens of beautiful, haunting, and unusual monuments dating to the late 1700s. Inscriptions range from the poignant to the bizarre; countless romantic, tragic, and downright spooky tales lie buried in the old graves. The Natchez City Cemetery comes alive each October during the popular **Angels on the Bluff** event, which features evening tours of the cemetery and living history performances by descendants of its "residents." Call (601) 446–6345 or (800) 647–6724 for ticket information.

Natchez's rich history includes a strong African-American heritage, showcased in the **Natchez Museum of African-American History and Culture.** The museum houses more than 600 artifacts depicting African-American culture in Mississippi from the 1890s through the 1950s. Located at 301 Main Street in Natchez, the museum is open Tuesday–Saturday 1:00–4:30 P.M. A historical marker at the intersection of St. Catherine and D'Evereux Streets designates the former site of the **Forks of the Road Slave Market,** one of the two largest slave markets of the antebellum South. African-American art is the focus of the **Mostly African Market,** a collection of regional arts and crafts displayed and sold in the gallery at 125 St. Catherine Street. The market is open seasonally; call (601) 446–9947.

One of the city's most famous African-American sons was William Johnson, "the Barber of Natchez." Born a slave in 1809, Johnson was freed by his owner

Prince among Slaves

Born near Timbuktu in 1762, Ibrahima was the son of a powerful African king. For twenty-six years Ibrahima lived as prince and celebrated warrior. But in 1788, Ibrahima was defeated in battle and sold to slave traders. He arrived in Natchez on a slave ship and was purchased by planter Thomas Foster.

After nearly twenty years in slavery, Ibrahima was recognized by a visiting doctor, John Cox, who had known Ibrahima's father in Africa. Cox tried to purchase Ibrahima's freedom, but Foster refused to sell his valuable slave. Cox did succeed, however, in making Ibrahima a national celebrity. Under public pressure, Foster finally agreed to free the former prince in the late 1820s. A local newspaper then launched a campaign to return Ibrahima to Africa. Prince Ibrahima sailed as far as the African coast, but died before making the final trip inland to his homeland.

The Goat Castle Murder

When eccentric, wealthy recluse Jennie Merrill was murdered in her Natchez mansion in 1932, suspicion immediately fell upon her neighbors, the even more eccentric Richard "Dick" Dana and Octavia Dockery.

Dana and Dockery lived next door to Ms. Merrill in Glenwood, a once-opulent mansion fallen into extreme disrepair. Once members of the Natchez aristocracy, Dana and Dockery had suffered a long, slow slide into abject poverty. At the time of the murder, they were barely supporting themselves by raising goats, chickens, cows, and pigs, all of which were allowed to roam freely through the deteriorating mansion. Their behavior was regarded as bizarre by the genteel folk of Natchez long before the time of the murder. Dockery, in fact, had had her own housemate, Dana, declared legally insane.

Bitter blood developed between the neighbors when the goats began wandering onto Ms. Merrill's property, and Ms. Merrill responded by shooting them. When Ms. Merrill's bullet-riddled body was found in a thicket behind her home, the police headed for Glenwood.

The utter squalor confronting them was more bizarre than any could have imagined. The huge, filthy mansion was overrun with livestock, its entire interior covered with dust, fleas, and animal droppings. Wallpaper peeled in sheets from the crumbling walls, framed pictures lay shattered on the floor, and banisters and balustrades hung at crazy angles. Goats had eaten an entire library of leather-bound volumes once perused by Robert E. Lee. The floors were strewn with piles of garbage, and the draperies were chewed as far up as the animals could reach. Dockery had been smoking goat meat in the fireplace in her bedroom; long strips of it were stretched over rusty bedsprings to "cure." The *Natchez Democrat* dubbed the foul mansion "Goat Castle," adding that the strangest thing about the place was that the goats could stand it.

Within weeks of Dana and Dockery's arrest, a transient confessed to Merrill's murder, and the two were released. They capitalized on their newfound celebrity, opening the squalid Glenwood for public tours. Fifty cents bought visitors a look at the decaying mansion and its famous goats. Dana and Dockery lived in the filthy wreck of a house until their deaths in 1948 and 1949.

Glenwood was razed in 1955, and a new subdivision, with streets named Dana Road and Glenwood Drive, was built on the property. Glenburnie, the scene of the murder, still stands adjacent to the subdivision, and is sometimes open for tours during pilgrimage. Jennie Merrill, Richard Dana, and Octavia Dockery are all buried in the Natchez City Cemetery, where Dockery's tombstone proclaims her the "Mistress of Goat Castle."

(who was more than likely also his father) as a young man. He trained as a barber, eventually buying his own barbershop and rising to prominence as a member of the free black aristocracy. Johnson, who himself owned some fifteen slaves, was a successful businessman, popular with both the white and black residents of Natchez. His detailed diary, begun in 1835, represents the most complete account of the daily life of a free African American in the antebellum South.

Johnson was murdered in 1851 over a land dispute. Despite public outcry from both blacks and whites and a trial that required a change of venue, Johnson's white murderer was acquitted. It was against the law for blacks to testify against whites, and all witnesses to the crime were black. The 1841 **William Johnson House** is now a part of the Natchez National Historical Park maintained by the National Park Service.

The rowdy riverboat landing at **Natchez Under-the-Hill** was once the notorious lair of gamblers, thieves, and ladies of the evening, a scandalous embarrassment to the decent citizens of Natchez. Many a boatman of the 1800s trekked up the Old Natchez Trace penniless and exhausted after a visit to the saloons and gambling houses Under-the-Hill, an area dubbed by an evangelist of the day as "the worst Hell hole on earth." Listed on the National Register of Historic Places, the landing is now a respectable, restored area of colorful shops, bars, and restaurants. More than a century after the last gaming house of the 1800s closed its doors, the landing is again home to a casino, **The Isle of Capri.** Merry calliope music and steamboat whistles ring through the area when the luxury riverboats *Delta Queen* and *Mississippi Queen* make their regular stops in Natchez.

Natchez Under-the-Hill relives its days as a red-light district every June during the **Steamboat Jubilee.** The *Delta Queen* and *Mississippi Queen* dock in Natchez during their neck-and-neck race down the Mississippi River, and the city welcomes them with a wacky festival that includes the highly competitive **Best Floozie Contest.** The river is also the backdrop for another popular Natchez festival, the **Great Mississippi River Balloon Race.** This October event features dozens of colorful balloons racing across the Mississippi River (duck when you get to the bridge!). Festivities include arts, crafts, entertainment, and balloon rides for spectators. Expect a champagne dousing after your first flight. For event dates, call the **Natchez Convention and Visitors Bureau** at (800) 647–6724.

Natchez is home to a number of colorful shopping areas offering one-of-a-kind gifts, specialty foods, local artwork, "southern" souvenirs that border on the politically incorrect, and too many antiques shops to list. The **Canal Street Depot and Market,** downtown Natchez, and the **Franklin Street Marketplace** are all excellent places to begin a shopping expedition. If you're in the

Little-Known Facts about the Heartland

The world's first human heart and lung transplants were performed in 1964 in Jackson at the University of Mississippi Medical Center.

Myrlie Evers-Williams, widow of assassinated NAACP field secretary Medgar Evers, went on to become the Chairman of the NAACP.

Jackson's Malaco Records is the world's largest gospel music recording label.

Neatniks worldwide owe a debt of gratitude to Harry Cole Sr., of Jackson, the inventor of Pine-Sol.

The Parent-Teacher Association (PTA) was founded in Crystal Springs in 1909.

On May 11, 1887, a most unusual object plummeted from the skies above Bovina during a hail storm—a 6-inch by 8-inch gopher turtle, completely encased in ice.

The Waterways Experiment Station in Vicksburg is the Army Corps of Engineers' largest research, testing, and development facility.

Tipping the scales at more than eighteen pounds, the state record largemouth bass was reeled in from Natchez State Park Lake.

The Easter Flood of 1979 caused more than $200 million in damages in the Jackson area. With the Pearl River 15 feet above flood stage, hundreds of homes were flooded, residents were forced to escape by boat, and much of downtown Jackson was under water.

In 1997, Mississippi Attorney General Mike Moore settled a $3.36 billion lawsuit against the nation's tobacco companies. Moore played himself in the 1999 tobacco whistle-blower saga, *The Insider.* The film was nominated for an Academy Award for Best Picture.

market for spirits, Natchez even boasts its own winery. Located just off US 61 at the northern outskirts of Natchez, the **Old South Winery** offers free tours and tastings of its muscadine wine from 10:00 A.M. to 5:00 P.M. Monday–Saturday and 1:00–5:00 P.M. Sunday. Ole South's most popular selection? A sweet rosé labeled "Miss Scarlett."

Living souvenirs of Natchez are available at **Stewart Orchids,** a nursery and orchid breeding operation just outside town. A leader in the orchid prop-agation business since the 1920s, Stewart Orchids moved its entire operation from California to Natchez in 2000. A tour of the facility includes a look at the orchid growing labs, a one-and-one-half-acre greenhouse, and thousands of exquisite orchids of every size and color. To get to the farm, follow US 61 North approximately 1 mile past the US 84/98 intersection. Turn left on Mor-gantown Road just before Jefferson College, and continue 1 mile to Foster

Mound Road. Take a right on Foster Mound Road and bear right at the fork. For more information, call (800) 621–2450 or visit www.stewartorchids.com.

Natchez offers several unique options for hungry visitors. Open for lunch year-round and lunch and dinner during the pilgrimage, the **Carriage House Restaurant** (401 High Street) behind Stanton Hall serves up traditional southern dishes and is famous for its homemade biscuits. **Wharf Master's Restaurant and Bar** (57 Silver Street) serves up American and Cajun cuisine in a refurbished shanty with a view of the mighty Mississippi River; **King's Tavern** (619 Jefferson Street) is the place for steaks, seafood, and a good ghost story; and **Monmouth Plantation** and **The Castle Restaurant and Pub at Dunleith** represent candlelight dining at its absolute finest (more on these elegant options follows).

The Natchez experience simply isn't complete without an overnight stay at one of the city's palatial bed-and-breakfast inns. The town is home to more than thirty exceptional bed-and-breakfasts, many of which have been featured on countless television shows and in national travel magazines.

Perhaps the most celebrated of these elegant inns is Monmouth Plantation, an 1818 beauty named one of the Top 10 Romantic Places in the USA by both *Glamour* magazine and *USA Today.* This breathtaking bed-and-breakfast also earns top honors from *Conde Nast Traveler,* which named Monmouth one of America's Top 25 Small Luxury Hotels and also lists the inn on its Gold List of the World's Best Places to Stay. Monmouth's most famous owner was John Quitman, Governor of Mississippi and a U.S. congressman during the 1860s. Today, the twenty-six-acre plantation is owned by Ron and Lani Riches, a couple from California who fell in love with the then-deteriorating property on a visit to Natchez. They purchased Monmouth and restored the home and gardens to their original splendor.

Marked by enormous azaleas in the spring, caladiums in the summer, brilliant fall foliage, and evergreens twinkling with white lights in the winter, Monmouth is a pleasure in any season. The lushly landscaped grounds are home to thirty luxurious guest cottages and suites, many featuring fireplaces, Jacuzzi tubs, private patios, and spacious sitting rooms. Pea gravel paths wind through the wooded property, past gazebos and pergolas draped with wisteria, fountains filled with koi, and two scenic ponds populated by what must be very contented ducks.

trivia

Author and Natchez resident Greg Iles used his hometown as the setting for the bestsellers *The Quiet Game* and *Sleep No More.* Iles confesses to using a few of his neighbors as the models for his unforgettable characters.

Cocktails are served each evening in Quitman's Study, or beside the fountain and under the stars in the courtyard. Dinner at Monmouth is a special treat, an affair marked by crystal, candlelight, and five delectable courses. Guests are seated at the General's Table in the mansion's formal dining room or at private tables in the parlor. Your dinner companions may be Natchez locals or travelers from around the world; either way, the setting is elegant and the conversation is sure to be lively. Dinner at Monmouth is $40 per person, exclusive of cocktails, wine, tax, and tip. You do not have to be an overnight guest to dine at Monmouth, but seating is limited and reservations are required.

Monmouth is located at 36 Melrose Avenue. For more information or dinner or room reservations, call (800) 828–4531 or visit www.monmouthplantation.com.

Equally opulent accommodations are available at **Dunleith,** a magnificent Greek Revival–style mansion built in 1856. Dunleith's massive columns and sheer size make this templelike palace one of the most impressive homes in Natchez— a superlative among superlatives. According to legend, the owner of the plantation hid his prize horses in the basement during the Civil War. Dunleith was so huge that Federal troops who searched the mansion had no idea the horses were there. The restored plantation carriage house is now The Castle Restaurant and Pub, an elegant establishment where the incredible atmosphere is upstaged only by the excellent food and service. The impossible-to-miss Dunleith is located at 84 Homochitto Street. For room or dinner reservations, call (601) 446–8500 or (800) 433–2445, or visit www.dunleithplantation.com.

Monmouth and Dunleith are just two examples of the bed-and-breakfast experience in Natchez. For more information about outstanding bed-and-breakfast inns or reservations in Natchez, call Natchez Pilgrimage Tours at (601) 446–6631 or (800) 647–6742 or visit www.natchezpilgrimage.com. Then prepare to climb into the down-filled comfort of a vast four-poster bed, where you're sure to dream of elegant cotillions, dashing men in uniform, and the merciless squeeze of an antebellum corset.

If you need a reminder that Mississippi history didn't begin with the antebellum South, stop at the **Grand Village of the Natchez Indians** just south of Natchez off US 61 South on the banks of St. Catherine's Creek. The culture of the Natchez Indian tribe reached its peak in the mid-1500s, with the Grand Village serving as the center of activities for the sun worshippers from A.D. 1200 to 1729. The fading journals of French explorers make reference to the ceremonial center at the Grand Village. The Natchez vanished as a nation following a hostile encounter with French settlers at the Grand Village in 1730. The Grand Village site was excavated in 1930, revealing a ceremonial plaza, burial mounds, and rare artifacts now housed in an on-site museum. The Grand Village is open 9:00 A.M.–5:00 P.M. Monday–Saturday and 1:30–5:00 P.M. Sunday.

The annual ***Pow-Wow at the Grand Village*** is two days of Native American dancing, music, and craft demonstrations. On-site camping is available. Call (601) 446–6502 for festival dates, which usually coincide with the Natchez Spring Pilgrimage.

As you head out of the area on US 61 South, you'll spot one last Old South icon just outside Natchez. In these days of political correctness, the sight of a 50-foot mammy smiling from the roadside is indeed a memorable one. Open the door in her bright red skirt and step into ***Mammy's Cupboard*** (555 Highway 61 South)

Mammy's Cupboard

for a southern-style lunch. Be sure to snap a photo of the towering, smiling mammy, complete with kerchief and outstretched arms holding a serving tray. If you're from anywhere north of the Mason-Dixon line, your friends back home will never believe such a place still exists. Mammy's Cupboard is open for lunch and gift-shop browsing Tuesday–Saturday.

The Natchez Trace Parkway

The Lower Natchez Trace is actually the parkway's beginning. The original Natchez Trace was a one-way route that began in Natchez, then ran north to Nashville. In the late 1700s and early 1800s, flatboats floated merchandise downriver to Natchez and New Orleans, but the return trip north was along the Old Natchez Trace. By 1800, as many as 10,000 "Kaintucks"—the local lingo for boatmen from anywhere north of Natchez—annually trekked the Trace, each armed with a rifle and a bottle of whiskey.

The terrain was rough, and a broken leg often spelled death for the lone traveler. Murderous bandits, savage Indians, ferocious wild animals, and other perils encountered along the way earned the Natchez Trace the nickname "Devil's Backbone."

The Lower Natchez Trace runs past a number of historic sites and nature trails, as well as many of the cities and towns listed earlier in this chapter. The nature trail at mile marker 122 in Madison winds through the deep green and heavy silence of the *Cypress Swamp,* where towering trees growing in an old riverbed form a lush canopy overhead. A short, boardwalked path through the swamp is easily explored in half an hour. Just north of Jackson, the Trace hugs the shoreline of the Ross Barnett Reservoir for 8 miles, with a scenic reservoir overlook located at mile marker 105. Beware of vengeful spirits as you explore a section of the *Old Trace* at mile marker 102. The dense wilderness surrounding the narrow trail is the perfect hiding spot for bandits or Indians. This section of the Parkway includes a stop at the Mississippi Crafts Center in Ridgeland before coming to a dead end just north of the capital city. To rejoin the Trace, take Interstate 220 to Interstate 20 West, which intersects the parkway south of Jackson.

This final leg of the Trace passes a number of picnic areas and historic sites. If you're traveling in the spring, you'll see a profusion of blooming dogwoods, redbuds, and an occasional patch of daffodils; the Trace's fall foliage display is equally impressive.

Any time of year, you're sure to notice the gray, gossamer substance dripping from the trees along this section of the parkway. That's Spanish moss, a native plant that looks dead, but keeps on growing, even if you move it indoors. Giant oaks laden with the stuff adorn the grounds of many of the area's antebellum homes, adding a gothic touch to the scenery. The farther south you travel, the more moss-draped trees you'll spot.

Forty miles south of Jackson, the *Rocky Springs National Park* offers a campground, picnic tables, and hiking and biking trails, all just a short walk from the forgotten settlement of Rocky Springs. A prosperous community of the 1800s, Rocky Springs was a center of agriculture and commerce, home to several businesses and large homes. The cotton that made the town rich, however, made the soil poor. Gradually the earth became depleted and eroded, and by 1930, Rocky Springs was a ghost town.

A stroll along the boardwalk through the preserved town site begins at a marker reading, THE TOWN OF ROCKY SPRINGS. POPULATION 1860—2,616. POPULATION TODAY—0. A church, cemetery, and rusting safe once filled with treasures are all that's left of the once-thriving community. The *Rocky Springs Methodist Church,* built in 1837, still overlooks the old town site and is open to the public. The Rocky Springs Methodist Church and cemetery were the scene of a grisly murder in Mississippi author Nevada Barr's bestseller, *Deep South.* Visitors can also hike along a section of the original Old Trace thick with ferns and bamboo and wade in the shallow waters of Little Sand Creek. A marker at the entrance to the nature trail invites explorers to WALK DOWN THE SHADED TRAIL AND LEAVE YOUR PRINTS IN THE DUST, NOT FOR OTHERS TO SEE, BUT FOR THE ROAD TO REMEMBER.

Take a moment to explore a section of sunken trace south of Rocky Springs at mile marker 41. This deeply eroded tunnel through the wilderness is another portion of the original road. A canopy of trees stretches across the dirt bed of the trail—a route perhaps still trekked by the ghosts of earlier adventurers.

South of Rocky Springs the Trace parallels US 61 and offers exits to the towns, cities, and attractions described earlier in this chapter, including **Port Gibson, Lorman, Fayette, Washington,** and, of course, **Natchez,** where the fabled parkway was born.

Places to Stay in the Heartland

The following is a partial listing of the many hotels, motels, and bed-and-breakfast inns in the area not mentioned in the text.

Lincoln Ltd. is a full-time reservation service for bed-and-breakfast inns statewide. For reservations in any area of Mississippi, call (601) 482–5483 or (800) 633–6477.

JACKSON
The Edison Walthall Hotel
225 East Capitol Street,
(601) 948–6161

Quarter Inn
1865 Lakeland Drive,
(601) 366–6661

NATCHEZ
Natchez Pilgrimage Tours provides reservation services for more than thirty antebellum and Victorian mansions and bed-and-breakfast inns in the area. For information and reservations, call (601) 446–6631 or (800) 647–6742, or visit www.natchezpilgrimage.com

The Radisson Natchez Eola Hotel
110 North Pearl Street,
(601) 445–6000

Ramada Inn Hilltop
130 John R. Junkin Drive,
(601) 446–6311

RAYMOND
Dupree House and Mamie's Cottage
(bed-and-breakfast)
2809 Dupree Road,
(601) 857–6051 or
(877) 629–6051

VICKSBURG
Vicksburg is home to more than a dozen historic bed-and-breakfast inns. For a complete listing of additional bed-and-breakfast inns in Vicksburg, call the Vicksburg Convention and Visitors Bureau at (800) 221–3536.

Anchuca
(bed-and-breakfast)
1010 First East Street,
(601) 661–0111 or
(888) 686–0111
www.anchucamansion.com

Cherry Street Cottages/Shlenker House
(bed-and-breakfast)
2212 Cherry Street,
(601) 636–7086 or
(800) 636–7086

Duff Green Mansion
(bed-and-breakfast)
114 First East Street,
(601) 638–6662 or
(800) 992–0037

Places to Eat in the Heartland

The following is a partial listing of the many restaurants in the area not mentioned in the text.

JACKSON
Nick's (fine dining)
1501 Lakeland Drive,
(601) 981–8017

Peaches (soul food)
327 North Farish Street,
(601) 354–9267

Rainbow Whole Foods Grocery/High Noon Cafe
(vegetarian, organic)
2807 Old Canton Road,
(601) 366–1602
www.rainbowcoop.org

NATCHEZ
Biscuits & Blues
(southern cuisine, live blues music)
315 Main Street,
(601) 446–9922

PORT GIBSON

The Old Depot Restaurant
and Lounge
(seafood, steaks, po'boys)
1202 Market Street,
(601) 437–4711

RIDGELAND

Pan Asia
(Asian fusion, stir fry)
862 Avery Boulevard
(The Promenade),
(601) 956–2686

VICKSBURG

Goldie's Trail Bar-B-Que
4127 South Washington
Street,
(601) 636–9839

ALSO WORTH SEEING

JACKSON

Dogwood Festival Market

The International Museum of Muslim
Cultures

Jackson Municipal Art Gallery

Jackson Zoological Park

LeFleur's Bluff State Park

Live performances by the Mississippi
Symphony Orchestra, Mississippi
Opera, and Ballet Mississippi at New
Stage Theatre

The Mississippi Arts Pavilion
(stages major international exhibitions
every other year)

Mississippi Museum of Art

Mississippi Sports Hall of Fame

Mynelle Gardens

Northpark Mall

Rapids on the Reservoir

Russell C. Davis Planetarium

State Capitol Building

War Memorial Building

NATCHEZ

Canal Street Coffee Roasters of
Natchez

Frogmore Plantation

Historic City Bus Tour

Lady Luck Casino

Natchez in Historic Photographs
exhibit

Natchez State Park

PORT GIBSON

Energy Central Visitors Center, Grand
Gulf Nuclear Reactor

VICKSBURG

Ameristar Casino

Harrah's Casino

Isle of Capri Casino

Rainbow Casino

Vicksburg Factory Outlets

Southern Mississippi and the Gulf Coast

Southern Mississippi is a contradictory blend of pioneer spirit and carefree coastal life, a region where rugged frontier land, thick forests, and tranquil beaches all lie within a couple of hours' drive.

Visitors to southern Mississippi can relive the adventures of early explorers, retreat to a quiet artists' colony, and roll the dice in a glitzy casino, all in the same day. This dynamic mix of cultures and lifestyles makes a single trip to southern Mississippi a multifaceted adventure.

The Old Southwest

The southwestern corner of the state is made up of towns and cities still proud of their frontier heritage and, for the most part, still living it today. Much of the area just south of Natchez remains undisturbed and unexplored, peppered with overgrown forts, old-fashioned mercantiles, and sturdy buildings largely unchanged since the first settlers erected them more than a century ago.

The 35-mile stretch of U.S. Highway 61 South between Natchez and Woodville is sprinkled with antiques shops, junk shops, and trailers housing businesses from dog grooming to

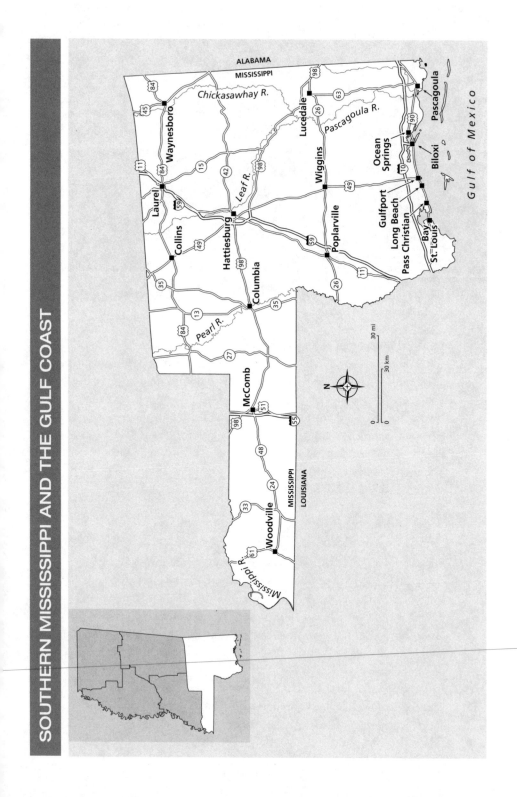

palm reading. You'll pass establishments like ***Relative Relics,*** a combination grocery store/antiques shop/cafe where you can purchase a cold soft drink, depression-era glass, or a ventriloquist's dummy, rent a movie, and sample the blue plate special, all in one stop.

But don't browse too long—you'll need at least a day to explore ***Woodville,*** the charming town Harvard University once described as "best typifying the Old South in appearance, customs, and traditions." That notoriety aside, Woodville remains for the most part an undiscovered treasure. Unlike Natchez, her tourist-oriented neighbor to the north, Woodville actually takes pleasure in remaining off the beaten path. At least for now, visitors can soak up the southern charm without calling for reservations, waiting in line, or catching a shuttle bus.

The town boasts a number of antebellum homes and churches, but Woodville's most famous link to the Old South is ***Rosemont,*** the childhood home of Jefferson Davis. As you come into town on US 61 South, follow the signs to the 300-acre plantation where the Confederate States of America's only president spent his boyhood. A sun-dappled gravel road winds through towering trees dripping with Spanish moss, ending at a shaded gazebo where visitors listen to a short recording before touring the main house.

Samuel and Jane Davis moved to this airy planter's cottage with their ten children in 1810. (It's interesting to note that Jefferson, the youngest child, was given the middle name "Finis.") Home to five generations of the Davis family over the next century, Rosemont remains much the same today as it appeared during Davis's childhood. Many of the furnishings and artwork are original

MARLO'S FAVORITE ATTRACTIONS IN SOUTHERN MISSISSIPPI AND THE GULF COAST

Rosemont,
Woodville

Clark Creek Natural Area,
Pond

Shopping in Old Town,
Bay St. Louis

The shade of the Friendship Oak in July,
Long Beach

The beaches of Ship Island,
accessible from Gulfport

Beauvoir,
Biloxi

The Ocean Springs Gallery District,
Ocean Springs

Sunset over the water,
Mississippi Beach

Fresh seafood,
Mississippi Beach

Hitting blackjack in any casino,
Mississippi Beach

Davis family pieces, including Jane Davis's spinning wheel, books inscribed with the family name, chandeliers fueled by whale oil, and champagne glasses once raised in presidential toasts.

A wall in the hallway bears the height charts of several Davis children, and Jefferson Davis's brother-in-law, Issac Stamps, scratched his name into one of the windows downstairs. Stamps was killed at the Battle of Gettysburg, and Davis's sister traveled all the way to Pennsylvania to bring his body home to Rosemont for burial. Davis issued a presidential pass allowing her to cross enemy lines.

Originally called "Poplar Grove," the plantation was renamed Rosemont in honor of Jane Davis's elaborate flower gardens. Many of the rose bushes still blooming on the grounds today were originally planted by Jefferson Davis's mother in the early 1800s. The property also includes the Davis family cemetery where many members of Jefferson Davis's immediate family, including his mother and Issac Stamps, are buried. President Davis himself is buried in the old Confederate capital of Richmond, Virginia. Photos displayed at Rosemont capture the throngs of Confederate supporters who attended Davis's funeral in New Orleans. Some 200,000 mourners came to pay their last respects—the largest funeral attendance in history prior to services for President John F. Kennedy.

The $7.50 admission includes the house, outbuildings, cemetery, and lavishly landscaped grounds. Rosemont is open March 2–December 14 Monday–Friday 10:00 A.M.–5:00 P.M. and on weekends during the Natchez Spring and Fall Pilgrimages. Call (601) 888–6809.

Head back to US 61 and go straight through the four-way stop to downtown Woodville, where you'll find the traditional town square and courthouse. A block south of the courthouse, the **Wilkinson County Museum** features changing exhibits related to local history. The museum is housed in a lovely, 1838 Greek Revival–style building that originally served as the offices of the West Feliciana Railroad Company. The museum is open 10:00 A.M.–noon and 2:00–4:00 P.M. Monday–Friday, and 10:00 A.M.–noon Saturday. For groups as small as four, the museum will put together a **Lost Architectural Treasures and Cemeteries Tour,** which includes a look at a number of centuries-old grave sites, crumbling columns, and other architectural relics around Wilkinson County. The tour can be as long, short, simple, or involved as the group would like and can include a picnic lunch. Call curator David Smith at (601) 888–3998 for details.

David can also point out a number of historic churches just off the town square. There's the 1809 **Woodville Baptist Church,** the oldest church in Mississippi; the 1823 **St. Paul's Episcopal Church,** a founding parish of the Episcopal church in Mississippi; and the 1824 **Woodville Methodist Church,**

MARLO'S FAVORITE ANNUAL EVENTS IN SOUTHERN MISSISSIPPI AND THE GULF COAST

BILOXI

Confederate Memorial Day at Beauvoir,
April,
(228) 388–9074

Blessing of the Fleet,
May,
(228) 435–5578

HATTIESBURG

Hubfest,
October,
(800) 238–4288

MISSISSIPPI GULF COAST

Cruisin' the Coast,
October,
(800) 466–9048

Mardi Gras,
February or March,
(228) 432–8806

OCEAN SPRINGS

Landing of d'Iberville,
April,
(228) 875–4424

Peter Anderson Arts and Crafts Festival
(In Marlo's opinion, the best art festival in Mississippi), November,
(228) 875–4424

the oldest Methodist church in Mississippi. Woodville is also home to the state's oldest newspaper and continuously run business, *The Woodville Republican.*

Just around the corner from the museum on First South Street you'll spot the two modest graves that make up the infamous ***Oswald Family Cemetery.*** It seems that Lee Harvey Oswald had a number of relatives in the Woodville area, and history buffs still come in search of these right-off-the-sidewalk-but-still-hard-to-spot tombs. The tour guide at Rosemont recalls an encounter with one group who asked about the grave sites. "I told them I knew where they were because, unfortunately, I was distantly related to Oswald myself. They didn't appreciate that—apparently they were related to him too, and *didn't* find it unfortunate."

If you're in Woodville around dinnertime, ask David Smith about his family's restaurant, ***South of the Border.*** Don't go in search of a taco—the border in question is the Mississippi–Louisiana state line. As David explains, the restaurant is located in Louisiana because "the idea was to create the last great Southern roadhouse, and Mississippi was dry." South of the Border serves a southern menu in a cheerful atmosphere Tuesday–Saturday 11:00 A.M.–10:00 P.M. and Sunday 11:00 A.M.–9:00 P.M.

History buffs and outdoor enthusiasts will find a side trip west of Woodville to the microscopic communities of **Pond, Pickneyville,** and **Fort Adams** a worthwhile adventure. Head west out of downtown Woodville to Mississippi Highway 24, then follow the Pond-Pickneyville Road 16 miles to the **Pond Store,** an old-fashioned general store in business since 1881. According to local records, the pond for which the store was named was manmade, dug by the county as a watering hole for oxen, horses, and mules used to haul cotton to Fort Adams for shipment aboard steamboats. The mules are long gone, but with hardwood floors, long rows of wooden shelves, and antique display cases, the Pond Store retains its original frontier charm. Proprietors Liz and Norman Chaffin live in back of the store and will give you a look at the traditional lifestyle of the merchant class for a small admission fee. The store sells sundries and provides information on the area seven days a week from 7:00 A.M. to 7:00 P.M. Call (601) 888–4426 to arrange a tour of the proprietors' house. Located on the store property, the **Pond Store Cabin** is a rustic, one-room cabin equipped with two beds, a sleeping loft, and a small kitchen. To inquire about a country getaway at the cabin, call Liz and Norman Chaffin at (601) 888–4426 or write to the Chaffins at Pond Store, 182 Fort Adams-Pond Road, Woodville, Mississippi 39669.

The Pond Store is located near the entrance to the 1,400-acre **Clark Creek Natural Area.** The terrain at Clark Creek is wild and rugged, made up of steep ravines, water-sculpted rocks, and sheer loess bluffs crisscrossed with hiking trails. The area is home to fourteen enchanting waterfalls, the highest of which tumbles some 50 feet down the bluff. This is not the place for a casual stroll. Reaching the waterfalls requires hiking boots, a healthy water supply, and most of all, stamina. Don't forget to pick up a trail map at the Pond Store—you'll need some help navigating this scenic but remote area. To avoid disappointment, call ahead to the Pond Store to be sure Clark Creek is open. Erosion problems occasionally present a safety hazard and cause the area to close for "repairs."

The Pond-Pickneyville Road continues into equally tiny Pickneyville, where you'll find the **grave of Oliver Pollack,** inventor of the dollar sign, and the **Desert Plantation,** a 1,000-acre plantation and bed-and-breakfast inn. The Desert Plantation is conveniently located 18 miles from both Woodville and **St. Francisville, Louisiana,** another town famous for its antebellum homes and pilgrimage tours. Call (877) 877–1103 or visit www.desertplantation.com for rates and reservations.

The neighboring community of Fort Adams is a virtual ghost town, home to little more than a handful of hunting and fishing camps. The 1700s fort that gave the town its name has long since been swallowed up by rampant vegetation.

Fort Adams's most famous resident was fictional. The town was immortalized in Edward Everett Hale's tale *The Man Without a Country* when character Philip Nolan, banished from American soil after denouncing the United States, did time in a Fort Adams prison. Fort Adams is just north of Pond at the end of Highway 24, but as one of the town's few residents puts it, "there's nothing much to do once you've gotten here except turn around and go back."

When you're ready to turn back, head east on Mississippi Highway 24, which turns into Mississippi Highway 48 just west of **Liberty** and the **Jerry Clower Museum.** The late Jerry Clower opened this small museum years ago to house an ever-expanding collection of memorabilia accumulated over his decades-long career as America's favorite country comedian. The collection includes the keys to forty-nine cities, an Indian headdress, numerous stuffed raccoons, and a plaque proclaiming Clower, "the World's Nicest Person." The museum is open Monday–Friday 8:30 A.M.–3:00 P.M., by appointment. Call (601) 684–8130 for directions and to arrange a tour time.

When you've had all the country comedy you can stand, continue on Mississippi Highway 48 East to **McComb.** A bit of musical trivia—the McComb area has been home to a number of renowned musicians, including the legendary Bo Diddley, blues guitarist Vasti Johnson, and most recently, triple platinum R&B singer and star of TV's *Moesha,* Brandy Norwood. And while pop superstar Britney Spears actually resided just across the state line in Louisiana, she attended school at McComb's Parklane Academy.

The best time to visit McComb is in late March or early April, during the **Lighted Azalea Festival.** Inspired by Japan's traditional lighting of the cherry blossoms, the first lighted azalea trail was staged in 1953. A drive through McComb provides a look at twinkling, decades-old azaleas of every size, shape, and color. The festival also includes the crowning of the Azalea Queen and a Spring Tour of homes. For dates and a map of the **Azalea Trail,** call the **Pike County Chamber of Commerce** at (601) 684–2291 or (800) 399–4404.

Lunch in McComb means a trip to **The Dinner Bell,** a bastion of southern cooking located on Fifth Street off U.S. Highway 51 North. Hungry locals and travelers alike have gathered on the front porch of this former private home since 1959 in anticipation of a home-cooked meal and a down-home good time. Diners sit at large, communal tables and take turns spinning a lazy Susan groaning with fried chicken, meatloaf, catfish, mashed potatoes, fresh beans and peas, casseroles of every description, and other hearty southern dishes prepared by cooks who've never heard the words "diet" or "cholesterol." Be sure to sample the house special, fried eggplant prepared with a super-secret recipe. Lunch includes your fill of sweet, sweet tea, fresh-baked biscuits or cornbread, and dessert. The Dinner Bell puts food on the table 11:00 A.M.–2:00

P.M. Tuesday–Sunday and 5:30–8:00 P.M. Friday–Saturday. Spin the lazy Susan as many times as your waistband will allow for a mere $9.00 Tuesday–Thursday, $10.00 Friday and Saturday, and $12.00 on Sunday. If you're confident your culinary skills are up to the challenge, pick up a copy of *Celebrating 50: The Dinner Bell Restaurant Golden Anniversary Cookbook,* and try preparing some of these southern specialties at home (sorry, the famous fried eggplant recipe is *not* included).

Shopping opportunities beckon from just across the street at the **Gulf South Gallery.** Showcasing Mississippi artists and craftsmen, the gallery offers paintings, pottery, jewelry, and other collectibles and gifts. The Gulf South Gallery is located at 228 Fifth Avenue. Call (601) 684–9470.

If you're in the area over the Memorial Day weekend, take a side trip up Interstate 55 North to U.S. Highway 84 East (about 40 miles total from McComb) and spend a day in **Monticello** at the **Atwood Music Festival.** A thirty-year tradition, the festival features golf and tennis tournaments, hot-air balloon races, children's activities, and an arts and crafts show; but Atwood's biggest draw is energetic performances by country music's hottest superstars. The festival is held at Monticello's Atwood Water Park. For this year's line-up of performers and events, call (601) 587–3007.

The steamy days of August heat up even more during the **Montipaloosa Music Festival.** Montipaloosa is also held at Atwood Water Park, but any similarity to Monticello's other music festival ends there. Geared toward young adults, this two-day extravaganza features as many as forty bands playing rock, alternative, blues, jazz, acoustics, and a smattering of other musical styles. While the Montipaloosa Web site warns, "August in Monticello at the Atwood Water Park may be akin to Satan's own sauna," the festival also promises a weekend of cutting edge entertainment, a generous flow of cold beverages, and an atmosphere in which no one is a stranger. In recent years, Montipaloosa has added children's workshops on drums and guitar playing. Kids of all ages are welcome, although the festival's Web site does suggest that "earplugs may be helpful in keeping this from becoming a learning experience for your five or six year old." Montipaloosa is held the first weekend in August. For this year's line-up of bands, visit www.montipaloosa.com.

Monticello is home to a unique restaurant. Painter Margaret Garrett converted an abandoned dry-cleaning establishment into a French-style bistro and decorated it with her own paintings and photographs and those of other local artists. The result is **Henri's,** a delightful dining experience revolving around seafood, po' boys, and gumbo. Henri's is open for lunch 11:00 A.M.–2:00 P.M. Monday–Friday at 321 West Broad Street.

It's a short drive along U.S. Highway 98 East from McComb to the small community of **Tylertown,** but a visit to Tylertown's **Merry Wood** wilderness resort seems a world away. Owners Ryck and Merry Caplan describe Merry Wood as "a setting where our guests can relax and experience the beauty, solitude, and inspiration of nature in luxury." Secluded Merry Wood is a haven for guests interested in painting, bird watching, and wildlife and nature photography, or for couples who simply crave a romantic getaway. The wooded property encompasses 5 miles of nature trails, a number of tranquil ponds, and organic vegetable and flower gardens. Overnight accommodations are available in the Merry Wood Cottage, a rustic bungalow complete with covered porch, or the Merry Wood Lodge, a contemporary house featuring upstairs and downstairs fireplaces and a deck ideal for stargazing. The Merry Wood Mouse House features a meeting room, exercise facilities, and a comfortable library lined with volumes on ecology, natural history, and philosophy.

Custom packages at Merry Wood include spa services, environmental education programs, guided nature walks, gardening demonstrations, picnics, and candlelight dinners. Rates are based on the number of guests and the length of stay, and begin at $100 per night. Only registered, adult guests are allowed on the property; Merry Wood does not allow children because "we cannot create a childproof wilderness." You'll find Merry Wood tucked into the forest at 26 Dillons Bridge Road. For more information or reservations, call (601) 222–1415 or (866) 222–1415, or visit www.merrywoodcottages.com.

From Tylertown, follow US 98 East into downtown **Columbia,** where the 100-foot-wide Main Street was designed to accommodate horse-and-wagon U-turns. Main Street's **Hill Hardware Company** stocks some 24,000 items, including plows, horse harnesses, and old-fashioned kitchen implements most modern homemakers would be at a loss to put to use. According to proprietor Leon Bohuslav, "If we don't have it, you probably don't need it." Tradition runs deep at Hill's; Bohuslav is only the third proprietor in the store's one-hundred-year history. Browse the goodies at Hill Hardware from an early-bird 5:00 A.M. until 5:00 P.M.

Main Street is also home to the **Marion County Museum and Archives.** This small, volunteer-run museum displays local artifacts but focuses primarily on Marion County genealogy. The museum also houses a Confederate library—the books written, as one volunteer is quick to point out, "by actual Confederates. Nobody from up North."

Columbia's most famous son is former Mississippi Governor Hugh White. Built in 1925, the beautifully restored **Hugh Lawson White Mansion** is the finest example of Spanish Colonial Revival architecture in the state. Located at

1 Governor Hugh White Place, the private home is not open for tours, but its striking architectural lines are visible from the street.

While exploring Columbia, keep an eye out for descendants of Governor White's cherished white squirrels. The governor introduced the squirrels to his estate on Keys Hill more than sixty years ago. The frisky, alabaster-colored animals have since raised several generations of descendants in the Columbia area, and the city has adopted an ordinance protecting the squirrels.

Early exploration maps of the Columbia area include **Red Bluff,** also known as *"Mississippi's Little Grand Canyon."* Formed by the natural erosion of the west bank of the Pearl River near Morgan Town, Red Bluff is made up of colorful layers of sand, gravel, soil, and clay plunging 200 feet into a creek that empties into the river. The landscape around Red Bluff changes constantly; the road atop the bluff has been pushed back twice to accommodate the ever-widening canyon. Hikers will be disappointed to learn that Red Bluff is located on private property, but the unusual formation is easily visible from Mississippi Highway 587 about 15 miles northwest of Columbia.

If you're in the Columbia area on a Saturday or Sunday, take Mississippi Highway 35 South to **Sandy Hook** and the **John Ford House.** Built in 1809, this sturdy structure served as a frontier inn, fort, and territorial post office. The house has withstood not only the ravages of time but the fury of Hurricane Camille to become the oldest building in the Pearl River Valley. The inn was a center of activity in Mississippi's frontier days. Andrew Jackson slept here en route to the Battle of New Orleans, but he was given the best room in the house only after promising to watch his language. Tours take visitors back to the early 1800s, when the inn provided a safe haven from the dangers of the uncharted territory that later became the state of Mississippi. The house is open weekends 2:00–4:00 P.M. Admission is $4.00 for adults and $2.00 for children— a modest sum today, but probably a good deal more than the room rates of the early 1800s. The John Ford Home is open by appointment during the week; call (601) 731–3999.

From Columbia, take Mississippi Highway 13 South to Interstate 59 and head straight for the Mississippi Beach, or continue on US 98 East to Hattiesburg and the Piney Woods.

The Piney Woods

The **Piney Woods** begin at the northern tip of the DeSoto National Forest and stretch south to the Gulf Coast, forming a thick green canopy over the cities and towns in their path. Towering loblollies dominate most of this region's landscape, earning the area the nickname, "the pine belt."

The largest city in this region, **Hattiesburg,** serves as a cultural dividing line. Towns north of Hattiesburg share the traditional southern personality of Jackson, while communities south of Hattiesburg lean toward the casual indulgence of the Gulf Coast. Life on the boundary line is a pleasant mix of both, with the spirited feel of a college town as an added bonus.

US 98 turns into Hardy Street in Hattiesburg, home of the **University of Southern Mississippi.** The campus is located at the intersection of US 98 and U.S. Highway 49, its main entrance marked by the multicolored, fragrant **All-American Rose Garden,** home to some 750 patented bushes.

Curious George and other beloved characters from childhood are preserved and celebrated in the University's **de Grummond Children's Literature Museum.** Housed in the McCain Library, the museum showcases rare children's books and original manuscripts and illustrations. Exhibits are taken

The Unexpected Philanthropist: Oseola McCarty's Gift

When Oseola McCarty died in 1999, she left a legacy of generosity that touched millions.

Ms. McCarty's name became a household word in 1995, when the eighty-six-year-old laundress with a sixth-grade education donated $150,000 to the University of Southern Mississippi.

The gift represented more than half of Ms. McCarty's life savings, earned through seventy-five years of washing and ironing. In August of that year, eighteen-year-old Stephanie Bullock became the first recipient of the Oseola McCarty Scholarship. Through her generous gift, Ms. McCarty had provided for others the education she herself had been denied.

Ms. McCarty received countless honors in recognition of her selfless gift, including the Presidential Citizens Medal, the Wallenberg Humanitarian Award, and an honorary doctorate from Harvard University. The *New York Times* described Ms. McCarty as "living proof to impatient young people that dignity and reward in work is what you make of it." *Newsweek* called her, "a reminder that even the humblest among us can leave the world a better place for having walked on it."

But fame never changed Ms. McCarty. When asked to comment, Mississippi's most famous benefactress said simply, "I'm just proud I'm leaving something positive in this world. My only regret is that I didn't have more to give."

Upon Ms. McCarty's death, Stephanie Bullock, now a USM graduate, said of her, "She was an inspiration, a blessing, a treasure to the entire earth. Heaven couldn't have gotten a better angel."

from the University's de Grummond Collection, one of the largest compilations of children's literature in the world. The de Grummond archives include original manuscripts and illustrations by some 1,200 authors and illustrators and more than 70,000 published children's books dating from 1530 to the present. The museum exhibits are open to the public Monday–Friday 8:00 A.M.–5:00 P.M.; the archives are open by appointment to teachers, librarians, and others with a special interest in children's literature. Call (601) 266–4349 to arrange a visit with some of your oldest and most beloved (albeit fictional) friends.

From the campus main entrance, follow US 49 South to the **Beverly Drive-In Theatre.** The Beverly's towering screen first lit up the south Mississippi night on May 29, 1948, inviting patrons to "dress comfortably and leave your worries behind you." The theater was originally owned and operated by Herby and Sue Hargroder and their young daughters Beverly and Suzette. To say the Hargroders spent their entire lives at the movies is no exaggeration—the family actually lived in a nine-room, 4,000-square-foot home beneath the silver screen. "Miss Sue" Hargroder was determined to run a classy theater geared toward family entertainment. "When you mention a drive-in, everyone thinks of young couples making out, but momma didn't have any of that," Suzette Hargroder recalls. "She would walk around, and if she didn't see two heads, she would ask them to sit up or get out." The Beverly continued to shine for more than thirty years, surviving hurricanes, movie theater multiplexes, and even the invention of the VCR. But following Herby's death in 1980, Sue Hargroder reluctantly admitted she wasn't up to running the theater alone, and the Beverly's gates closed. Other than two unsuccessful attempts by new management and an occasional private screening, the drive-in was dark for the next two decades.

Today, the Beverly once again invites you to "dress comfortably and leave your worries behind you." In 2001, the classic drive-in reopened under the management of N&S Theatres. The refurbished Beverly shows first-run double features 365 days a year; show times vary according to season. For the latest on what's showing at the Beverly, call (601) 544–4101. For performance information plus vintage photos and ads, visit www.beverlydriveinn.com. Then stop by the concession stand for a tub of hot buttered popcorn, settle into the comfort of the family Ford, and enjoy a nostalgic night of entertainment under the stars.

Military buffs and veterans should continue on US 49 South about 12 miles past the Hattiesburg city limits and follow the signs to the **Armed Forces Museum at Camp Shelby.** The $4.5 million museum houses artifacts—most donated by Mississippians—representing every branch of the military and every war in which the United States has fought since the War of 1812. Many of the displays go beyond interactive, actually immersing the visitor in "combat." The disturbingly realistic Trench Experience recreates a battlefield trench from

World War I, complete with life-size soldiers, ear-splitting machine-gunfire, and the acrid scent of smoke and blood. Other exhibits include a signed copy of Hitler's *Mein Kampf,* life-size dioramas, blood-stained maps, thousands of photographs, weapons of every description, and a number of military clocks and watches, all set at just past five o'clock—the hour when officers go off duty.

The Armed Forces Museum is open Tuesday–Saturday, 9:00 A.M.–4:30 P.M. Visitors must agree to a security search before proceeding to the museum, which is located in the heart of Camp Shelby. For more information, call (601) 558-2757.

Head back into Hattiesburg on US 49 North, then west on US 98/Hardy Street to Southern Avenue and the *Hattiesburg Historic Neighborhood District.* The 115-acre area includes a number of architectural marvels built between 1884 and 1930. The focal point of the historic neighborhood is the *Tally House,* a 13,000-square-foot, turn-of-the-nineteenth-century home featuring eleven fireplaces and a two-story, wraparound porch. The grounds are planted with blooming plants and flowers, including more than one hundred colorful species of daylilies.

A mix of well-preserved and restored architectural styles including Neoclassical Revival, Italian Renaissance, and Art Deco earned downtown Hattiesburg inclusion in the National Register of Historic Places as the *Hub City Historic District.* Main, West Pine, Forrest, and Front Streets showcase several public and private buildings reflecting these striking architectural styles.

The district is also home to a number of eclectic galleries and eateries. Browse the contemporary art and jewelry at *A Gallery* (512 Main Street); shop for quilts, photography, sculpture, or paintings at *Gallery RX* (101 Walnut Street); study the contemporary works of William Dunlap, Ed McGowin, and Andy Warhol at *Space 119* (119 East Front Street); see works by Mississippi artists at the *Hattiesburg Arts Council Gallery* (723 Main Street); or browse the weavings, pottery, and stone sculptures at *Impressions Gallery* (113 Newman Street). Follow your taste of the arts with lunch at *Shelby's Coffee Café* (631 North Main Street), *Coney Island Lunch Stand* (400 Main Street), or *206 Front* (206 Front Street), or a treat from the old-fashioned ice-cream bar at the *Walnut Square Pharmacy* (124 Walnut).

If you're more a flea market hound than a gallery buff, spend your shopping time in Hattiesburg at the *Calico Mall,* Mississippi's largest indoor daily flea market, featuring fifty-three shops in a 13,000-square-foot area. Browse the glassware, clocks, clothing, furniture, jewelry, linens, and antiques Tuesday–Friday 10:00 A.M.–5:00 P.M., Saturday 9:00 A.M.–5:00 P.M., or Sunday 1:00–5:00 P.M.

Hattiesburg offers a number of diverse dining options, as well as an active nightlife geared toward the college crowd. Excellent choices for discriminating diners include **The Purple Parrot** and **Crescent City Grill,** both owned by renowned chef and syndicated food columnist Robert St. John. Be sure to pick up a copy of *The Southern Palate,* a mouthwatering coffee table cookbook produced by St. John and gifted Mississippi watercolor artist Wyatt Waters. This delectable volume includes thirty-five Waters watercolors, 130 contemporary southern recipes, and thirteen essays by St. John—a tasty combination Waters describes as "salivational."

Overnight visitors will want to book a room at **Dunhopen Inn.** This elegant bed-and-breakfast is owned and operated by Pat and Billy Allen, who so fell in love with the concept of bed-and-breakfasts as travelers, they decided to build one of their own. The inn's name is drawn from Pat's family history. When her grandfather built his dream home decades ago, he told young Pat he was "done hoping for a home." When construction was completed on her Colonial-style inn in 1997, Pat announced that she was "done hoping for her B&B." Dunhopen offers ten guestrooms, some with fireplaces, furnished with family heirlooms and antiques. The property includes a swimming pool and hot tub. The inn's Grill Room Restaurant serves dinner Tuesday–Saturday and an elegant Sunday brunch. You'll find Dunhopen at 3875 Veterans Memorial Drive (Highway 11). Rates begin at $85. For more information, call (601) 543–0707 or (888) 543–0707.

Hattiesburg is the southern end point of the **Longleaf Trace Rails to Trails,** a 39-mile walking, biking, and roller-blading trail. The Longleaf Trace winds north to south from **Prentiss** to Hattiesburg, following the route of an abandoned Illinois Central Railroad Line. About 80 percent of the 10-foot-wide, paved trail runs through dense forest land, yet hikers and bikers are never more than 4 miles from a house or rest stop. A 26-mile equestrian trail runs adjacent to the paved surface. Dogwoods, wildflowers, and tranquil lakes and ponds line the Longleaf Trace, which is generously populated with beavers, otters, deer, raccoons, possums, and other native wildlife.

canoeblackcreek

Black Creek, Mississippi's only National Wild and Scenic River, winds through Lamar, Forrest, and Green Counties and flows through the Wilderness Area of DeSoto National Forest. Black Creek attracts canoeists and campers from all over the country. For canoeing and canoe rental information, call (601) 582–8817.

Future plans for development along the Longleaf Trace include rest stops, horse stables, snack shops, and mileage and historic markers. An official brochure and map of the trail is available by calling (800) 638–6877 or visiting www.longleaftrace.com.

The trail access and parking lot for the Longleaf Trace in Hattiesburg is located at Jackson Road, just north of West Seventh Street. Adventurers may also access the trail at parking areas in the towns of *Prentiss, Carson, Bass-field, Sumrall,* and *Epley.*

From Hattiesburg, take a short drive north on Mississippi Highway 11 to *Petal* and the *International Checker Hall of Fame* (220 Lynn Ray Road). Yes, the *Checker* Hall of Fame. This museum honoring the venerable board game is housed in the enormous (35,000 square feet) private residence of Robert Walker, the undisputed checkers world champion. The Hall of Fame also houses the Ripley's Believe-It-or-Not largest and second-largest checker-boards in the world. Checkerholics from around the globe travel to Petal to compete in nail-biting tournament play. Competitors make their moves on regulation-size checkerboards, but large pillows positioned on the oversized, checkerboard floor allow visitors to observe every jump from the second-story viewing balcony.

In addition to checkers memorabilia, the Hall of Fame houses an eclectic collection of artifacts and displays related to everything and nothing at all. Exhibits include everything from stuffed game animals to a full suit of armor. The Hall of Fame is open during tournaments and for tours by appointment. Call (601) 582–7090 for directions and to schedule a friendly match with the checker master.

The section of US 49 north of Hattiesburg is punctuated with flea markets, fruit stands, and "outposts" offering canoe trips down *Okatoma Creek.* Billed as Mississippi's only "white water," the Okatoma runs through a series of small waterfalls and rapids as it flows through forests and farmlands. Canoe rentals are about $25 a day and include shuttle service to and from the water. For more information or to book a trip, contact the *Okatoma Outdoor Post* at (601) 722–4297 or *Seminary Canoe Rental* at (601) 722–4301.

Tiny *Seminary* is home to acclaimed potter Claudia Ka Cartee, whose jewel-toned dinnerware and decorative pieces have been shown throughout the South. Claudia's home studio is open by appointment, and with a little advance notice, she usually welcomes drop-ins. Call (601) 722–4948 for directions and to arrange a visit.

From Seminary, continue north on US 49 until you spot the bright yellow wall adorned with lions, tigers, and bears. The *Collins Exotic Animal Orphanage* is exactly what its name implies—a refuge for exotics purchased as "pets," then abandoned when they became too large to manage. As the owner explains, "Foolish people buy a lion cub or a panther and expect to lit-ter box train it. When it weighs several hundred pounds and starts eating their furniture and climbing the walls, they don't want it anymore. If the animals couldn't come here, they'd be destroyed." The $3.00 admission buys a look at lions, tigers, panthers, alligators, and other exotics housed in tiny cages. The view is more close-up-and-personal than in the average zoo, and it's hard to imagine anyone thinking of these powerful, enormous animals as "pets." This is one trip to the zoo that's almost as sad as it is educational.

Take the downtown *Collins* exit off US 49 North to Main Street and *Pope Company.* This grand old department store has survived the Great Depression, two World Wars, and the most serious threat of all—Wal Mart. Pope Company opened for business in 1913 and has remained in the Pope family for three generations. Shoppers find modern-day merchandise from clothing to appliances displayed alongside horse collars, corn cutters, and mule feed. At one time, Pope Company even sold tractors. The hardwood floors, wooden display cabinets, and old-fashioned cash registers are reminders of a time when shopping was more a social event than a hassle; they create a warm, folksy atmosphere that's not for sale at any price. Pope Company welcomes browsers Monday–Friday 7:00 A.M.–5:00 P.M., and Saturday 7:00 A.M.–2:00 P.M.

An interesting dining option awaits down Highway 35 South near the Covington County/Jefferson County line. The tiny Prentiss community is home to *Cowboy Jim's Riverside Restaurant,* a colorful seafood and steak house in a remodeled barn. Nestled between the Bouie River and a tranquil lake graced by cypress trees, Cowboy Jim's picturesque setting is as big an attraction as its steaks and seafood. Patrons are welcome to feed the fish in the lake, watch as the restaurant's flocks of ducks waddle up for a cracked corn treat, or simply relax to the rhythm of the slowly turning water wheel.

Complimentary fish food and fishing poles are provided for younger diners; the property even includes a "worm farm" for kids who prefer to dig their own bait. Located on Highway 35 South in Prentiss, Cowboy Jim's is open Thursday 4:00–9:00 P.M. and Friday–Saturday 4:00–10:00 P.M. Call (601) 765–3125.

It's just a short drive from Collins to *Mt. Olive,* but a visit to the *Old Order German Baptist Community* feels more like a trip through time. Practicing a lifestyle similar to the Amish, the families who work these small farms live a simple life far removed from the hectic pace of the modern world. The German Baptists grow or raise virtually everything they eat, make their own clothing and furnishings, and rely on bicycles or horses for transportation.

You'll discover examples of the German Baptists' fine craftsmanship at *Diehl Bros. Furniture,* which specializes in hand-crafted, custom-made furniture and cabinetry. Owner Bill Diehl will sketch a one-of-a-kind design during your visit, then ship the finished piece home to you. Diehl Bros. also accepts orders by mail. For more information, write to Bill Diehl at 337 Highway 532, Mt. Olive, Mississippi 39119.

If you're traveling with a group of twelve or more, sit down to a memorable lunch or dinner at **Martha's Kitchen.** Meals are served on the Diehl family farm and include fruits and vegetables grown on the property, homemade breads and pies, and freshly churned butter.

Martha's Kitchen also showcases the work of another fine craftsman. Roger Jamison hand weaves distinctive baskets in every shape and size from local wood. The baskets are available in two finishes, natural or a reddish brown that comes from homemade pecan shell dye. Finished baskets are available for sale at Martha's; Roger will also custom-weave a basket in the shape or pattern you prefer. There is no telephone at Martha's Kitchen. For more information about Roger's baskets or to make lunch or dinner reservations, write to Bill and Edith Diehl at 1462 Highway 532, Mt. Olive, Mississippi 39119.

Back on US 49, head just past the Mt. Olive exit to the intersection of US 49 and Jaynesville Road and **Carol's Realistic Dolls & Company.** Housed in the charming white Victorian with the red roof, this antiques, floral, and gift shop is best known for its custom-made dolls. Proprietor Carol Bush creates exquisite, one-of-a-kind dolls made to look exactly like their one-of-a-kind owners. Travelers interested in a look-alike playmate for their daughter or granddaughter have only to provide Carol with photographs; the completed doll will be shipped to their door. Carol's Realistic Dolls & Company also carries several lines of collectible dolls, including Adora, Seymour Mann, Lee Middleton, and the classic Madame Alexander line. Carol's shop is located at 309 Jaynesville Road. For more information or to order a custom doll, call (601) 797–5995.

From Mt. Olive, continue east on Highway 532 to the tiny community of **Hot Coffee.** In the 1800s, weary travelers often parked their horse-drawn carriages at an inn in the area. The innkeeper's wife was known for her homebaked cakes and strong, piping-hot coffee. The inn was referred to as "the Hot Coffee," and eventually, the surrounding area adopted the moniker as well.

Two old-fashioned general stores in Hot Coffee are worth a quick stop. **McDonald's Store** serves up hand-dipped ice cream, R. C. Cola, moon pies, hoop cheese by the slice, and plenty of—you guessed it—hot coffee. McDonald's is closed on Saturday. The **J&H Harper Grocery** in "downtown" Hot Coffee has served the area since the early 1900s and offers souvenir T-shirts, caps, and cups. J&H Harper is closed on Sunday. Both stores are located on Mississippi Highway 532.

Continue east on Highway 532 to US 84, then head east 20 miles to **Laurel.** Along the way you'll pass the Leaf River Church Road turnoff to **Mitchell**

Farms, a pick-your-own vegetable farm operated by Dennis and Nelda Mitchell. As many as 400 people a day show up to pick fresh veggies during June and July, harvest peanuts August through December, and watch Nelda create wood sculptures year-round. Call (601) 765–8609 to find out what's in season.

Entering the elegant, timber-money town of Laurel, continue straight on U.S. Highway 84 East across Sixteenth Avenue until it turns into Fifth Street (streets and avenues are both numbered in Laurel; streets run east-west, avenues north-south). Veer left at Sixth Avenue onto Carroll Gartin Boulevard, then take a left on Fifth Avenue. At the end of the block you'll find the **Lauren Rogers Museum of Art,** Mississippi's oldest and arguably finest art museum. Permanent collections include eighteenth-century paintings and sculpture, an extensive collection of Georgian silver, eighteenth- and nineteenth-century Japanese Ukiyo-e wood block prints, and more than 800 baskets from around the world. The museum was founded as a tribute to Lauren Rogers, a twenty-three-year-old newlywed who died in 1922 following an appendectomy. His family chose his unfinished homesite as the location for a library and museum honoring his memory. The Lauren Rogers Museum of Art is open Tuesday–Saturday 10:00 A.M.–4:45 P.M. and Sunday 1:00–4:00 P.M. Incredibly, there's no admission fee. For information about the museum's collections, changing exhibitions, and special programs and events, call (601) 649–6374 or visit www.lrma.org.

The museum is located in the heart of Laurel's oak-shaded **historic district,** which features the largest collection of turn-of-the-twentieth-century homes in the United States; the entire neighborhood is listed on the National Register of Historic Places. **Wisteria,** one of these lovely homes located just across the street from the Lauren Rogers Museum, is open for tours. This elegant, lavender-hued house features exquisite handmade window glass and period antiques. Tours are by appointment; admission is $3.00. Call (601) 649–6374.

Overnight accommodations are available in the historic district at the **5th Street Bed-and-Breakfast** (601–649–5197), **Hatfield House Bed-and-Breakfast** (601–649–0227), **Laurel Inn Bed-and-Breakfast** (601–428–8773), **Magnolia Oaks Bed-and-Breakfast** (601–425–5561), and **The Mourning Dove** (601–425–2561 or 800–863–3683).

From the museum, take Seventh Street east to Mississippi Highway 15 South and **Landrum's Country Homestead and Village.** This detailed re-creation of an 1800s settlement includes a water-powered gristmill, blacksmith shop, pioneer cabin, schoolhouse, general store, Indian village, and more than thirty-five other painstakingly re-created buildings and displays, all nestled on ten tranquil, landscaped acres. Members of the Landrum family are on hand to conduct personal tours of the village and talk you into sampling a sugary funnel cake or a slice of fresh bread slathered with freshly churned butter. Take a stroll through the past Monday–Saturday 9:00 A.M.–5:00 P.M. Admission is $8.00 for adults and $7.00 for children. Group and package rates are available.

The Homestead began as a project to amuse and educate the Landrum grandchildren. The Landrum family's first love and original business is furniture making. **Landrum's Showroom** on the property is 6,000 square feet of hand-crafted pine furniture, antique reproductions, and unique gifts and home accessories. For more information on Landrum's Country Homestead and Village or Landrum's Showroom, call (601) 649–2546 or visit www.landrums.com.

Continue on Highway 15 South to **Trapper's Gator Farm,** a menagerie of alligators, bobcats, raccoons, snakes, and other native species. Call (601) 428–4967 and ask owner "Trapper" Parker what time he'll be serving dinner at the gator pond—the sight of thirty hungry reptiles devouring whole chickens is one you won't soon forget. But Trapper's isn't all scary—there's a petting area where some of the tamer animals socialize with curious children. In fact, petting is allowed for most of the animals who reside at Trapper's—even some of the gators. Visit them Saturday 10:00 A.M.–4:00 P.M. Admission is $5.00.

From Trapper's, take Highway 15 North back to Laurel and pick up I–59 South to the Gulf Coast. Just south of Laurel you'll see the exit to **Ellisville,** once the capital of the **Free State of Jones.**

Confederate deserter Newt Knight shot Major Amos McLemore, a Confederate soldier sent to capture him, in the living room of the **Deason House** in Ellisville. McLemore's blood seeped into the pine floors, staining them so badly the residents finally covered them with new boards. The ghost of the murdered major is still said to roam the halls of Deason House and the bloodstain occasionally reappears on the floor. Decide for yourself whether Deason House is truly haunted—call the **Ellisville City Hall** at (601) 477–3323 to arrange a tour of the murder scene.

trivia

Mississippi boasts more churches per capita than any other state.

If you're visiting Ellisville overnight, book a room at the historic **Hotel Alice.** Originally opened as a fine hotel in 1902, the Alice played host to timber barons and cattle drivers and was the center of activity in Ellisville, Jones County's first seat. Over the next century, the property served as a boarding house, apartments for World War II veterans, and a boys' dormitory, gradually falling into disrepair. By the time current owners Jan and Eddie Malone bought the Alice in 1999, the once-fine hotel had become a crack house.

The Free State of Jones

The small farm owners of 1860s Jones County resented the notion of fighting a "Planters' War" and sent a representative to the 1861 Mississippi state assembly to vote against secession from the Union. But once in Jackson, the representative was overwhelmed by the near-hysteria sweeping the capital city and instead cast his lot with the secessionists.

Back home, the good citizens of Jones County burned the representative in effigy, formed an independent government, and actually seceded from the Confederacy. Declaring Ellisville their capital and Confederate deserter Newt Knight their leader, renegades from "the Free State of Jones" raided both Union and Confederate supply bases, supposedly practicing such atrocities that Union POWs quartered in Meridian were given arms to protect themselves.

When the city of Laurel dedicated a monument to the soldiers of the Confederacy decades later, most of the money was provided by a northern-born businessman. The benefactor noted the irony of the occasion, remarking, "You see here a handsome monument, erected with Yankee money to the Confederate dead of the Free State of Jones, which seceded from the Confederacy after the Confederacy seceded from the Union."

"I drove by there one afternoon and saw a boy who couldn't have been more than fifteen come out with a bag of drugs," Jan Malone recalls. "I watched him pass them around to his friends, and it broke my heart. I started praying about it, then starting asking other people to do something about it, then finally realized that the Lord wanted *me* to do something about it."

Unfazed by their complete lack of experience in the hotel business, the Malones bought the Alice and began an extensive restoration project. One year and nine 35-yard dumpsters of debris later, they opened the hotel's **Alice Café,** which once again became the center of activity in downtown Ellisville. A year after the cafe served its first meal, Hotel Alice reopened. Restored to its original glory, the inn features nine charming guest rooms, each with a unique theme and distinctive decor. The hotel's original third-floor ballroom is used for parties and other special events. The Malones salvaged the Alice's original windows and skylights, and left a few cracks in the walls to "preserve her character." You'll find Hotel Alice and the Alice Café at 110 Front Street, in the heart of downtown Ellisville. The cafe is open for lunch and dinner. For reservations at this classic, reborn hotel, call (601) 477–9871 or visit www.hotelalice.com.

Continue on I–59 South past Hattiesburg and through pastoral **Poplarville,** where actor and Mississippi native Gerald McRaney and his wife, actor Delta Burke, own a ranch. When you reach the outskirts of **Picayune,** follow the signs to the **Crosby Arboretum**, home to one hundred acres of native plants and trees. Walking trails wind through a savannah filled with carnivorous plants, a wetland thick with cypress trees, and shaded woodlands where azaleas bloom under loblolly pines. The arboretum's Pinecote Pavilion is the first—and so far the only—building in Mississippi to win the American Institute of Architecture's Honor Award for Design Excellence. Get back to nature at the Crosby Arboretum Wednesday–Sunday 9:00 A.M.–5:00 P.M. Admission is $4.00 for adults, $2.00 for children. The Arboretum also hosts a full calendar of lectures, tours, identification classes, plant sales, and workshops covering everything from pine needle basket weaving to bird watching to gardening. For a schedule of events and programs, call (601) 799–2311 or visit www.msstate.edu/dept/crec/camain.html.

Before you leave Picayune for the Mississippi Beach, stop by **Paul's Pastry Shop** (Highway 43 North), the nation's largest shipper of king cakes. These cream cheese and fruit-filled pastries topped with green, gold, and purple frosting are a staple of Mardi Gras celebrations in New Orleans and throughout the South. Each cake is baked with a tiny plastic baby inside; whoever bites the baby has to host the next party, or at least buy the next king cake. Call (601) 798–7457, or to place an order after you've returned home, call (800) 669–5180 or visit www.paulspastry.com.

The Mississippi Beach

From Waveland to Ocean Springs, a chain of resorts, casinos, artists' colonies, and fishing villages is linked by 26 miles of sugar-white sand, the longest man-made beach in the world.

The French, Spanish, English, and Irish have all influenced the Gulf Coast area, resulting in a cheerful, vibrant mix of cultures that encourages and celebrates individuality. The coastal culture also borrows heavily from neighboring **New Orleans,** making an appreciation of food, festivals, and fun virtually mandatory.

Before you reach the beach, you'll have the opportunity to explore outer space with a trip to **NASA's John C. Stennis Space Center** and the **StenniSphere** exhibit center. If you prefer to skip this adventure in favor of heading straight for the shore, take I–59 South from Picayune to Mississippi Highway 43 South, which intersects with U.S. Highway 90 at the beach.

Tours to StenniSphere depart from the Mississippi Welcome Center west of Bay St. Louis on Interstate 10 at exit 2.

StenniSphere exhibits include Fred Haise's Apollo 13 space suit, moon rocks, and a replica of the space shuttle. "Space Believe" offers interactive exhibits for kids, and "1 Main Street, Mars" shows what the future may hold for space pioneers.

The high point of the tour is heading out to the bleachers to experience the deafening roar and earthshaking force of a space shuttle main engine test firing. A single space shuttle engine weighs 7,000 pounds, stands 14 feet tall, and generates enough horsepower to fly two and a half 747 airliners. Prepare to get wet—the *1 million gallons* of water used to cool things down turns to steam quickly, then showers onlookers with a fine, cool mist. StenniSphere is open for free tours daily 9:00 A.M.–6:00 P.M. Memorial Day–Labor Day, and 9:00 A.M.–5:00 P.M. the remainder of the year. If it's the test firing you're really interested in, call (800) 237–1821 to be sure you schedule your visit for a testing time and day.

Following the noisy, high-tech excitement at Stennis, a visit to tiny **Waveland** is quite a contrast. From I–10, take Mississippi Highway 607 South until it turns into US 90 at this pretty little fishing village, your first stop on the beach. Waveland was once a haven for pirates, and much of the local lore revolves around notorious swashbucklers complete with parrots, wooden legs, and buried treasure. It's this cutthroat legacy that gave Waveland's **Buccaneer Bay Waterpark** and **Buccaneer State Park** their names. Summers find the Buccaneer **wave pool** packed with more children than treasure seekers. Buccaneer State Park is located 2 miles off US 90 on South Beach Boulevard. Call (228) 467–3822 for camping information.

It's little wonder that a favorite pastime on the Gulf Coast is cruising oak-studded US 90, the busy scenic route that parallels the beach. From Waveland, follow US 90 East, nicknamed "The Hospitality Highway," into **Bay St. Louis.** Take a right off US 90 at the Casino Magic sign, then take a right onto Main Street and into the heart of Bay St. Louis's **Old Town.**

"Quaint" may be an overused adjective, but there's simply no better word to describe this charming, 3-block area of galleries, shops, and restaurants that earned Bay St. Louis a listing in John Villani's book, *The 100 Best Small Art Towns in America.* The motto here is "Spend a Day in the Bay," and it's a more than welcome assignment.

The forty or so boutiques and eateries in Old Town truly live up to the promise of "something for everyone." Retro fans should make their first stop **Paper Moon** (220 Main Street). Owner, artist, and self-proclaimed pack rat Vicki Lever has accumulated an eclectic collection of vintage goodies, ranging from hats, clothes, and shoes to small appliances, posters, and an impressive collection of rabbit ears, sans their TV sets. Vicki uses these rescued bits and pieces to make one-of-a-kind shadow box collages, paper sculptures, and jewelry. Choose from tray after tray of vintage buttons, charms, and beads, then

Praline Alley

The stretch of US 90 between Bay St. Louis, Mississippi and New Orleans, Louisiana, is marked by countless roadside stands, souvenir shops, and country cafes all hawking one thing—pralines.

Sinfully caloric and sweet enough to make your teeth ache, the praline (repeat after me, "praw-lean") is a staple in every southern cook's repertoire and a mandatory treat when visitingMississippi. Whether your personal preference is gooey, crunchy, or somewhere in between, Mississippi has a praline that's just right for you—that perfect mating of sugar and nuts that will have you buying (and devouring) them by the bagful.

Of course, the best pralines are homemade. So after you've sampled a few of the Mississippi-made variety, test the recipe below in your own kitchen.

Mississippi Pralines

2 cups sugar

1 cup buttermilk

½ teaspoon baking soda

2 tablespoons Karo syrup

2 tablespoons butter or margarine

2½ cups pecans (repeat after me, "puh-cahns")

Cream sugar, milk, soda, salt, and Karo. Boil five minutes, stirring often. Add butter and pecans. Stir for five minutes. Remove from heat. Cool one minute. Beat until creamy, then drop by the teaspoon onto waxed paper. Let sit for five minutes before serving. Enjoy in moderation.

browse among the retro clothing and decorative items while Vicki makes you a pin, bracelet, or pair of earrings. And when she tells you, "It'll be 25," chances are good she means 25 cents, not $25. You'll want to stock up for yourself and do your Christmas shopping here—an original pair of delightfully quirky Paper Moon earrings, handmade while you wait, sells for as little as $5.00.

Other shops worth a visit include ***Bay Crafts*** (107 North Beach Boulevard), where you'll find upscale pottery, jewelry, and artwork created by more than 250 craftspeople; ***The Purple Snapper*** (209.5 Main Street), which bills itself as "a plethora of real cool artists," and carries mosaic tiles, stained glass, metal work, jewelry, and paintings; ***The Sun Porch*** (113 North Second Street), packed with imported pottery and decorative candles; ***Bluewater Beads*** (211 Main Street), where you can purchase handmade jewelry or enroll in a class and make your own; and ***North Beach Interiors*** (104 North Beach Boulevard), purveyor of such necessities as "Wash Away Your Sins" and "Dirty Girl" soaps and bubble baths and "Virgin/Slut" lip gloss sets.

Most of Old Town's shops open around 10:00 A.M. and close around 5:00 P.M., but the second Saturday of every month Old Town stays open into the evening, allowing for browsing under the stars and often featuring live entertainment.

From Old Town, drive (or if the weather's pleasant, stroll) down Beach Boulevard a few blocks east, go past the church, and take a right down Union Street to the **Historic L&N Depot District.** Built in 1928, the old depot is a two-story, mission-style building surrounded by parklike grounds. The restored depot hosts special events, meetings, and private parties. The area surrounding the depot is home to yet more galleries, shops, and restaurants.

Perhaps the most colorful of these attractions is waiting inside the blue house at 214 Bookter Street. This is the former home of the late folk artist Alice Moseley, one of Bay St. Louis's finest treasures. Once Ms. Moseley's Studio, the house is now a museum displaying her work. Ms. Moseley first picked up a paintbrush at the age of sixty-one. Her whimsical scenes of everyday life in the rural South struck a chord. People began purchasing her work, and soon the retired English teacher and Birmingham resident was pursuing painting as a second career.

Ms. Moseley came to Bay St. Louis for a 1989 art show, and never left. She made her home and studio in the little house on Bookter Street until her death in 2004 at the age of ninety-something.

Visitors to the museum see quirky paintings with equally quirky titles, like *Living High, Low, and Middle on the Hog, Three Sheets in the Wind,* and *Coons in Heaven Better Hide Tonight.* Ms. Moseley turned down an offer of $10,000 for her favorite painting, a depiction of her bird dog being welcomed into pet heaven, titled *Until Today, I Thought I Was Folks.*

Ms. Moseley's most popular work is a self-portrait that shows the artist dancing in the street in front of her house, clad in her trademark red beret and patchwork artist's vest. The piece is titled *The House is Blue, but the Old Lady Ain't.*

You can pick up limited edition prints of Ms. Moseley's work, but the originals are no longer for sale. In fact, her son Tim has launched a campaign to buy back her original paintings for the museum established in her honor. Ms. Moseley's former home and museum is open 10:00 A.M. to 4:00 P.M. Monday through Saturday. Call (228) 467–9223 for more information.

Bay St. Louis's restaurants are as varied as its shops and galleries. The depot area is home to a row of eateries serving everything from po' boys to pasta to gourmet coffee. **Benigno's Grocery, Bay City Grill,** and **Flying Cups and Saucers** are all sound dining choices.

More restaurants wait back in Old Town, where you can nosh with the pink flamingoes at **Amelia's on the Bay;** savor the fresh seafood and learn how the po' boy got its name at **Trapani's Eatery;** enjoy lunch or dinner overlooking the water at **Dock of the Bay;** or indulge in a superb cut of meat at **New York New York.** The preferred attire at all Bay St. Louis restaurants (even the fancier ones) is "coast casual."

Located at the eastern edge of the Old Town district, the **Bay Town Inn** is the only area bed-and-breakfast boasting an unobscured view of the water. From the moment you step through the door of this elegant, turn-of-the-twentieth-century inn, owner Ann Tidwell (aided by her toy poodle, Tudor) and innkeepers Roy and Debbie Lain (aided by their Chinese crested powder puff, Jo Jo) will go out of their way to make sure your stay is a pleasant one. Take a close look at the paper sculptures and collages on the walls downstairs—they're original pieces created by Ms. Tidwell's daughter Vicki, proprietor of the Paper Moon. The Bay Town Inn's ten guest rooms are spacious and comfortable, but the inn's real attraction is a breezy front porch shaded by a centuries-old live oak tree that offers a soothing view of the bay. Call (228) 466–5870 or (800) 533–0407, or visit www.baytowninn.com for rates and reservations.

Other bed-and-breakfast inns located in or near Old Town include the **Blue Meadow Inn** (877–952–2900), **The Calais** (888–702–2686), **Captain's Quarters** (228–467–1380), **Heritage House** (888–702–2686), and **The Palm House** (866–467–7256 or www.palmhouse.org). Bed-and-breakfast accommodations are also available in the historic depot district at **The Trust** (800–331–9046).

Before leaving Bay St. Louis, pause for a moment of quiet contemplation at the **Marian and Agony Grotto** on the grounds of **St. Augustine's Seminary.** This inspirational structure was designed and built in 1944 by Thaddeaus Boucree, an artistically gifted, African-American bricklayer. Boucree used debris from a hurricane as his raw material. The words WATCH AND PRAY hang over the arched entrance to the gray stone grotto. Inside, the filtered sunlight illuminates scenes of Jesus in prison prior to the Crucifixion; the Last Supper; and the Resurrection. The exit is adorned with the words PEACE BE TO YOU. The seminary and grotto are located at 122 Seminary Drive just off US 90 in Bay St. Louis. For more information, call (228) 467–6414.

Further inspiration awaits at the **St. Rose De Lima Catholic Church,** where the 9:30 A.M. Mass combines Roman Catholic tradition with uninhibited southern Gospel music. The celebrated church choir performs annually at the New Orleans Jazz Festival. The St. Rose De Lima altar is adorned with an original mural painted by Auseklis Ozols, founder of the New Orleans Academy of Fine Arts. *Christ in the Oak* depicts the Crucifixion and Resurrection. The church welcomes visitors; call (228) 467–7347 for more information.

Across the bridge east of Bay St. Louis, US 90 continues through the equally charming town of **Pass Christian.** (Don't give yourself away as a tourist—it's pronounced "Kris-chee-ann.") This section of US 90 is particularly picturesque, bordered by the beach on one side and stately mansions overlooking the water on the other. Many of these palatial homes were once mere summer retreats, built by wealthy southern planters and New Orleans aristocrats who fled to the Gulf Coast to escape the summer heat and the threat of malaria. Surrounded by ancient live oaks and generations-old camellias and azaleas, most of the homes feature open balconies and wide porches designed to catch the coastal breeze.

Watch for the left turn off US 90 onto Scenic Drive (the road gets a little tricky here—be careful not to wind up headed into traffic). The first building you'll spot is the **Harbour Oaks Inn,** a quaintly weather-beaten bed-and-breakfast that's stood watch over the Pass Christian Harbor since 1860. Call (800) 452–9399 for rates and reservations. You'll pass a handful of upscale art, antiques, and gift shops before arriving in downtown Pass Christian, a tiny cluster of pastel-painted buildings. Just outside downtown you'll discover another bed-and-breakfast, the **Inn at the Pass.** Call (800) 217–2588 for rates and reservations.

When you spot the MERMAID CROSSING sign you'll know you've arrived at **Hillyer House,** Pass Christian's most popular shopping spot. A favorite haunt of *Southern Living* magazine, Hillyer House showcases the work of 200 potters, jewelers, and painters from around the United States. The gallery/shop is open 10:00 A.M.–5:00 P.M. Monday–Saturday and noon–5:00 P.M. Sunday.

Back on US 90, you'll pass still more elegant old homes as you cross into **Long Beach,** another coastal community marked by blue sky, warm breezes, and sun-spangled waters. The beaches here are uncrowded and quiet, dotted with fishing piers stretching far into the Mississippi Sound. Take the exit to the University of Southern Mississippi-Gulf Coast, then drive straight ahead on campus to Hardy Hall and the **Friendship Oak.** According to legend, those who step into the shadow of this 500-year-old live oak tree must "remain friends through all their lifetime, no matter where fate may take them." At 50 feet tall with a 151-foot spread of foliage, the tree casts an enormous shadow indeed. The average length of the Friendship Oak's enormous limbs—which are supported by heavy cables and rest on blocks—is 66 feet from the trunk. A platform nestled high in its branches is a popular spot not only for photos, but for wedding ceremonies. If estimates of its age are accurate, the Friendship Oak was a sapling when Christopher Columbus set sail for the New World. The Friendship Oak is the most famous of the many live oak trees found along the coast. Many of the trees bear names indicating age and wisdom ("Councilor" and "Patriarch," to name a couple) and are registered with the Live Oak Tree Society.

As US 90 crosses into **Gulfport,** the quiet artists' colonies and rustic fishing piers are replaced by the glitz and glitter of floating **casinos** and the hustle and bustle of the Port of Gulfport. Gift shops here sell more T-shirts and seashells than fine art, and the beaches are packed with sunbathers. Gulfport is home to a number of well-marked, modern beach pleasures, including jet ski rentals, pleasure-boat rides, and sailing and deep-sea-fishing charters. Indulge in a banana split in honor of the Port of Gulfport—America's number one banana import terminal. A navigational note—the section of US 90 that runs through Gulfport and neighboring Biloxi is also referred to as Beach Boulevard.

Follow the signs near the Port of Gulfport to the **Marine Life Oceanarium,** where you'll see the trained dolphins, sea lions, and tropical birds put through their paces. The Oceanarium also offers a half-hour train tour of the port, including a look at one of the largest banana terminals in the world. Call (228) 863–0651 for show times and admission prices.

Gulfport also offers excursions to **West Ship Island** 12 miles off the Mississippi mainland. The Mississippi Sound meets the Gulf of Mexico at Ship Island, one of four natural barrier islands that are part of the **Gulf Islands National Seashore.** Clear waters and constant surf make Ship Island the most popular spot for sunbathing and beachcombing on the coast; in fact *USA Today* named the beach at Ship Island one of the top ten in the United States. Snacks, beverages, and chair and umbrella rentals are available, and lifeguards may be on duty

Friendship Oak

Hurricane Camille

Thirty years later, the mere mention of her name still evokes images of death and destruction.

She was Camille, the most violent hurricane in United States history, a furious, howling hussy who tried—almost successfully—to wipe the entire Mississippi Gulf Coast off the map.

The night of Sunday, August 17, 1969, Camille slammed into the Mississippi Gulf Coast, packing 20-foot tides and 205-mile-an-hour winds—the highest in the history of the Western Hemisphere.

Though some 75,000 coastal residents evacuated, hundreds more stayed behind to ride out the storm. After all, the coast had weathered hurricanes before, and few could imagine just how monstrous Camille would be.

The stories of those who stayed behind to battle Camille have become Gulf Coast legend. There was the couple who remained at home "to put out pots and pans in case the skylights starting leaking." They wound up riding out the hurricane atop a 60-foot television antenna after Camille swept their entire house into the sea.

The residents of the Richelieu Manor Apartments in Pass Christian refused to evacuate, despite two visits from the chief of police. Instead they poured cocktails in anticipation of a "hurricane party." According to one of the survivors, there was more praying than drinking going on when Camille finally hit. The three-story Richelieu simply disintegrated; nothing was left but the cement foundation. Twenty-three party-goers joined the death toll.

In Hattiesburg, more than 70 miles north of the Gulf Coast, winds reached 140 miles per hour as Camille flattened most of the pinebelt. Two hundred miles from the storm's

in season. The boardwalk leading to the gulf side of the island is about one-third of a mile, so travel lightly. A word of warning—take *plenty* of sunscreen.

Ship Island is also home to **Fort Massachusetts.** Under construction from 1859 to 1866, the Fort saw limited action during the Civil War. Ship Island, however, was the site of a Confederate POW camp. The island even housed one female prisoner, a New Orleans housewife charged with laughing at a Union officer's funeral procession and teaching her children to spit on Union officers. Guided tours of the fort are available daily March–October, and history buffs can explore the structure anytime on their own.

Excursion boats bound for Ship Island leave the Gulfport Yacht Harbor daily March–October. Call (228) 864–1014 or (866) 466–7386 for the day's schedule. Round-trip excursions are $20.00 for adults and $10.00 for children landfall, Jackson took gusts of up to 67 miles per hour. Camille tore through Tennessee, Kentucky, North Carolina, and into Virginia's Blue Ridge Mountains, where she dumped 27 inches of rain in eight hours—a deluge so heavy, people actually drowned trying to walk in it.

Monday morning, a shell-shocked Mississippi coast awoke to a level of destruction that defied imagination. Pass Christian, Gulfport, and Biloxi had been virtually erased. Four thousand homes had been simply wiped away, leaving nothing but their foundations and an occasional flight of stairs leading heavenward. Dozens of palatial southern mansions that had withstood not only centuries of storms, but the Civil War, were reduced to rubble. The luxury hotels that had looked out over the Mississippi Sound had vanished—1,600 rooms, gone in the blink of Camille's eye.

Shrimp boats rested in sand-filled front lawns up and down the coast. More than 5,000 cars and trucks were damaged beyond repair, including nearly all of the coastal police fleet. What hadn't been washed into the Sound was piled haphazardly in the middle of what was left of U.S. Highway 90.

The coast had been reduced to 260,000 tons of debris, and 129 Mississippians were dead.

But even amidst the terrible wreckage and chaos, there were signs of hope, indicators of a resilient people who would not be beaten by a mere hurricane. As early as one day after Camille's rampage, handwritten signs rose from the debris proclaiming, WE ARE COMING BACK AND WE'LL RISE AGAIN.

And rise again the coast did. A decade later, the *Biloxi Sun Herald* issued a special Camille anniversary edition which juxtaposed photos of the 1969 devastation with shots of rebuilt, better-than-ever roads, homes, businesses, and hotels.

The headline? "Hurricane Camille. She won the battle, but we won the war."

---

ages three–ten. The hour-long ride to the island is an adventure in itself—playful dolphins usually accompany the ferry to its destination.

If you'd prefer a pelican's eye view of the islands, book a flightseeing tour with **Wings of Anglers.** Passengers board a four-seat Cessna 172 for a one-hour flight over the Gulf Islands National Seashore, beachfront casinos, and other coastal landmarks. An experienced, FAA-licensed commercial pilot doubles as your tour guide, providing information on the islands and their history as you soar above the sea. Flights are approximately $45.00 per person, and depart from the Gulfport–Biloxi airport. For more information or to reserve a flight, call (228) 547-3474 or visit www.wingsofanglers.com.

If you're back on the mainland (or back on the ground) by dinnertime, buzz on over to the **Blow Fly Inn,** "where people swarm for fine food." Don't let the name scare you—the Blow Fly is neat and tidy, nestled in a cove over-looking peaceful Bayou Bernard. The family-style restaurant's steaks, ribs, and seafood are indeed tasty, but it's the name that attracts the most attention. The walls are adorned with crayon-colored blow fly cartoons, and each plate comes with a plastic blow fly garnish. You can even purchase a souvenir Blow Fly Inn T-shirt. The Blow Fly Inn is open 11:00 A.M. to 9:00 P.M. Sunday–Thursday, and 11:00 A.M. to 10:00 P.M. Friday–Saturday. Take US 90 to Teagarden Street, turn right on Pass Road, then go left on Washington (watch carefully; it's hard to spot the street sign after dark), which dead-ends at the water and the restaurant.

You'll hardly notice you've left Gulfport and crossed into *Biloxi,* your next stop on US 90. Once a quiet community frequented by families in search of a budget beach vacation (and hung with the unfortunate nickname "Redneck Riviera"), Biloxi is now a hopping resort town offering twenty-four-hour *casino gaming.* Today Biloxi's beaches are packed towel-to-towel and lined with T-shirt shacks, hotels, eateries, miniature golf courses, and tattoo parlors. The steady flow of traffic along US 90 includes colorful casino shuttles and stretch limousines. This is also the place to rent a jet ski, charter a deep-sea-fishing boat, or play golf year-round.

Resort development in Mississippi reached a new level in 1999 with the opening of the palatial *Beau Rivage Casino.* The $650 million "Beau" was designed to be a quintessentially southern resort, complete with an indoor mag-nolia grove. Coastal residents whose yards boasted prize magnolias were offered as much as $80,000 per tree. Money changed hands, yards were re-landscaped, and dozens of the towering, flowering trees, some nearly a century old, were lowered through skylights into the Beau Rivage's spacious atrium.

Alas, the magnolias were not impressed with the Beau's glitz and glam-our. The trees voiced their displeasure, first by shedding their leaves all over the floral carpets, then by dying, despite the best efforts of a team of emer-gency horticulturists.

Today the lobby of the Beau is beautifully landscaped with more casino-friendly trees. Of course, you can still stop and smell the magnolias—you'll just have to leave your seat at the slots to do it.

Like everything else at the Beau, dining here is a rarefied experience. Along with the obligatory casino buffet, the Beau houses a microbrewery, a barbecue joint, an atrium cafe, an Asian noodle factory, an ice-cream parlor, a coffee house, and a couple of snack bars. The Beau's *La Cucina* Italian restau-rant serves up its pasta and pizza on dinnerware custom-designed for the Beau Rivage by renowned Mississippi potter Gail Pittman. More than 4,000 pieces of bamboo were imported from Malaysia to form the walls of the Beau's elegant

Jayne Mansfield's Last Performance

Hollywood bombshell Jayne Mansfield gave her final performance at Biloxi's Gus Stevens Supper Club on June 28, 1967. Patrons from a four-state area flocked to Biloxi to see Mansfield's show, never imagining it would be her last.

In the early hours of June 29, Mansfield was killed on US 90 when the car she was riding in slammed into an eighteen-wheeler. Rumors that Mansfield was decapitated in the wreck persist to this day. A witness to the accident reported seeing a "flying head," which was actually Mansfield's blond wig placed upon a hat form.

sushi bar, **Mikado** (the name means "bamboo veil"). And perhaps the most unusual dining atmosphere on the Coast is found at the Beau's **Port House,** where patrons dine on the finest cuisine while surrounded by a floor-to-ceiling, 120-foot wraparound aquarium populated by more than 4,000 tropical fish and sharks. Accommodations at the Beau are as posh as the restaurants. *Conde Nast Traveler* named Beau Rivage to its annual Gold List of the World's Best Places to Stay and *Travel and Leisure* selected the Beau as the fourth-best leisure hotel in North America.

Fortunately for nongamblers, not everything in Biloxi revolves around a slot machine. Just as you come into town from Gulfport, you'll spot a sign directing you to **Beauvoir,** the last home of Confederate President Jefferson Davis. Davis purchased this seaside estate from a family friend in 1879 for $5,500. Once you step onto the quiet grounds, it's easy to understand why the former president chose to spend the last years of his life writing his memoirs and enjoying the peace and solitude of the coast.

Davis was revered by southern patriots, and in the years following the war, Beauvoir ("beautiful view") hosted a constant parade of veterans and well-wishers—so many visitors, in fact, that neighbors had to lend the Davis family enough food to entertain them. Following Davis's death in 1889, his widow Varina rejected an offer of $100,000 for Beauvoir, instead selling the property to the Mississippi Division of the Sons of Confederate Veterans for $10,000 with the stipulation that Beauvoir be used as a home for Confederate veterans and their families. More than 2,000 residents signed the roster of the Beauvoir Confederate Soldiers' Home, including several former slaves who fought for the Confederacy. In 1941, the main house was opened as a shrine honoring Jefferson Davis. In 1957, the last two war widows were moved to a nursing home, and Beauvoir, its outbuildings, and grounds became a museum. The estate is still owned and managed by the Mississippi Division, United Sons of Confederate Veterans, who operate the attraction under the name "Beauvoir, the Jefferson Davis Home and Presidential Library."

The Beauvoir tour begins in the Presidential Library, which houses exhibits about the life of Jefferson Davis, a theater that screens the film *Jefferson Davis—An American Son,* and a research library. Artifacts and exhibits give visitors a complete picture of Davis's life, tracing his sorrowful journey from American war hero to Confederate president to war criminal. Prior to the southern secession, Davis was a revered U.S. senator who also served as the U.S. Secretary of War. He had no inkling that the fine army he built would soon march against him. At the war's end, Davis was imprisoned and indicted for treason. In 1868, charges against him were dropped and he was released from prison. Pardon was an option, but Davis refused to ask for a pardon for "an offense I have not committed." Jefferson Davis remains the only former U.S. Secretary of War whose death has not been marked by the lowering of the U.S. flag to half-mast.

Davis was finally restored to U.S. citizenship in 1978, during the presidency of Jimmy Carter. The joint resolution restoring his status as an American citizen is displayed in the Presidential Library. Other artifacts include clothing and personal belongings; first editions of Davis's published memoirs; letters and manuscripts penned by Davis and his beloved wife Varina; funeral programs and flowers; and Davis's death mask. Words from many of Davis's speeches are stenciled on the walls. In his last public address in 1888, Davis appeared to have reconciled not only with the Confederate defeat, but with his own painful past, telling the crowd: "The past is dead; let it bury its dead, its hopes and aspirations. Before you lies the future—a future of golden promise, a future of expanding national glory, before which all the world shall stand amazed. Let me beseech you to lay aside all rancor, all bitter sectional feeling, and to make your places in the ranks of those who will bring about a consummation devoutly to be wished—a reunited country."

The Beauvoir mansion itself contains original and antique furnishings and Davis family possessions, including several Davis family portraits. The fifty-seven-acre property includes a cemetery where nearly 800 soldiers who followed Davis in life are buried. Davis's father, Samuel Emory Davis, was re-interred in the Beauvoir cemetery in 1942. The ***Tomb of the Unknown Confederate Soldier*** stands just outside the cemetery. An inscription on the tomb written by Father Abram Ryan, poet laureate of the Confederacy, reads, AND TEARS SHOULD FALL FORE'ER O'ER ALL WHO FELL WHILE WEARING THE GRAY FOR US. Located at 2244 Beach Boulevard, Beauvoir is open daily 9:00 A.M.–5:00 P.M. March 1–October 31, and

9:00 A.M.–4:00 P.M. November–February. Admission is $7.50 for adults; $6.75 for AAA members, active military personnel, and visitors sixty-five or older; and $4.50 for·students.

The troops march again each October during the Beauvoir **Fall Muster,** which features military drills and Confederate campsites. Be warned—the crowd of observers is highly partisan. Shouts of "Go get 'em Rebs!" fill the air, and those in Yankee garb are sometimes subjected to cheerful heckling. Call (228) 388–9074 for this year's reenactment date, or check the Beauvoir Web site at www.beauvoir.org. Civil War buffs may also want to stop by Biloxi's **Church of the Redeemer,** where Davis's pew is still preserved.

As you continue east on US 90, you'll pass another Civil War–era landmark, the **Father Ryan House.** Now a bed-and-breakfast inn, the house is hard to miss—it's the one with a towering palm tree growing out of the front steps. Built in 1841, the house was the home of Father Abram Ryan, poet laureate of the Confederacy. It was here that Father Ryan composed his best-known poems, *Sea Rest* and *Sea Reverie.* A well-known and revered figure during the Civil War, Father Ryan even made an appearance in the epic novel *Gone With the Wind.* Author Margaret Mitchell wrote that, "Father Ryan, the poet-priest of the Confederacy, never failed to call when passing through Atlanta. He charmed gatherings there with his wit and seldom needed much urging to recite his *Sword of Lee* or his deathless *Conquered Banner,* which never failed to make the ladies cry." The house and grounds of the Father Ryan House have been painstakingly restored and furnished in keeping with the

Father Ryan House

antebellum and Civil War period. Rates at the bed-and-breakfast begin at $100; tours of the house are free. For reservations, call (228) 435–1189 or visit www.frryan.com.

Continuing on US 90 you'll spot the 65-foot *Biloxi Lighthouse,* the only lighthouse in the United States beaming from smack in the middle of a four-lane highway. Built in 1848, the 48-foot structure has survived not only the Civil War, but sixteen hurricanes. Take a left at the lighthouse and follow the signs to the *Biloxi Visitors Center,* operating in the 1895 Brielmaier House. Leave your car at the visitors center and enjoy a stroll through the city's historic district.

Begin your tour at the *Ohr–O'Keefe Museum of Art* located on the second floor of the Biloxi Public Library. The building is easy to spot—it's the angular, thoroughly modern structure in the middle of the historic district, and its entrance is marked by a giant, mustachioed archway labeled "Mr. Ohr's Neighborhood." George E. Ohr was a colorful Biloxi folk artist of the 1890s whose eccentric behavior and two-foot-long mustache earned him the nickname "the Mad Potter of Biloxi." Ohr supported his wife and ten children through sales from his small shop, aptly named the "Pot-Ohr-E." His contemporaries described Ohr as "one fork short of a place setting," a reputation he cultivated in order to draw attention to his art. Photos of Ohr would seem to indicate that his talent for facial contortioning was on par with his gift for throwing pots.

Ohr was frustrated by critics who didn't appreciate his "mud babies," and at one time even buried a cache of pots in hopes a more "enlightened" generation would unearth them. That future generation has arrived. In 1968, a respected art and antiques dealer purchased 7,000 pieces of Ohr's pottery and offered it for sale in New York, turning the art world on its collective ear. Ohr came to be known as the "father of American pottery," recognized for his innovative sculptural vessels with unusually thin pinched, crimped, and fluted walls. Dismissed by his contemporaries, Ohr is now celebrated as a genius; his pots have sold for as much as $100,000.

The Ohr Cultural Center houses a permanent collection of 250 of the Mad Potter's original works, the largest public collection of Ohr pottery in the world. A gift shop—appropriately known as Ohriginals—sells pottery and art. Join the madness at the Ohr Center Monday–Saturday 9:00 A.M.–5:00 P.M. Admission is $6.00 for adults, $5.00 for seniors, and free for children under twelve.

Ground has been broken for a new Ohr–O'Keefe Museum campus designed by Pritzker Prize–winning architect Frank Gehry. The $16 million, 25,000-square-foot museum will feature African-American folk art and history and contemporary regional art as well as works by the father of American pottery. The *Pleasant Reed House,* currently located in downtown Biloxi, will be moved to the Ohr–O'Keefe campus. Born a slave, Pleasant Reed was the first African American to build and own his own home in Mississippi. On an interesting side note, Ohr's grandson, Joe Moran, operates **Moran's Art Studio** in Biloxi near the visitor center. The studio gallery displays original paintings by Joe Moran, whose work has been exhibited in the Smithsonian, as well as Ohr pottery and prints of coastal scenes.

From the Ohr–O'Keefe Museum, stroll through the **Rue Magnolia Walking Mall**. The oak-shaded complex is home to **Mary Mahoney's Old French House**, the coast's legendary courtyard restaurant. The building and old slave quarters remain much the same as when they were originally constructed in 1737; the towering **Patriarch Oak** in the courtyard is estimated at 2,000 years old. And if the ambience isn't enough to inspire a visit, the seafood and steaks at Mary Mahoney's are nothing short of delicious. Ms. Mahoney once catered a party for President Ronald Reagan on the White House lawn; an autographed photo of Mary with the President still hangs in the restaurant.

> ## trivia
>
> Mary Mahoney's Old French House restaurant is featured in John Grisham's bestsellers *The Runaway Jury* and *The Partner*.

In 1985, the city of Biloxi even hosted a "Mary Mahoney Day" in honor of its most famous restaurateur. The restaurant complex includes several dining rooms in the main house, open-air dining in the brick-walled courtyard, two lounges (one in the old slave quarters), a sidewalk cafe open twenty-four hours a day, and the Magnolia Memories gift shop. Call (228) 374–0163.

Across the mall from Mary Mahoney's you'll spot the **Magnolia Hotel**, a fashionable coastal retreat built in 1847 for a cost of $2,500. The oldest hotel on the Gulf Coast no longer rents rooms, but does house the **Mardi Gras Museum**, a collection of colorful costumes and memorabilia donated by royalty of the coast's Mardi Gras krewes. The museum is open 11:00 A.M.–4:00 P.M. Monday–Saturday. Admission is $2.00 for adults, $1.00 for seniors and students. You can see the krewes in action each February or March, when **Mardi Gras** parades roll through Biloxi and other coastal communities. Mardi Gras on the Gulf Coast is equally colorful but a little more family-oriented (read "tame") than the same celebration in neighboring New Orleans. For dates and parade routes, contact the Gulf Coast Carnival Association at (228) 432–8806.

Back on US 90 you'll spot one of the coast's antebellum summer homes, **Tullis-Toledano Manor.** Built in 1856 by a wealthy New Orleans cotton broker, the manor is now open for tours 11:00 A.M.–4:00 P.M. Monday–Saturday. Admission is $2.00 for adults, $1.00 for seniors and children. The house shares the two-and-a-half-acre property with the 600-year-old ***Councilor Oak,*** which once provided shade for Indians and early explorers.

Continue on US 90 to Point Cadet Plaza and the ***J. L. Scott Marine Education Center.*** The $5.00 admission buys a look at some forty aquariums, including the 42,000-gallon Gulf of Mexico tank. Point Cadet is also home to the ***Maritime and Seafood Industry Museum,*** where exhibits depict not only the history and growth of the seafood business along the coast, but how the industry influenced the culture and lifestyle of its people. A film on devastating Hurricane Camille plays on the hour. Admission is $5.00 for adults, $4.00 for seniors and $3.00 for children. The museum is open Monday–Saturday 9:00 A.M.–4:30 P.M. The museum operates two replica sailing schooners, the *Glenn L. Swetman* and the *Mike Sekul,* both of which are available for daylong, half-day, or sunset cruises on the Mississippi Sound. Call (228) 435–6320 for cruise information and reservations. Another testimony to the significance of seafood to coastal history is ***St. Michael's Catholic Church,*** where the roof is a giant oyster shell and stained-glass windows depict the apostles as fishermen.

For an up-close-and-personal look at the seafood industry, head to sea on the ***Biloxi Shrimping Trip.*** You'll sail into coastal waters on a real shrimping expedition with an experienced crew, who'll identify specimens caught during the voyage. The Biloxi Shrimping Trip leaves from Slip #104 at the Biloxi Small Craft Harbor. For sail days and times, rates, and reservations, call (228) 385–1182 or (800) 289–7908.

Seafood's contribution to the local economy is celebrated each spring during the ***Biloxi Shrimp Festival and Blessing of the Fleet.*** The festivities begin with a mass at St. Michael's Catholic Church, followed by a huge shrimp festival at Point Cadet Plaza. Following the crowning of the Shrimp King and Queen, activities move to the Biloxi harbor, where commercial vessels and pleasure boats parade past a "blessing boat." The Catholic bishop sprinkles each gaily decorated craft with holy water to ensure a safe and plentiful fishing season. Call (228) 435–5578 for this year's blessing and festival dates.

The Gulf Coast is home to a number of other festivals celebrating everything from antiques to sand castles. One of the largest parties is the annual ***Cruisin' the Coast.*** Thousands of classic cars descend on the Coast every October for this five-day event featuring classic auto shows and competitions, parades, and big-name entertainment. Approximately 4,000 registered cars from thirty-five states cruise Beach Boulevard en route to celebrations in Bay St. Louis, Long Beach, Gulfport, D'Iberville, Biloxi, and Ocean Springs. Call (228) 385–3847 for dates and details.

Overnight accommodations in Biloxi range from posh casino resort hotels to vacation cottages to historic inns. Splendid bed-and-breakfast

Little-Known Facts about Southern Mississippi and the Gulf Coast

The world's first can of condensed milk was produced in Liberty, Mississippi, by inventor Gail Borden.

A plane carrying the rock group Lynyrd Skynyrd crashed just south of McComb on October 20, 1977, killing six.

The Pioneer Aerospace Corporation of Columbia is the world's largest manufacturer of parachutes.

Columbia's Walter Payton was the first football player ever featured on a Wheaties cereal box.

Hattiesburg's Camp Shelby is the largest National Guard Training facility in the United States.

Leontyne Price of Laurel was the first African American to achieve international stardom in the world of opera, performing with the New York Metropolitan Opera.

Before monster storm Camille in 1969, the Mississippi Coast weathered major hurricanes in 1893, 1901, 1915, and 1947.

Astronaut Fred Haise of Biloxi was aboard the ill-fated flight to the moon immortalized in director Ron Howard's *Apollo 13*.

Confederate President Jefferson Davis was restored to U.S. citizenship in 1978—during the presidency of Jimmy Carter.

Barq's Root Beer was invented in 1898 by Edward Barq of Biloxi.

New Orleans may have made it famous, but Mardi Gras was first celebrated in the New World in Mississippi. The original "Fat Tuesday" was observed in 1699 by explorer Pierre LeMoyne d'Iberville and his crew at Fort Maurepas in Ocean Springs.

The rarest of North American cranes, the Mississippi sandhill crane lives in a protected area in the grassy savannahs of Jackson County. The county's annual Crane Festival attracts naturalists from around the country.

accommodations await at ***Green Oaks*** (580 Beach Boulevard), a lovely antebellum retreat believed to be Mississippi's oldest remaining beachfront residence. Owner Jennifer Diaz has completely renovated this elegant southern mansion, creating a *Gone With the Wind* experience with the added pleasure of a tranquil beach view. Nestled on two acres of beautifully landscaped grounds, Green Oaks' amenities include a breezy balcony facing the sea, comfortable rooms furnished in antiques, and mint juleps guaranteed to take the edge off. Green Oaks has been featured in more than twenty national magazines, including *Southern Living, Travel Holiday, Travel and Leisure,* and Delta Airlines' *Sky.* Rates begin at $140. Call (888) 436–6257 or (228) 436–6257, or visit www.gcww.com/greenoaks.

Cross the bridge east of Biloxi and you'll find yourself in **Ocean Springs,** a tranquil artists' colony so peaceful and so serene it's as if the crowded resorts just 3 miles to the west don't even exist.

Take a right off US 90 (known within the Ocean Springs city limits as Bienville Boulevard) onto Washington Avenue and you'll find yourself in Ocean Springs's charming business district. Washington Avenue crosses Robinson Avenue and Government Street, then runs 4 more blocks before dead-ending at the beach. An easy stroll, on these three streets you'll discover dozens of quaint shops, restaurants, galleries, and artists' studios.

Choose a striking and useful piece from the **Magnolia Bay Craft Mall** (902 Washington Avenue); take care of all your Christmas shopping at **Salmagundi Gift** (922 Washington Avenue); browse the antiques at **Minerva's Antiques and Fine Arts** (619 Washington Avenue); or try on the distinctive ladies' apparel at **Bayou Belle** (622 Washington Avenue). Enjoy the paintings and prints at the **Local Color Gallery** or **Local Color Too** (1101 and 1141 Robinson Avenue); admire the glazes at **Mississippi Mud Works** (1009 Government Street); watch as pewter smiths meld original tableware and sculptures at **Ballard Pewter Ltd.** (1110 Government Street); or shop for one-of-a-kind home accessories and gifts at **Art and Soul** (1304 Government Street).

Kids and grown-ups alike will enjoy a fun-filled visit to **Miner's Toy Stores** (927 Washington Avenue), five-time winner of the Playthings National Award, the highest honor in the toy industry. In addition to virtually every game, toy, and doll imaginable, Miner's sells collectible Civil War toy soldiers, handcrafted of pewter by local artist and historian Ron Wall. According to owner Maryalice Miner, "We can't keep enough of Robert E. Lee, but we've got plenty of Grants."

A co-op gallery operated by the Ocean Springs Art Association, **The Art House** features hand-painted rugs, sculpture, pottery, paintings, and weavings by thirty working artists, with two artists in residence every day. A tour of The Art House doesn't stop indoors; the outdoor sculpture garden features whimsical statues made entirely of found objects. Located at 921 Cash Alley, The Art House is open Monday–Saturday 10:00 A.M.–4:30 P.M. Call (228) 875–9285.

If all that shopping and strolling leaves you hungry, you're still in the right place. Downtown Ocean Springs is home to several eateries and snack shops every bit as eclectic and charming as its boutiques and galleries. **Martha's Tea Room** (715 Washington Avenue) offers sandwiches, salads, and homemade desserts in a cozy atmosphere; the **Bayview Gourmet** (1210 Government

Street) serves scrumptious breakfast and lunch specials on a sunny outdoor patio; and the ***Tato Nut Shop*** (1114 Government Street) is the state's sole purveyor of doughnuts made from potatoes. Sinful treats are also available at the ***Candy Cottage*** (702 Washington Avenue), where the pralines are made fresh in the front window, and at ***Le Croissant French Bakery Café*** (612 Washington Avenue), where the owner's accent and the enormous French pastries are guaranteed to make you think you've awakened in gay Par-eee.

You'll appreciate Ocean Springs's artistic legacy even more after a visit to the ***Walter Anderson Museum of Art*** (510 Washington Avenue). Creative types have been drawn to Ocean Springs for centuries, but the town's most famous son was eccentric painter Walter Inglis Anderson (1903–1965). Anderson was known for his vivid paintings and block prints depicting the rich plant and animal life of the Gulf Coast, its marshes, and wetlands.

The artist spent much of the last eighteen years of his life on Horn Island, one of a group of barrier islands that now make up the Gulf Islands National Seashore. Anderson would row the 12 miles from the mainland to the island in a small skiff, carrying minimal necessities and his art supplies. He lived on the uninhabited island for weeks at a time, working in the open and sleeping under his boat in blistering summers, freezing winters, and through hurricanes. Anderson painted and drew a multitude of the island flora and fauna species, crawling through wild thickets on hands and knees and lying submerged in lagoons to more fully "realize" his subjects.

trivia

Artist Walter Anderson's son, John, was the first park ranger assigned to the Gulf Islands National Seashore. This national park includes Horn Island, Walter Anderson's greatest source of inspiration.

In the early 1950s, Anderson began retreating for weeks at a time to a tiny cottage in Ocean Springs to work in solitude. When his family opened the cottage after his death in 1965, they discovered brilliant murals painted on every inch of the walls and ceiling. The entire "little room" mural, which depicts a coastal day from sunrise to sunset crowned with a brilliant zinnia on the ceiling, has been moved to the museum. Hundreds of Anderson's watercolors, drawings, oils, block prints, ceramics, and carvings are all represented in the museum's permanent collection. *The Islander,* an award-winning film shown in the museum theater, reveals more about Anderson's unusual life and timeless art.

The museum adjoins the ***Ocean Springs Community Center,*** the interior walls of which Anderson adorned with brilliant murals. Anderson worked on the spectacular, 3,000-square-foot murals from 1951 to 1952, charging the community $1.00 for his efforts. The murals are appraised today at more than $1 million. Look for the slightly darker blue jay in the upper left corner as you face the stage. It was painted by Anderson's wife, Sissy.

The Walter Anderson Museum of Art is open Monday–Saturday 9:30 A.M.– 5:00 P.M., and Sunday 12:30–5:00 P.M. May–September; and Monday–Saturday 9:30 A.M.–4:30 P.M., and Sunday 12:30–4:30 P.M. October–April. The museum stages changing exhibits, many featuring the work of other significant artists, and offers a full calendar of workshops, lectures, and special events. For more information, call (228) 872–3164 or visit www.walterandersonmuseum.org.

If you'd like to take a piece of Anderson's genius home, choose a print from the museum gift shop, the *Local Color Gallery,* or *Realizations, the Walter Anderson Shop* (1000 Washington Avenue), which also carries clothing featuring Anderson's work. *Threadneedle Street* (619-A Washington Avenue) carries Anderson designs for cross-stitch kits and needlepoint.

Walter Anderson is the most famous member of an entire family of gifted artists. Walter's talented brother Peter established *Shearwater Pottery* in 1928. Shearwater is still a family affair, now run by Peter's son James. The very picture of an artists' colony, the twenty-four-acre Shearwater compound includes a studio and gallery housed in rustic cabins and surrounded by thick green woods. The pottery collection includes dinnerware, vases, and sculpture. Pieces and table settings can be custom ordered, but don't expect to receive your shipment in the usual five to seven business days. Each piece is an individual work of art, and Shearwater Pottery doesn't do rush orders. Art lovers from around the world have sought out the remote colony in this tiny seaside village. Comments in the guest book include, "I loved the woods," "I could have stayed all day," "Dazzled," and "Expensive, but worth it."

Follow the signs from Washington Avenue past the Ocean Springs harbor and across the bridge to the Shearwater complex, located at 102 Shearwater Drive. The showroom is open Monday–Saturday 9:00 A.M.–5:30 P.M. and Sunday 1:00–5:30 P.M. The workshop is open weekdays from 9:00 A.M.–noon and 1:00–4:00 P.M. Ocean Springs honors Shearwater's founder the first weekend of November during the spectacular *Peter Anderson Arts and Crafts Festival.* Fine artists from eighteen states display and sell paintings, pottery, woodcrafts, jewelry, and furniture in downtown Ocean Springs. For more information call the Ocean Springs Chamber of Commerce at (228) 875–4424.

The work of yet another talented Anderson descendant graces the wall at Washington Avenue and Bowen Avenue in downtown Ocean Springs. Christopher Inglis Stebly, Walter Anderson's grandson, was commissioned to paint a mural commemorating Ocean Springs' 300th anniversary. Titled **Ocean**

Springs: Past, Present, and Future, the 80-foot mural is a bright, joyous tribute to life in this vibrant coastal city.

No trip to Ocean Springs would be complete without a visit to **Crooked Feather.** In 1976, Hungarian sculptor Peter Toth presented the city of Ocean Springs with a massive carving of an Indian head christened "Crooked Feather." Toth spent four months in Davidson Park on US 90 carving the 30-foot-tall monument out of a 2,000-year-old cypress log.

Crooked Feather was one of a family of sixty-seven Indian sculptures carved by Toth throughout North America. The artist traveled the continent from 1982 to 1988, carving at least one statue in every state in the nation and two in Canada. Toth referred to the sculptures collectively as the "Trail of the Whispering Giants." Each statue was a gift to the community in which it was carved; Toth expected no pay for his work.

Crooked Feather faithfully guarded the entrance to Ocean Springs at Davidson Park on US 90 for twenty-four years. Alas, time and weather took their toll on the cedar carving, and in 2000, Ocean Springs officials chose to replace it. Ocean Springs sculptor Thomas King was given the honor of creating the new Crooked Feather. Following two months of King's hard work, a new Crooked Feather carved of cypress was unveiled on the same site as the original.

Founded in 1699, Ocean Springs is one of the oldest cities in the United States. Three centuries ago, Pierre LeMoyne d'Iberville stepped ashore at Ocean Springs and claimed the area for France. The annual **Landing of d'Iberville** celebrates this momentous event with a spring historical ball and pageant and a full-scale reenactment of the landing at a replica of the French **Fort Maurepas** located on the beach at the foot of Jackson Avenue (1 block west of Washington Avenue).

Those interested in a more in-depth study of Ocean Springs' three-century history can take a narrated walking tour through time. **Ocean Springs Historic Walking Tours** guide visitors down oak-shaded streets, past historic homes and churches, and deep into this seaside city's storied past. Walking tours are $8.00 for adults and $4.00 for children under twelve. Call (228) 875–4424 or (228) 872–1289 to arrange your stroll through history.

More active visitors may prefer to bike their way through Ocean Springs along the **Live Oaks Bicycle Route.** This 15.5-mile route departs from the Old L&N Train Depot, winds through the streets of downtown, and leads to the Davis Bayou Area of Gulf Islands National Seashore before returning to the depot. Bikers can pick up a map of the route at the Ocean Springs Chamber of Commerce (1000 Washington Avenue) or simply follow the green-and-white designated bike route signs located on the right side of the city streets.

The Heat Is On

Mississippi is hot.

Oh, forecasters may try to soften the blow with euphemisms like "sultry," "balmy," or the highly understated "very warm," but take my word for it, the best description for Mississippi in the summertime is "sweltering."

Temperatures reach the upper nineties before noon. The sun is relentless, the breeze, nonexistent. And humid? You almost need scuba gear just to breathe.

When we describe summer conditions in Mississippi to our friends "up North," they invariably ask (with a look of horror), "How on earth can you live there?"

So, how do Mississippians cope with a summer heat index that seems perpetually stuck at 110? Well, from June through September we pretty much stay indoors and give thanks for air conditioning and iced tea.

But when October rolls around, we breathe a sigh of relief and celebrate the crisp days and brilliant colors of fall. Come January, we marvel at the plight of northerners up to their eyeballs in snow and wonder if we'll really need to take a jacket with us on our daily stroll. And in early March, when most of the country is still looking forward to another six weeks of snow and ice and slush, we see the first of our spring flowers in bloom.

Truth is, while we may complain about it, Mississippians have long since made peace with the heat. It's a small inconvenience that's simply part of life here in the Deep South—a life most of us would never trade for an existence in a winter wonderland.

Let a little heat and humidity run us diehard southerners out?

When Mississippi freezes over.

Ocean Spring hosts several popular festivals and annual events. Held every March, the **_Herb and Garden Festival_** features plant sales, herbal crafts, foods, remedies, nature walks, and live entertainment. During the Labor Day weekend **_Art Walk_**, downtown businesses, galleries, and restaurants host artists displaying their work and demonstrating their crafts. And in the fall, the highly original **_Scarecrow Contest_** finds the town populated by themed straw men. For specific dates and more information on all Ocean Springs events, contact the Ocean Springs Chamber of Commerce at (228) 875–4424.

Ocean Springs is home to a number of restaurants welcoming hungry travelers, most specializing in—you guessed it—fresh seafood. Enjoy lunch or dinner with a view at **_Anthony's Under the Oaks,_** an elegant eatery nestled among 400-year-old oaks overlooking Fort Bayou. The upscale menu includes steak, seafood, and veal. Anthony's serves dinner Tuesday through Saturday and kicks off the week with a Sunday champagne brunch—the corks start popping at 11:30 A.M. Anthony's is located at 1217 Washington Avenue north of US 90.

Another local favorite is *Jocelyn's,* housed in the hard-to-miss, bright fuchsia cottage on US 90. When the popular Ocean Springs restaurant known as Trilby's changed hands some years ago, cook Jocelyn Mayfield decided to take her recipes and strike out on her own. She transformed her in-laws' small house into a restaurant, painted it pink, and opened her doors to diners hungry for her sophisticated approach to seafood, beef, and chicken. Jocelyn's is open for dinner 5:00–9:00 P.M. Wednesday–Thursday and 5:00–10:30 P.M. Friday–Saturday.

Other excellent dining choices include *Al Fresco's Italian Bistro* (708 Washington Avenue), where the "pastabilities" are endless and the bar is described as the "classiest on the Coast"; *Aunt Jenny's Catfish Restaurant* (1217 North Washington Avenue), where the catfish, fried chicken, and shrimp are served with a bayou view; *Germaine's* (1203 Bienville Boulevard), a Coast fine-dining classic; and *Phoenicia Gourmet Restaurant* (1223 Government Street), the place to go for an authentic Greek or Lebanese lunch or dinner.

Continue on US 90 East to the well-marked entrance to the Mississippi headquarters of the *Gulf Islands National Seashore.* The national seashore extends some 150 miles from Mississippi to Florida. The Mississippi portion of this national park begins at *Davis Bayou* on the mainland, then stretches into the Mississippi Sound to include the *Barrier Islands of West Ship, East Ship, Horn,* and *Petit Bois.* West Ship and East Ship Islands were originally one; Hurricane Camille split the island in two in 1969. Horn Island—a favorite inspiration of artist Walter Anderson—and Petit Bois Island have been designated wilderness areas by the U.S. Congress. Protected from development and human interference, these islands provide habitats for uncommon species of birds, animals, and marine and plant life.

The headquarters at Davis Bayou includes miles of secluded marshlands brimming with wildlife, a campground, picnic shelters, nature trails, and boat launches. Misty mornings are prime time for bird-watchers, photographers, and fishermen. The marsh provides a home for creatures representing every level of the food chain. From industrious fiddler crabs to stately great blue herons to inquisitive alligators, you're sure to spot something scurrying, splashing, or flying in every corner of the bayou at every hour of the day. The Davis Bayou visitors center houses exhibits describing the flora and fauna of the mainland marshes and the islands.

There's no beach at Davis Bayou, but excursion boats departing from Gulfport transport visitors to the swimming and recreational beaches at West Ship Island daily during spring, summer, and fall. Information about charter boats licensed to ferry adventurous explorers and campers to the wilderness islands is available at the visitors center and at the Ocean Springs Chamber of Commerce.

Ocean Springs is home to several tranquil bed-and-breakfast inns that provide a welcome break from the road. The *Acorn Cottages at Centennial Oak* (228–875–4963); the *Carriage House at Bayou Oaks* (228–818–2946); *The Eaves* (228–875–8173); *Oak Shade* (228–872–8109 or 888–875–4711); *Shadowlawn* (228–875–6945); or the *Wilson House* (228–875–6933 or 800–872–6933) are all excellent choices.

Travelers with a daredevil streak may want to make a side trip to *Moss Point* for an adventure that's both off and *above* the beaten path. *Gold Coast Skydivers* promises a spectacular view of the Mississippi Gulf Coast from 14,000 feet in the air. The company offers a variety of skydiving thrills for beginners and experienced jumpers. Their most popular is the tandem jump—following a mere ten minutes of instruction, you'll be strapped to an instructor and the two of you will jump out of a perfectly good airplane. A videographer is on hand to document your plummet from the skies. Jumps are generally offered weekdays by appointment and weekends 9:00 A.M. until sunset. The plane leaves from Trent Lott International Airport, 8301 Saracennia Road. For more information or to take the plunge, contact Gold Coast Skydivers at (228) 474–1144 on weekends or (800) 796–7117 weekdays, or visit www.goldcoastskydivers.com.

If you prefer to keep your feet on the ground, leave Ocean Springs on US 90 East and drive through the quiet community of *Gautier* (Go-shay). When you spot the giant shipyards lining the beach, you'll know you've arrived in *Pascagoula.* Follow the signs to the *Scranton Floating Museum,* a retired shrimp boat docked in the Pascagoula River Park. The free tour includes a look at the tiny galley, cramped crews' quarters, and aquariums and dioramas displayed in the hull. The entire tour takes less than ten minutes. Visitors who find themselves feeling a bit claustrophobic are sure to leave with a new respect for the shrimpers who worked the boat—not many people would volunteer to spend two weeks at sea in such spartan quarters. The museum is open 10:00 A.M.–5:00 P.M. Tuesday–Saturday and 1:00–5:00 P.M. Sunday. From the river park, head south on Highway 63 to the *Scranton Nature Center* for a look at the wildlife exhibits. The Nature Center is located at *I.G. Levy Park,* where the tranquil grounds offer a nice break from the road. The Nature Center and park are open Tuesday–Saturday 10:00 A.M.–4:00 P.M. and Sunday 1:00–4:00 P.M.

Back on US 90 East you'll cross the *Pascagoula River,* also known as the *"Singing River"*. The river has apparently been musically inclined for centuries; French explorer d'Iberville referenced the "Singing River" in journal entries dated 1699. A young member of d'Iberville's crew, Joseph Simon de la Pointe, became the master of Pascagoula a few years following d'Iberville's landing. In 1718, de la Pointe built what is now known as the **Old Spanish Fort** on the original town site. The oldest building in the Mississippi Valley, the fort features 18-inch-thick walls made of oyster shells, moss, and mud. A museum on the grounds displays artifacts from Pascagoula's Indian era as well as relics from the eighteenth century. Follow the signs from US 90 East to the Old Spanish Fort at 4602 Fort Drive. The fort and museum are open Monday–Saturday 9:30 A.M.–4:30 P.M. Admission is $3.00 for adults, and $1.00 for children.

One of the most historically significant landmarks in Pascagoula is ***Scranton's Restaurant and Fire Engine Room Lounge.*** Operating in Pascagoula's original 1924 fire station/city hall/city jail, the restaurant is also a mini-museum, displaying memorabilia and photos from Pascagoula's history. The fire engine lounge still features the original fire door, lifted when the trucks raced out to battle fiery disasters. Scranton's is open Monday–Friday for lunch and Wednesday–Saturday for dinner. But be warned before you go—the restaurant has been struck by lightning not once, but twice. Scranton's is located in the downtown plaza near the old depot. Call (228) 762–1900 for reservations.

Continuing east on US 90 you'll reach the Mississippi Highway 63 junction. Take Highway 63 North to Lucedale, or continue a few miles farther on US 90 to the ***Gulf Coast Gator Ranch.*** The self-proclaimed "fastest, most furious, fun-filled extravaganza in Mississippi," the Gator Ranch offers airboat tours of

The Legend of the Singing River

Legend has it that centuries ago, a young princess of the Biloxi Indian tribe was betrothed to a hot-tempered Biloxi warrior. The princess, however, fell in love with a young chieftain of the peaceful Pascagoula tribe, and the two ran away together.

The spurned Biloxi warrior then led his braves in an attack on the Pascagoula. Rather than face death or slavery at the hands of the enemy, the entire Pascagoula tribe linked hands and walked into the Pascagoula River, singing a traditional tribal death chant as they surrendered their souls to the waters.

How much of the legend is true will forever remain a mystery, but whether the source is Indian ghosts or scientific phenomena, the Pascagoula River does sing. The music has been likened to everything from buzzing bees to the strains of a harp, and it usually reaches its highest volume on late summer and early autumn evenings. In fact, the river's song has been so loud, it has actually stopped traffic on the bridge.

Is it a trick of the sand and silt, or the last sad song of a people long extinct? Spend a summer evening listening to the concert firsthand, then decide for yourself.

Fruitland Park

The small community of Fruitland Park had its origins in a plan to attract prosperous Yankee farmers to the South.

In 1914, F. B. Mills, owner of a vegetable seed business in New York state, bought 20,000 acres in south Mississippi to develop as a planned community he christened "Fruitland Park." Mills distributed brochures to northern farmers describing a rich, fertile land with a pleasant climate, and a variety of "orchard home packages." For a mere $1,250, the Mills Company would build you a fine "Mississippi Style Orchard Cottage," complete with six spacious rooms and indoor plumbing.

Frostbite-weary farmers poured in from Ohio, Wisconsin, Michigan, and Minnesota, dreaming of a new life in the blessed warmth of the South. Alas, a series of disasters befell Mills's little utopia. A hailstorm wiped out the watermelons and a hard freeze zapped nearly 300 acres of figs. The Northern transplants had expected winter to last only a week or two, and were shocked to discover that 30 degrees in Mississippi wasn't any warmer than 30 degrees above the Mason-Dixon line. Residents soon became discouraged and left. His dream failed, Mills sold Fruitland Park in 1917.

One of the few remaining buildings from the original Fruitland Park is the 1914 **New York Hotel,** which is listed on the National Register of Historic Places. The hotel's register lists some of the disappointed farmers who failed to tame a land designed by Mother Nature to grow pine trees.

a marshland area populated by alligators, beavers, and other creatures that call the swamp home. The tall marsh grasses provide camouflage for hundreds of the scaly gators—keep your fingers out of the water! Airboat tours and a stroll through the gator farm are $25.00 for adults, $12.50 for children, and free to kids five and under. Walking tours of the gator farm only are $5.00 and free to kids five and under. A gift shop sells gator skulls, teeth, rubber impostors, and other gator memorabilia. Call (228) 475–6026 or stop by for a tour Monday–Saturday 9:00 A.M.–6:00 P.M. and Sunday 1:00–5:00 P.M.

From the Gator Ranch, double back toward Pascagoula on US 90 West to Mississippi Highway 63 North, the shortest route to the Holy Land. You'll find the cities and geography of the Bible duplicated in miniature 12 miles north of **Lucedale** at the **Palestine Gardens.** Built by a Presbyterian minister who believed people had to understand the Bible's geography in order to understand its stories, the gardens re-create the Holy Land on twenty wooded acres. The scale in relation to the real Holy Land is about 1 yard per mile. Signs identify major cities and landmarks, including Bethlehem, Nazareth, Joseph's carpentry shop, and Golgatha, site of the crucifixion. Stroll the Holy Land Tuesday–Friday 9:00 A.M.–4:00 P.M., Saturday 9:00 A.M.–5:00 P.M., and Sunday 1:00–4:00 P.M. The gardens are located 6.5 miles east of US 98. Follow the signs from Lucedale or from US 98, or call (601) 947–8422 for directions to this out-of-the-way inspiration.

Head back into downtown Lucedale, a quiet hamlet described by *Arkansas Democrat-Gazette* columnist Paul Greenberg as "the way small towns are supposed to look, and still do in storybooks."

While Lucedale is home to the obligatory small town Main Street, the local diner, and a handful of quaint little shops, the town also boasts the unusual amenity of a back-scratching post. No one seems to remember how, when, or why **Bailey's Scratching Post** ended up in the middle of downtown, but when you've got an itch, it really doesn't seem to matter. Celebrities from Ronald Reagan to Dizzy Dean have unabashedly scratched their backs right there on Main Street.

From Lucedale, take Mississippi Highway 26 West to **Wiggins** and **Archie Batson's aquaculture, blueberry, and fish farm.** Batson's offers a genuine, down-home country experience guaranteed to charm and relax harried city folk. In addition to acres of ponds used to grow catfish, crawfish, and fresh-water shrimp, Batson's offers an open-air petting zoo—home to the largest assortment of domestic livestock since Noah.

Batson's aquaculture products are sold by the pound; for a small fee, visitors can pick their own blueberries or try their luck in the fish ponds, which are home to monster catfish, bass, and rainbow trout. Archie Batson also gives guided tours of his parents' cabin, which overlooks the property. Surrounded by carefully arranged pieces of petrified wood, the rustic cabin is packed to the rafters with antique farm tools and Indian artifacts collected at nearby Arrowhead Springs. A waterwheel below the cabin provides the home with fresh spring water.

Batson's is located off Highway 26, about three miles west of the U.S. Highway 49 intersection. Batson's is open for fishing and tours Friday and Saturday year-round and for blueberry picking in season. To make reservations for group tours or check on the availability of aquaculture products, call (601) 928–5271.

Places to Stay in Southern Mississippi and the Gulf Coast

The following is a partial listing of the many hotels, motels, and bed-and-breakfast inns in the area not mentioned in the text.

Lincoln Ltd. is a full-time reservation service for bed-and-breakfast inns statewide. For reservations in any area of Mississippi, call (601) 482–5483 or (800) 633–6477.

BILOXI

The Old Santini House
(bed-and-breakfast)
964 Beach Boulevard,
(228) 436–4078 or
(800) 686–1146

CENTREVILLE

The Centreville House Bed and Breakfast
146 West Howard Street,
(601) 645–6119

GULFPORT

Grand Casino Oasis Resort and Spa
3215 West Beach Boulevard,
(228) 870–7777 or
(800) 946–7777

HATTIESBURG

Ash-Leah Manor
(bed-and-breakfast)
3885 Veterans Memorial
Drive (Highway 11),
(601) 584–8050

LONG BEACH

Red Creek Inn
(bed-and-breakfast)
7416 Red Creek Road,
(228) 452–3080 or
(800) 729–9670
www.redcreekinn.com

MAGNOLIA

The Coney House
(bed-and-breakfast)
204 South Clark Avenue,
(601) 783–3000 or
(800) 340–4487

OCEAN SPRINGS

Pelican's Roost Beach House
7213 Belle Fontaine Drive,
(228) 872–5634 or
(888) 600–1413

WOODVILLE

Carnot-Posey House
(bed-and-breakfast)
417 Church Street,
(877) 810–9489
www.carnotposey.home
stead.com

Places to Eat in Southern Mississippi and the Gulf Coast

The following is a partial listing of the many restaurants in the area not mentioned in the text.

BAY ST. LOUIS

Fire Dog Saloon
(burgers, appetizers, steaks, gumbo)
120 South Beach Boulevard,
(228) 467–8257

BILOXI

Alberti's Italian Restaurant
2028 Beach Boulevard,
(228) 388–9507

The Fountain (seafood)
111 Rue Magnolia,
(228) 435–1106

COLLINS

Covington House Restaurant (steaks, seafood)
Highway 49 North,
(601) 765–1684

GULFPORT

Chimneys Restaurant
(steaks, seafood)
1640 East Beach Boulevard,
(228) 868–7020

Vrazel's
(French, Italian, steaks, seafood)
3206 West Beach Boulevard,
(228) 863–2229

HATTIESBURG

Grill Room at Dunhopen
(upscale dining, Sunday brunch)
3875 Veterans Memorial
Drive (Highway 11),
(601) 543–0707

OCEAN SPRINGS

Manhattan Grill Steakhouse
(steaks, chicken, ribs)
705 Washington Avenue,
(228) 872–6480

ALSO WORTH SEEING

BAY ST. LOUIS
Casino Magic

McLeod Water Park

BILOXI
Biloxi Tour Train

Casino Magic

Grand Casino Biloxi

Imperial Palace Casino

Isle of Capri Casino

Palace Casino

President Casino

Treasure Bay Casino

GULFPORT
Copa Casino

Grand Casino Gulfport

Grass Lawn Tour Home

Lynn Meadows Discovery Center
(children's museum)

Prime Outlets at Gulfport

HATTIESBURG
Canebrake Golf Course
(ranked number 2 public course in the
U.S. by *Golf Digest* magazine)

Hattiesburg Zoo

University of Southern Mississippi
Museum of Art

MCCOMB
Bogue Chitto Water Park

Percy Quin State Park

Pike County Speedway

OCEAN SPRINGS
All Veterans Walkway

Mississippi Vietnam Veterans
Memorial

Index

About the Author

Freelance writer Marlo Carter Kirkpatrick lives in Madison, Mississippi, with her husband, wildlife photographer Stephen Kirkpatrick.

Marlo is also the author of *Extreme Exposure, the True Story of a Photo Expedition Lost in the Amazon*. She and her husband collaborated on the coffee-table books *Romancing the Rain, Wilder Mississippi,* and *To Catch the Wind.* Both *Extreme Exposure* and *Romancing the Rain* were winners in the 2003 International Self-Published Book Awards. *Wilder Mississippi* was the winner of the 2002 National Outdoor Book Award and was the Southeastern Outdoor Press Association's 2002 Book of the Year. Marlo's latest book, *Lost,* will be released by W Publishing Group in June 2005.

The Kirkpatricks' work has taken them to destinations throughout North, Central, and South America. Their current projects focus on tropical locations and underwater photography.

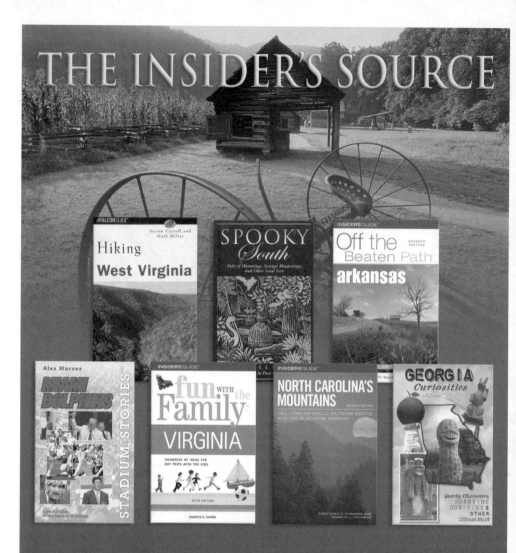
 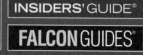